MUTE ICONS

—and Other Dichotomies of the Real in Architecture

MUTE

Marcelo Spina & Georgina Huljich
with Constance Vale

ICONS

—and Other Dichotomies
of the Real in Architecture

This book is for Ona and Anju, who are simply the best part of us.

ACKNOWLEDGMENTS

A book on such precise subject matter as this requires a commitment to rigorously articulated viewpoints; nevertheless, architectural discourse doesn't grow in a vacuum, but develops rather within a living sphere of ideas. We owe our gratitude to a loosely formed network of friends, colleagues, and confabulators who have instigated and nurtured the foundation of this book over the years.

Our cultural context wouldn't be the same without David Ruy, Mark Gage, Ferda Kolatan, David Erdman, Tom Wiscombe, Todd Gannon, Marcelyn Gow, and Andrew Zago. In ways known and unknown to them, they all have had an impact on our thinking. Early conversations with Michael Osman, Timothy Hide, and Rodolfo Machado were essential in the gestation of the concepts that led to *Mute Icons*. Guillermo Martinez, along with his novels and writings about dialectics, has been an influential instigator. Aside from their critical contributions, Brett Steele and Ciro Najle offered essential insights into the nature of books, monographs, and manifestos at two pivotal moments: during the conception and conclusion of this book. Sara Herda and the Graham Foundation for Advanced Studies in the Fine Arts supported *Mute Icons* with an important grant, which transformed this project from a crazy weekend idea into a book.

SCI-Arc, UCLA AUD, PennDesign, Syracuse School of Architecture, Yale School of Architecture, and all of their incredible students with whom we had the pleasure of working during these years, allowed our thinking, and therefore the content of this book, to grow and mature. Within these institutions, the support of Hernan Diaz Alonso, Eric Moss, Hitoshi Abe, Winka Dubledam, Michael Speaks, and Robert A. M. Stern has been critical. We are indebted to our fantastic colleagues at SCI-Arc and UCLA AUD, our second homes. Among many and for different reasons, we especially want to thank Joe Day, Casey Rehm, Anna Neimark, John Enright, Ming Fung, Russell Thomsen, Maxi Spina, Florencia Pita,

Elena Manferdini, Wonne Icks, Mohamed Sharif, Neil Denari, and Craig Hodgetts. For their energy, support, motivation, and stimulating spirit, we want to acknowledge Deborah Irmas, Kristy Edmunds, Jesse Reiser, Nanako Umemoto, Nader Tehrani, Jeff Kipnis, Richard Koshalek, Kimberly Meyer, Megan Steinman, and Stephen Phillips. Over the years, the personal support, mentoring, and friendship of Thom Mayne have been both relentless and unwavering.

The rigorous and comprehensive writing, editing, as well as personal commitment of Constance Vale was essential in the development and realization of *Mute Icons*; most particularly, the History Section would simply not exist in its present form without her involvement. Special thanks go to James Vincent, whose evolving photorealist outlook of our work gave it a new life and pushed us to reconceive and recalibrate our assumptions about the aesthetic and material being of our projects. In Nephew and Shimahara, we found keen likeminded collaborators interested in pursuing similarly uncharted paths in the narrative power of images.

Ramon Pratt, Ricardo Devesa, and everyone at ACTAR Barcelona, believed in and trusted in this project when others did not. Jessica Fleischmann of Still Room asked the right questions and convinced us of the need for restraint, and generated a clear and timeless concept for the graphic design. Carrie Paterson's insightful editing, copyediting, and proofreading, was essential in assuring that our vision could be conveyed unmistakably to a wide audience.

At PATTERNS, Daniela Atencio, Adrian Wong, Dylan Krueger, and Mahyar Naghshvar deserve a special mention for their relentless efforts in making this book and its content, through its many iterations, a beautiful visual reality.

Furthermore, the work of many, many young people during the last six or seven years, including employees, students, and collaborators who participated in projects and/or specifically in the book include Adin Rimland, Adrian Wong, Adriana Hinojosa, Agustina Alaines, Albert Kos, Alexis Peneff, Alberto Alfonso, Alex Blugerman, Andrew Choi, Anthony Stoffella, Arditha Auriyane, Ashley Sholder, Carlos Navarro, Cheryl Lin, Chris Cui, Chris Chen, Claudia Wainer, Connor Covey, Corie Saxman,

Dan Lu, Danial Mahfoud, Daniela Atencio, Daniele Profeta, Diandra Rendradjaja, Diastika Lokesworo, Dylan Krueger, Eda Yetim, Elias Arkin, Evaline Huang, Fatma Gonca Tunc, Fefei Zhang, Garet Ammerman, Harrison Steinbuch, Henry Yang, Huaiming Liao, Isabel Socorro, Ivan Zhang, Jacky Hoang, Jacob Waas, Jeff Guiducci, Jingyi Jiang, Yensu Kim, Josh Shultz, Juan Benavides, Julia Spackman, Julio Perez, Junxi Peng, Justin Tan, Laura Baobao, Mahyar Naghshvar, Manying Wang, Maria Clelia Scutteri, Matthew Kendall, Maya Alam, Melissa Peter, Melissa Pomsztein, Michelle Sugeng, Mike Wang, Mun-Yi Cheng, Muotaz Abbas, Namku Kim, Negar Jazbi, Rachele Sipione, Rajwa Alseif, Renata Galan, Robert Panossian, Shawna Meng, Siyao Zheng, Sophie Lauriault, Stan Lin, Stefan Svedberg, Tal Dotam, Tom Ferrer, Treya Yano, Vasilisa Sokolova, Viola Ago, Wei Qiu, Wenxin Lin, William Maya, William Patrick Adams, Xingtai Sun, Xiaonan Yang, Yosephine Anglingdarma, Yipeng Liu, You Wu, Zaina Sweidan, Zhang Avon, Zhuoxian Deng, and Zixiao (Kiwi) Zhu.

Finally, we want to thank our partners and collaborators, who allowed us to carry on projects and maintain our capacity to practice globally across scales, geographies, and cultures: John Spence; Alexis Tzakos; Lars Jan; Jose Herrasti / MUTUO; Sharif, Lynch: Architecture; SOM LA; Juan Rincon / Taller Paralelo; Guillermo Banchini / BArqs; Nones+Nones; Chris Reed / Stoss; Matthew Melnyk / NOUS; and Casey Reas and Bill Pearson / North Sails.

FOREWORD:
Mute Icon—
Architecture's Duplicitous Realities
Brett Steele

1. Past Realities

"Dichotomies of the Real," appended to the title of *Mute Icons* on the book before you, is something of a tell regarding the architectural project this publication foregrounds. The subtitle points to a long-running preoccupation of this book's talented and imaginative authors, architects Georgina Huljich and Marcelo Spina (PATTERNS), regarding one of the most important questions architectural careers must eventually address regarding an architect's life work: what constitutes 'the real' in architecture?

How should architects define 'reality' in a discipline and profession that is built upon the task of imagining and giving form to the most unreal of all human ideas: the idea of the future? It is, of course, the future that architects' work is most directed toward: taking a world as found and giving it new form, organization, and arrangement, in anticipation of new human activities, needs, and ambitions. How surprising and welcome it is, then, to read a monograph like *Mute Icons* — produced by architects in a futurist era like ours, one dominated by research and technological cultures of all kinds and indebted to illusory images of the future that are mostly defined by an endless array of new and startling technologies. The book foregrounds something else entirely: the longer history; not of architecture so much as architectural form, which this book brings alive again in new and unexpected ways.

The various ironies, dilemmas, or just torn allegiances of what constitutes the construction of new architectural realities today are presented in *Mute Icons* in a manner that is both persuasive and timely; most especially, by Huljich and Spina's decision not just to study, but also to model and to render so many compelling episodes, doing so in high-resolution, technicolor detail, and in ways that — while bringing them close to us for our own renewed consideration — nonetheless distance such examples from the cultural and historical accounts previously attached to such icons. Huljich and Spina draw (literally — make rendered detailed architectural models and images) in order to depict episodes of adjacent architectural epochs. This remarkable catalog of ancient and modern examples of a very specific kind of architecture that has long existed, but has as well long eluded, recent architectural description, let alone projective (even instrumental) architectural histories, is a smart, even ingenious, historiographic (more than technological) move. The layered complexities of architects' current, contemporary condition regarding the potential of form — let alone iconic form — to order and assemble our world and lived experiences are clearly at the forefront of the thinking of Huljich and Spina.

Mute Icons is a book confident in its rendering of the extraordinary in architecture: those entirely unique, one-off architectural worlds humans have imagined and built across millennia that have been deliberately conceived as distinct from and exceptional to the world surrounding them. In a very real sense, this book makes the case for an architectural icon whose greatest quality isn't that of a particular form, shape, or appearance (of a building, structure, or place), so much as one having an instrumental image able to be used by architects for unexpected purposes in the creation of their own, further (future) projects. As such, the idea of 'mute' icons on display here is remarkably *anti*-formalist in the modern and contemporary sense of image- and form-making, which places paramount importance on a viewer's or user's confrontation with a shape, material, and appearance, including how that confrontation *affects* its user. In the book's ultimate aims to be far more social and instrumentalist and of use to someone (like an architect looking at such images) in their own contemplation, it wouldn't be going too far out on a limb here to note the considerable connection between this interest and now nearly completely forgotten, Byzantine forms of painting and image-making practice related to the making of icons, whose role in many different cultures and religious orthodoxies stressed the ways in which certain kinds of icons were to be used as part of highly ordered, social and cultural forms of practice.

The idea of an architectural 'icon' today is one so fraught with complexity and compromise that most contemporary forms of critical (no less than professional) practice avert their attention elsewhere. The willingness of this book to elevate this very topic anew addresses the enduring potential of iconic form as a projective possibility, offering our contemporary forward-driven forms of practice the convergence of historically-remote, culturally- and geographically-distant projects as well as those of PATTERNS' own recent portfolio. This book is unlike any other in recent years; most especially, given previous publications on the work of these architects that have tended to foreground technological and material dimensions of Huljich and Spina's own considerable professional and academic expertise.

That architects actually 'make' the real world has long been a differentiating aspect of their discipline, a distinct field of human knowledge compared to those of other forms of cultural production. Architects, we should remember, don't actually 'build' their worlds, in the everyday sense of making a thing (like a painting, or sculpture, shaped by the artist's own hands), or 'perform' their work (in the bodily sense of how a dancer, for example, undertakes their performance in 'real', lived, ways). Architects, by contrast, work at a dimension removed from the eventual making or building of their worlds, working instead in an intermediary, mediating space of drawings, models, and other translatory communication (like scribbles, sketches, and calculations), whereby their ideas are ultimately converted into instructions for others (like builders, for example) to eventually realize their work.

As many have observed before, architecture is almost unique as a creative discipline, not only owing to its practitioners' focus almost entirely on this wholly intermediary space within which architects live and work on future worlds, but as well, to the privileged role of past architectural experiences in that undertaking. The question this poses then is this: *why* for architects is the opposite of the future — the past — of such importance to their work? The answer to which would be this: a recognition that it is past knowledge and experience — in this case, for architects interested in re-considering the potential and possibilities of form-making today, past examples of iconic form — which provide a meaningful way to counter the inherently episodic, serial aspects of any architectural practice, by knowingly posing it as part of a deeper, longer, and shared discipline.

Architectural pasts, when assembled by architects in new and unexpected ways, remain the most enduring of building materials, precisely for the ways in which they continue to assemble — to genuinely discipline — architectural knowledge itself. The construction of alternative architectural pasts and imagined genealogies, including the sort of expansive and generous genealogy of iconic forms included in this book, provide real means by which architects situate their own current and urgent architectural preoccupations within a field of co-conspirators and like-minded projects. Making this book, then, needs to be seen as an act of architectural world-building; reality-making in the most meaningful, enduring, and human sense of the term. As so many of the culturally significant precedents included in the opening catalog of examples show, projects that were undertaken, whether in ancient or more modern times, were created in close proximity to long-established human ritual and social significance.

Here, we see iconic architectures not only selected and studied by Huljich and Spina and their collaborators as if they were their very own projects, but also rendered and drawn in incredibly original, precise ways (usually oblique, and with an emphasis on these projects' surface qualities), the techniques of which we can then see are used in the representation of their own catalog of projects during the past decade. This method is what demonstrates the decidedly valuable, instrumental undertaking this book has been for two architects hitting their stride at this mid-career stage of their own work, thinking, and experience. With considerable clarity of purpose, and of the kind that gives legitimacy above all else to revealing the role form and its knowing re-description continues to play in the creation of new architectural realities, what comes across here is a confidence and certainty that turns our attention to the most unlikely of questions in critical architectural practice in the 2020s: meaningful, iconic, form-making. It's a bold move, one dependent upon a belief in architectural realism, and more specifically, upon forms conceived without expectation of their qualities communicating or traveling beyond the features of their own culturally unique, let alone architectural, specificities. This is formalism at its best, for precisely the ways in which it brackets off and sets boundaries around architectural or other expectations regarding how any one kind of architecture might offer itself — form asserted by knowing, and understood as the result of highly unique, one-off circumstances.

2. Future Forms

As already mentioned above, we need to recall that to a remarkable degree, architectural lives are spent chasing a thing that's not actually real at all: the future. This includes future arrangements of spaces, building materials, infrastructures, as well as the social lives of humans that architects imagine their work will bring into being — again, not now: in the future. So, however else architects comprehend and treat the shaping of 'reality' as the crucial, even urgent, reason for their work, what they know most about reality is this: it is malleable. Architectural practice, above all else, is undertaken to change reality. In the truest sense, architects expect to change the world as found, into something their work makes better; into something that better fits the needs of a world that will inhabit their built worlds. In other words, for architects, 'reality', it turns out, is the least stable, the one thing their work will inevitably change. No wonder then why concepts like form — most especially iconic form — can be seen to be such a meaningful, tangible, enduring concept within the discipline — such a concept provides, in a very real sense, a potential for (at least a degree of) permanence within a discipline that has, at its core, the exact opposite: incredible instability.

It's this instability of architecture's presumed realities — in the subtitle of this book, its 'dichotomous' features — that *Mute Icons* is most focused upon, and examines in so many different and compelling, and contemporary ways. From its opening pages, *Mute Icons* literally turns on its head the expectations of today's emergent architectural generation that recent digital and computational design and visualization technologies are enough alone to justify the making of new and interesting 'iconic' form. That's the false pretense of certain of PATTERNS' professional peers, who so regularly evidence such little interest in architectural histories (the work of which is now too often relegated to the growing field of historical professionals, operating at increasing distance from today's robust design cultures). What is presented here by contrast to a scholarly assumption of architectural histories is instead an opposite kind of architectural realism created in the most unlikely, but instrumentalist ways: by Huljich and Spina and their collaborators' utilization of advanced image-making and visualization software. As they model, represent, and render historical examples of iconic form, this process in turn provides the means by which to engage in form-making for their own purposes — in the creation of yet more iconic form.

It's a noteworthy project, and one that owes much to the years of research and development of representational (and not only building) expertise by these two architects who, working with talented graduate students at UCLA's department of Architecture & Urban Design as well as the Southern California Institute of Architecture (SCI-Arc), have created a treasure trove of supporting research and visual materials for the more immediate and pressing design projects and commissions undertaken by this Los Angeles-based office during the past few years. That architectural objects — historical as well as contemporary — can be seen in such startling and inventive new ways is one of this book's many exceptional achievements.

3. An Atlas of World-making

Mute Icons presents an open, optimistic resource, a toolbox and catalog that allows the reader to imagine the making of new built forms/realities, a kind of atlas in book form. Atlases emerged in the 17th and 18th century, initially as cartographic surveys documenting the cultural, scientific, or literary differences comprising large amounts of human or natural geographies. Unsurprisingly, this form of compilation was necessarily dependent upon its author/editor's experience directly gained from physical travel, movement, and survey across vast distances and times. As such, what we might think of the atlas is itself both a record of and tool for those forms of European 'enlightenment' we associate with early modern and modern histories. More recently, the atlas evolved into a very different instrument, by which individual modern artists and creative minds sought to provide a similar summary overview and survey — of the materials defining and enabling their own careers. Notable and highly influential examples by contemporary artists include the atlases of German painter Gerhard Richter; the American conceptual and appropriation artist Cindy Sherman; and the Los Angeles painter, photographer, and documentarian, the artist Ed Ruscha.

Since the 1960s, Gerhard Richter has been methodically collecting, arranging, and archiving ephemera that include newspaper clippings, photographs, and his own sketching, in order to compile his open-ended *Atlas* that today consists of 50-plus years of systematic self-description, archiving, and recording of materials the artist has referred to as "somewhere between art and garbage." Cindy Sherman's atlas-instincts, by contrast, consist of the serial collection, presentation, and installation of pieces in surveys such as her *Film Stills* series from the late 1970s, which brings together over 70 of the staged photographs she made of herself embodying different kinds of female characters, identities, and imagery, through which her work has so successfully engaged the visual and cultural codes of female identity — including those of the artist and even her own celebrity. Ed Ruscha, has, arguably, made at times the atlas itself a direct model with select examples of his own output and production, which spans from the painting and re-painting of iconic Los Angeles or Southern California post-war imagery into sets of variations on the same view (then installed in systematic, atlas-like arrangements of this production) to, at the other extreme, the production of photographic surveys made by the artist compiled and presented (in book and other graphic form) providing atlases of such overlooked, everyday spaces as those of Sunset Boulevard, or parking lots throughout Los Angeles.

An examination of this contemporary idea of the atlas is one of the ways *Mute Icons* engages that most enduring of all architectural concepts, architectural form; here, by challenging our expectations of the contents, and form, of an architectural monograph. For those readers who already know the work of Huljich and Spina, *Mute Icons* is spectacularly different in organization and purpose from *PATTERNS Embedded* (ACDCU, 2011), their previous publication documenting the first decade of these architects' work and thinking. That book was arranged in a more tried-and-true, serial and chronological format, and was organized and focused in the more conventional way on a chronological presentation of a series of self-contained building/design projects. By contrast (and I suspect, *by design*), *Mute Icons* is a more self-aware, deliberate mixing of parts; fragments, partial observations, historical and even formal coincidences, here uncovered in a more fluid, even instinctive way. As we encounter both historical and contemporary works, we see depicted surface alongside structure; parts presented as if wholes. Over and over, a reader's expectations are confounded, and the serial and episodic order of a conventional monograph upended. The effect of this assemblage/montage is that we are able to see a series of preoccupations that cut across the various individual examples and projects by which an architectural, and not just formal, sensibility emerge. *Mute Icons* isn't just a catalog or a document. For its authors, it's what the best monographs always should be for those undertaking the effort to survey an overview of otherwise busy parties and studio: it's a big, career- and not only discipline-defining leap.

Mute Icons gives the well-established genre of the architectural monograph new energy, purpose, and appearance. It returns to the genre of books documenting an architect's career, something that's been sorely missing from a post-digital generation so far: a belief in the necessity of imaging, and not only imagining, architecture's own past as part of one's own. This is an architecture of genuine realism; one grounded in examining, and comprehending the limitations and not only potentials of architecture's — not architects'! — ongoing, even enduring, preoccupation with formalism. About the ongoing disciplinary importance of *that* project, this book is anything but mute. Architecture's ongoing confrontation with the circumstances of its own making and re-making of reality, even of the most vital, that is *iconic* kind, endures.

Los Angeles, January 2020

1 Concept — Introduction

Mute Icons is, at its core, a book that interrogates images: historical, contemporary, and — more importantly — speculative. This examination concentrates on the increasingly dichotomic state of architectural practice, discourse, and contemporary culture at large. Through the analysis of images that exist and some that we propose, we aim to develop a language and a sensibility for discovering simultaneous, contradictory, and even unexpected readings of images in architecture.

1 Concept — Introduction

An Argument for the Mute Icon

The term *mute icon* is, in itself, a dichotomy: *mute*, referring to the inability to speak, express, or represent, and *icon* as a sign, symbol, or representation that speaks clearly. The mute icon neither deftly communicates, nor is it wholly inhibited and silenced. *Mute Icons* operates and finds significance within this dialectic. As architects, we have become accustomed to iconicity through various formal tropes and imageable features, many of which are now pervasive in our culture. This book offers an attempt to identify a progressive reaction to collective, established expectations of icons. Arguing for a redefinition of the project of the icon and therefore the image in architecture, *Mute Icons* aims to construct a viable alternative to the icon's simple cliché and exhausted form of communication, positing one that is decidedly introverted and withdrawn. Furthermore, it aims to carve out a niche in contemporary culture and history by suggesting that architecture, far from being a crowd-pleaser, can persist within society as a cultural and social irritant that can engender critical thinking via the multiple indeterminate readings of its image.

Placing so much emphasis on images seems almost imprudent at a time when images have questionable value due to their atomic distribution via social media, their dubious factuality, and their perceived banality in a world under so much social, political, and environmental turmoil. However, two critical arguments define the importance of addressing images today. First, we must learn how to look at images — architectural or otherwise — to challenge the truth of their content or the significance of their authenticity. Second, and more crucially, there is a new kind of architectural image, one that is not simply about legibility. Instead of banking on the "shock and awe"[1] of an occupying force, these architectural images suggest introspection and muteness.

In 2013, when we started thinking about this book — even though its actual writing officially commenced and continued later — the discussion was very different from what it is today. At that time, if there was a straw man to beat down, it was the one representing the perceived excesses of the digital avant-garde, to which we once belonged. Now, only six or seven years in the future, the situation could not be more different. After so much obsession with the new, the spectrum of reactionary historical revisionism that we see today, strongly present in American academia, in hindsight appears inevitable. As robust as it is confusing and with no clear end game in sight, its purveyors will soon find nothing else to oppose. This is precisely why the tradition of reactionary opposition and hostile antagonism in our field is as significant in its scope as it is futile in its agenda. In thinking about these particular issues of the present along with the atemporal problems of architecture, we believe it is crucial not only to contest problems and agendas but also to make arguments for the persistence of architectural culture by focusing on ideas and projects[2] that both nurture and challenge it.

Contending with the Icon

The icon has obvious associations in art history. The word icon, or Greek *eikōn*, is defined as an "an image, figure, or representation."[3] The storied past of icons in history as gilded iconographic panel paintings is far more illustrious and less populist than their life in the present as icons riddle our digital devices.

From Virgin Mother to Virgin Mobile, the icon's integrity has been tied to its immediacy of signification, establishing a static, symbolic realm in order to maintain its blunt legibility.

In stark contrast, muteness indicates an inescapable and absolute silence or a selective unwillingness to speak in a particular context. A mute silence is intellectually engaged but socially withdrawn. Sound, in the form of language or noise, activates the interior, but the interior remains unresponsive or hidden. Hovering near but not on the collective ground, muteness outlines the enigmatic realm between extroverted exteriority and introverted interiority.

The term "mute icons" implies different associations within an art historical realm than the word "icon" might alone. This combination of terms brings to mind Suprematism and later Minimalism but in particular Kazimir Malevich's *Black Square*. With its singular image occupying the room's corner — a position traditionally reserved in Russian Orthodox homes for the paintings of saints — *Black Square* displaced the religious icon and replaced it with an abstraction. This radically challenged the status of painting as a mimetic or representational system and produced a non-icon or, more provocatively, an icon that is unambiguously mute.

The didacticism and immediacy of icons have long been their virtue but in equal measure their fault. At one time they were propaganda of religious organizations and more recently have become the idols of online commerce, and as such, they carry the burden of precarious political associations. To invoke the word "icon" inspires a sense of dread that one may be attempting to summon the ghosts of the linguistic turn and revisit society's preoccupation with signification. Entrenched in its past, the icon offers a highly charged ground. To render an icon mute requires that it shed its static sensibility and become ambivalent toward meaning.

Black Square, at the corner of the original exhibition by Kazimir Malevich

A Categorical Expansion: Misuse and Provocation

In architecture, the word "icon" suggests a categorical generalization of buildings and projects that appear iconic. In this book, our use of the word does not intend to continue its simple deadpan denotation that was prevalent in the late '90s, but rather to instill it with new meaning. Therefore, readers should dispatch any a priori notion of the icon as a straw man that can be quickly knocked down. We are not interested in the icon's abhorrent incarnations, neither the one-liners and the clichés, the generic — with or without its cynicism — nor the exuberantly iconic with all its social and cultural naiveté. Rather we are invested in architecture that has been able to produce a constructed tension between legibility and reticence.

"Iconic" here refers to a category of projects that are visually distinct and legible, whether by association or through levels of abstraction. Given the categorical expansion — not just an icon, but a mute icon — this book revisits and positions projects which are decidedly opposed to any traditional understanding of iconicity by detailing how they undermine it. In these examples, the icon and the mute are married in a perpetual dialectic. The two do not cancel each other out but produce a sense of perpetual irritation.[4]

China Central Television Headquarters in *The Simpsons*

Antecedent 1: Charles Jencks and the Lineage of the Icon

> An icon always has a trace of sanctity about it, the aura of a saint; by definition it is an object to be worshipped, however fitfully.[5]
>
> —Charles Jencks,
> "The Iconic Building Is Here to Stay"

In arguing for the icon, postmodern theorist Charles Jencks suggests the importance of sublimating iconography through abstraction. Jencks refers to this move away from literal iconography as "calculated ambiguity" or creating "an icon without a clear iconography, an enigmatic signifier."[6] Jencks attempts to position and categorize icons with the understanding that not all built imagery is productive. However, he goes on to point out that beneficial aspects will never allay the icon's detractors: "One should not underestimate the desire of the public for good iconic buildings. They still make people leave home to enjoy the expressive aspects of the public realm. The complaint about their very real problems — the simplified image, the stupid one-liner, the a-contextual building, the destruction of the city — has been made for many years."[7]

In the contemporary and recent past, icons have exercised geopolitical power. That is, an act of architecture can be powerful enough to put a city, region, or country on the map. However, as we know well enough already, architects make buildings; only culture and time turn buildings into icons. Therefore, this issue is one of cultural absorption far more than it is about design speculation and has often forced unnecessary excesses into architecture.

While Jencks advises against the simplistic one-liners,[8] he also has words for self-canceling messages. In all his celebration and exaltation of difference, Jencks recognizes the weight of irritation in iconic buildings. "The news lesson is clear: if an iconic building is not hated enough — like the Eiffel Tower was at its inception — it will never inspire enough negative energy to be noticed by the public or to go on to be debated and, perhaps, defended."[9] Here he touches on one of the deep and complicated truths of the genre. The experience of iconic buildings, according to Jenks, is as diverse as it is paradoxical and even contradictory; icons are architecture in "the shape of something uncanny, fascinating, horrible, lovely."[10] However, Charles Jenks' turn-of-the-century approach may seem now from a more contemporary, socially engaged, and culturally attuned perspective, his argumentation and defense of the icon is still a relevant one for architecture.

Antecedent 2: Monolithic Architecture as a Form of Muteness

While not referring to the issue of iconicity in any direct way, Rodolfo Machado and Rodolphe el-Khoury's book *Monolithic Architecture*, including the introduction by the authors and Detlef Mertins' essay "Open Contours," is an essential predecessor to *Mute Icons*; its theoretical positions seeded our initial ideas.

While *Monolithic Architecture* went relatively unnoticed when published in the late-'80s as the catalog of an eponymous exhibition, it has since become an extremely relevant source for those interested in the tradition of solidity in architecture. Arguing for a paradoxical understanding of architectural form — one that could be as much about representation as about physicality — *Monolithic Architecture* proposed a radical new lens through which to look at and conceive of architectural projects and objects. Not just the idea that architecture could be constructed with a single material or carved out from a solid rock, but the notion that its legibility could somehow represent issues such as solidity and impenetrability. It is precisely in the paradoxical aspect of architecture, more than in the possible literality of its idea, where Machado and El-Khoury's *Monolithic Architecture* gains traction.

In a conversation with Rodolfo Machado in our class "Whole Dichotomy: Monolithicity in Architecture" that we taught at Yale School of Architecture in 2013, Rodolfo recalled the cultural context of the time and described his positioning of the exhibition and its catalog as a reaction to the rise of extreme fragmentation and collage that was being promoted by Deconstructivism.[11] Although far from becoming mainstream, Decon was certainly the predominant discourse in academia in its time. Interestingly enough, thirty years plus later, *Mute Icons* could be positioned as an alternative to both, the remains of the positivist morphology-driven, excess-producing, digital avant-garde and the often-negative, irony-propelled neo-postmodernism.

The Mute Icon

Haunted by vast processes taking place outside itself, architecture, like culture, appears to be at a significant crossroads. The past two decades have been shaped by events like 9/11, the financial collapse, the continued effects of climate change, and by sociopolitical movements, including the Arab Spring, Occupy Wall Street, the climate movement, Black Lives Matter, and the #MeToo movement, as well as Brexit, MAGA, ongoing refugee crises, and the rise of authoritarianism and populism worldwide. Meanwhile, each new epoch of economic austerity is followed by yet another economic bubble. In this era, the oft-proclaimed "death of the icon" and the specific declaration "no more weird buildings"[12] are naive responses to the impulse for increased social responsibility and the search for common sense and common ground in architecture as well as culture. While sociopolitical context can-not

"Globalization and Its New Discontents"
Occupy.com, August 12, 2016

be the only driver for architectural production nor any other cultural practice, it is a significant factor with which to reckon. In light of these societal shifts, the status and role of the architectural icon is under scrutiny, and its cultural relevance is under stress. While culture at large will always identify and promote new icons, the question here is: what constitutes a contemporary icon?

The mute icon — a kind of anti-monument — may provide an answer as architecture's most challenging and provocative response to the cultural tensions of our time. Unconcerned with either narrative excesses of meaning and communication, or with the shock and awe of sensation-making, the mute icon in architecture must do what it does best: express its virtues through volume, mass, surface, and aesthetics with all its social and cultural implications. By suppressing the now expected aesthetic teasers, the mute icon becomes intriguing in its ambivalence towards context and apathy towards the body. Balanced between object and building, the mute icon is defined by a dialectic legibility; strange silhouettes, strong postures, constructive brutality, uncommunicative nature, and apparent autonomy from the surrounding ground and context in spite of being partially embedded within either or both. Its attitude is absolute and unstable, anticipated and strange, manifest and withdrawn. Elusive and fleeting, mute icons entice enduring attention by delivering persistent irritation.

Theoretical defenses for these illegible architectural irritants can be found in the work of author and scholar Timothy Hyde, who argues for their legitimacy, stating, "The passive manner of irritation, or any ugly feeling, can only be overcome by a complete transformation of the situation from which that feeling emerges. In the absence of that transformation, irritation persists as a simultaneous pulling-together and pushing-apart of person and architecture."[13] Along similar lines, Reyner Banham insisted that a Brutalist building should produce an affecting "image," defined as "something which is visually valuable" and "'*quod visum perturbat*' — that which seen, affects the emotions [...] with pleasure, displeasure, or, pointedly, an admixture of the two."[14] By limiting legibility and visual pleasure, the mute icon demands closer scrutiny. Its resistance conveys resilience, and its introversion stimulates communication.

Both Hyde and Banham's arguments tie to the problem of estrangement, as pioneered by Russian literary theorist Viktor Shklovsky and his essay "Art as Technique." Shklovsky famously argues, "Art exists so that one may recover the sensation of life; it exists to make one feel things, to make the stone stoney."[15] To make the stone stony is to carve away the inscription already imprinted on it; it is to turn signs back into things, form into abstraction, and building into object. To make the stone stony, architecture must now appear "strange and wonderful."[16]

1 "Shock and awe" is a phrase developed by the U.S. Military to describe rapid dominance in warfare. The phrase was famously used by President George W. Bush at the start of the Iraq War in 2003, where American troops bombed and effectively invaded a country while the world watched on CNN and other satellite TV networks. The saying is inextricably linked to spectacle and the power of images.
2 We think of projects as both the dedicated and life-long research of architects who are bent on speculating and building in relation to a specific problem or narrow subset of problems, as well as those individual attempts to deal with specific situations.
3 "icon, n.", OED Online, *Oxford University Press*, June 2019, (accessed July 25, 2019).
4 This is related to a sense of "pulling together and pushing apart between subject and architecture" described by Mark Cousins when arguing for "The Ugly" (*AA Files*, Vol. 29 [Summer 1995], 3–6) and which Timothy Hyde quotes when addressing "architectural irritants" (Timothy Hyde, "Piles, Puddles, and Other Architectural Irritants," *Log*, No. 27 [2013], 76).
5 Charles Jencks, "The Iconic Building is Here to Stay," *City*, Vol. 10, No. 1 (April), 4.
6 Jencks, 13.
7 Ibid., 10.
8 Ibid., 8–10.
9 Ibid., 12.
10 Ibid., 13.
11 Philip Johnson and Mark Wigley, *Deconstructivist Architecture* (New York: Museum of Modern Art, 1988), accessible at moma.org/calendar/exhibitions/1813.
12 In 2014, the President of the People's Republic of China, Xi Jinping, famously declared, "no more weird buildings" would be built in China, describing the beginning of a new cultural era for the country. Using various buildings as negative examples, including the Rem Koolhaas' designed CCTV by OMA, he argued in favor of a Chinese nationalist agenda in his country's cultural production. He did so by saying that Chinese art should "disseminate contemporary Chinese values, embody traditional Chinese culture, and reflect Chinese people's aesthetic pursuit." Rory Stott, "Why China's President Says 'No More Weird Buildings'," *ArchDaily*, October 21, 2014, archdaily.com/559456/why-china-s-president-says-no-more-weird-buildings (accessed March 15, 2019).
13 Hyde, 76. Hyde is referring to "ugly feelings" as characterized by Sianne Ngai, *Ugly Feelings* (Cambridge, MA. Harvard University Press, 2007).
14 Reyner Banham, "The New Brutalism," *The Architectural Review* (Dec. 1955): 358, quoted in Timothy Hyde, "Piles, Puddles, and other Architectural Irritants," *Log*, Vol. 27 (2013): 73–74.
15 Viktor Shklovsky, "Art as Technique," *Theory of Prose* (Normal, IL: Dalkey Archive Press, 1991, [o.p. 1925]).
16 According to Aristotle, poetic language must appear "strange and wonderful." (Aristotle, *Poetics*, trans. Anthony Kenny [Oxford: Oxford University Press, 2013], 70.) Shklovsky refers to Aristotle's claim that "poetic language ought to have a character of something foreign, something outlandish about it" (Shklovsky, 27).

TOP: PATTERNS' League of Shadows with wildfires in the background @Paco1227
ABOVE: PATTERNS' League of Shadows, as seen within a dystopian fictional sight of DTLA, *The Walking Dead*, AMC

2 History — Timeline, Constance Vale, Co-Author

The History section aims to construct a lineage of mute iconicity in architecture by focusing on buildings and projects that over a vast period of time have transcended their type, form, and aesthetics and which have become poster children of architectural irritation, autonomy, and even estrangement. Organized chronologically and described by means of orthographic representations, the subsequent antecedents are rendered familiar and yet strange, appealing to a new life while communicating clearly their paradoxical nature as mute icons.

ABOVE: Precedent juxtapositions, worm's-eye isometric close-up

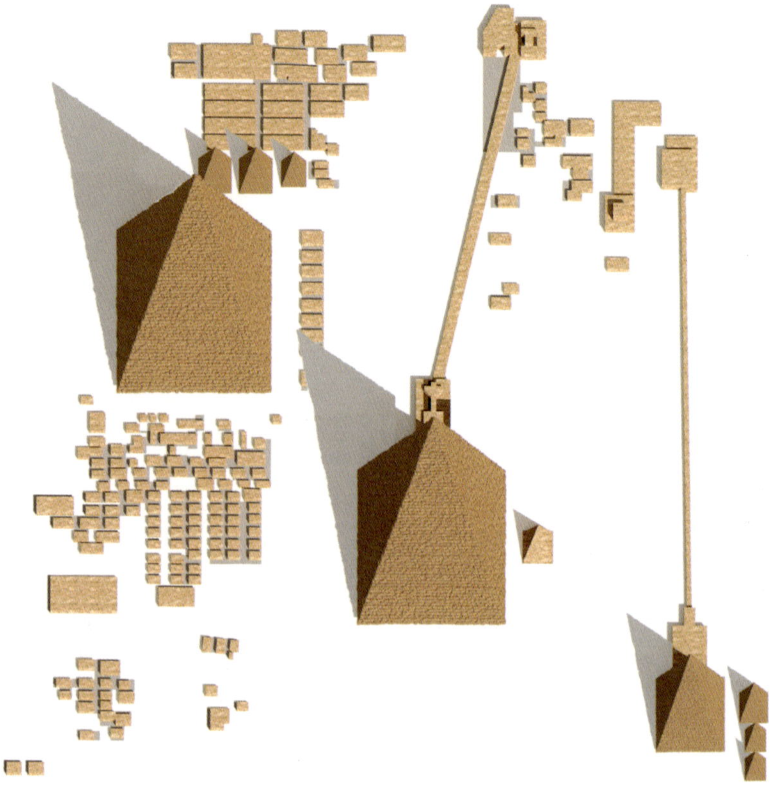

TOP: Plan oblique masterplan, **BOTTOM:** Oblique elevation

2.01 Great Pyramid of Giza, c. 2675–2565 B.C.

Architect: Unknown Location: Giza, Egypt
Project Type: Tomb Material: Limestone

The Great Pyramid of Giza is a recognizable image from the history of architecture, so much so that we may assume we already know it well. Built to entomb and safeguard the Pharaoh Khufu's body and belongings to facilitate his passage into the afterlife, its definitive role was as an icon that projected the authority and wealth of ancient Egypt and its Pharaoh. However, a close reading reveals this cultural icon is not entirely stable. That is, what would seem to be the most singular form and fixed image in this book is also profoundly indeterminate. Its legibility is progressively dissolved, muted by layered qualities of formal distortion and scalar ambiguity, and deformed through texture, color, and shadow. All of these contribute to the rewriting of its image.

As a Platonic form, the Great Pyramid is simple and readily comprehensible. In elevation, its three-dimensionality collapses into a flat triangular silhouette. The bold and singular profile can be read clearly against the sky, like a reductive symbol of a mountain. This abstract and otherworldly geology is the mountainous backdrop for the contemporary cityscape and residential enclaves that surround it to the east, north, and west. However, what appears at a distance like a mountain is a human-made construction. Further, what seems at first glance to be a perfect square pyramid is, in fact, an eight-sided figure that is distorted by a slight concavity in each face, visible in aerial view.[1] Neither pure geometry nor geology, the Great Pyramid is caught between two orders.

The clarity of the Great Pyramid's silhouette is further chipped away by its context. While the relationship between the Pyramid and the ground is stable in terms of its massing and structure, the ground destabilizes its form in a visual sense, entangling it with its background and obfuscating its autonomy. Looking to the south of the Giza Plateau, the dusty yellow structure blurs into the endless sandy backdrop of the Libyan Desert. As part of a vast necropolis, the Great Pyramid is joined by a suite of buildings: two other slightly smaller pyramids that are dedicated to Khufu's successors, Khafre and Menkaure; as well as the Sphinx, a series of smaller satellite pyramids, tombs, mortuary temples, and workers' housing — all of which also match the amber colored ground. This monochromatic wash visually eats away at the Great Pyramid's defined delineation from its surroundings.

The conflation of the material with the surrounding ground is authored not by an architect or builder, but by time. Once clad in polished white limestone from Tura with hairline joints and likely to have been completed by a sizable gold-plated capstone at its pinnacle, the Great Pyramid of Giza must have looked like a shimmering pentahedral sun.[2] Over time, it has been dramatically eroded, exposing the underlying granite megaliths that were quarried on site.[3] Made of the same material as the ground, the stones blend in with the surrounding bedrock and sand and assume its temporality. The weathered rustication of the facade situates the structure and complex in a geologic timetable, suggesting that the entropic winds of time will one day convert it into the anonymous particles of the desert floor.

When seen at a distance, the imprecise material approximation is rendered negligible, and the pure geometry comes into soft focus, subtly blurred by the textured surfaces. Floating in the emptiness of the desert, without its composite parts visible, the Great Pyramid does not explicitly reveal its scale. However, when viewed from the middle distance, the individual megaliths can be seen, and the image of the Platonic geometry pixelates. These stones could be read to determine scale, but each stone could be mistaken to be the size of a brick that fits in a human hand, even though it is far larger than a person. So the stone blocks work not as indicators of size relative to a human, but instead as obfuscators of this relationship that cause the structure's scale to be dramatically misread.

Further dissolving the clarity of the Great Pyramid's pure form is its sublimity, in the Kantian sense of its "formlessness" and "limitlessness."[4] Up close, its magnitude is overwhelming. Jeffrey Kipnis defines the "architectural sublime" through a mystified onlooker's reaction: "I didn't know man could build such things."[5] As the largest pyramid ever built, the Great Pyramid of Giza evokes this very astonishment at man's capacity to construct. It is composed of 2.5 million stone blocks that weigh 2.5 to 15 tons each, measuring roughly 760 feet at its base, and reaching a staggering 455 feet tall. So through its material and coloration, the structure subsumes the incomprehensible vastness of the desert into its form. The precision of its planning is equally astounding; all three pyramids are carefully situated in perfect alignment, such that each directs one face due north.

As a result of the three pyramids' orientation, shadow and illumination play into the misreading of form, scale, and distance. The northern faces are in perpetual shadow with the grid of blocks and rusticated texture visible only at the edges of the large black silhouettes. These faces cast large shadows across the site to the east and west and, despite the significant distance between them, the pyramids' heights are so great that the shadows even project the silhouette of one figure onto the next. Conversely, when two faces are fully illuminated the deteriorated corners are made more difficult to read, and the figure similarly flattens. However, for most of the day, the roughness of the stone creates mottled shadows, and light is dappled across the forms, creating the effect of a fuzzy image.

The surrounding pyramids shift in parallax on the horizon to produce ever-changing compositions that confuse any hierarchical differences. Due to the considerable distance between the main pyramids and the many satellite pyramids that surround them, there is a lack of information with which to establish scalar relationships, or that might clarify what is in the foreground, middle ground, and background. Distance becomes evident only at points where one figure passes in front of or behind another and betrays the relative sizes and elusive spatial relationship. For instance, from a single vantage point in the northeast, the three primary pyramids all collapse into one triangle, with Khafre and Menkaure hidden behind Khufu. At the northwest or southeast, they all fan out in a neat row with Khufu and Menakaure nearly symmetrically bounding the central Khafre. Viewed again from a vantage of subtle irregularity, the arrangement of the forms in space becomes apparent with layering and shadow revealing depth.

The muteness of the Great Pyramid's exterior is reified in section. Monolithic in the most literal sense, it has a solid stone core set on bedrock that forms its base. That said, it is not entirely solid; narrow passages and small interior chambers punctuate the mass. Flush-closure stone doors block any point of entry from the exterior or threshold to the interior, thereby reinforcing the structure's apparent solidity.

The interior is organized along this oblique such that it is best understood in section, with the predominant organization driven by moving up and down through the interior. Not unlike Boullée's Cenotaph for Newton, deep channels carve through the thick facade, piercing from the exterior to the Great Pyramid's center at The King's Chamber. These tunneling apertures cut through an astounding thickness, making apparent the monolithic nature of this structure.

Every quality and effect layered onto the Great Pyramid of Giza's Platonic geometry recasts it, silencing its pronounced image. What we might overlook as generic and simple is actually riddled with complexity and masked by lies about its purity, scale, and relationship to its surroundings. This project makes apparent the mute icon's duplicitous nature; the Great Pyramid exists as a contradiction of its perceived idealized form.

TOP: Oblique elevation close-up, BOTTOM: Diagrams, plan oblique

2.01. Great Pyramid of Giza

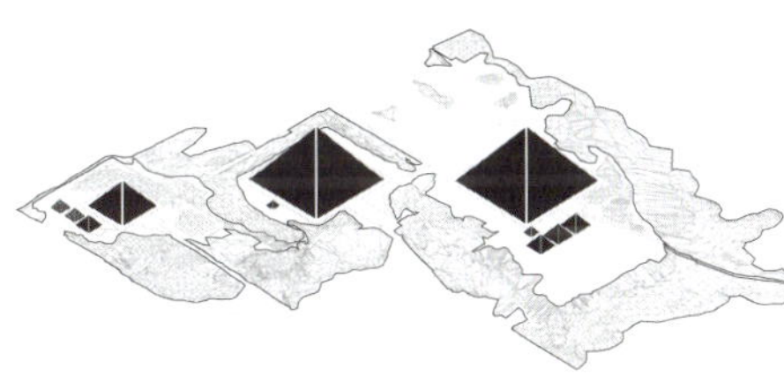

1 J.P. Lepre, *The Egyptian Pyramids: A Comprehensive, Illustrated Reference* (Jefferson, NC: Mcfarland, 2006), 65.
2 Ibid.
3 Ibid., 68. In addition to the weathering of the facade, historians suspect the casing was removed and tossed down the face of the Pyramid to be used for other buildings.
4 Immanuel Kant, trans. Werner S. Pluhar, *Critique of Judgment* (Indianapolis: Hackett, 2010), 128.
5 Jeffrey Kipnis, Thomas Ball, and Brian Neff; producer Jennifer Frutchy, *A Constructive Madness: Wherein Frank Gehry & Peter Lewis Spend a Fortune and a Decade, End up with Nothing and Change the World* (Cleveland: Telos Video Communications, 2003). Quoted from clip of Ridley Scott, *Gladiator* (Los Angeles: DreamWorks Distribution, 2000). In the clip the gladiator Juba is speaking to fellow gladiator Maximus as the two stare up in amazement at the Colosseum.

TOP: Worm's-eye isometric, BOTTOM: Oblique elevation

2.02 Qasr al-Farid Tomb, c. 1–75 A.D.

Architect: Unknown
Location: Mada'in Saleh, Saudi Arabia
Project Type: Monument Material: Carved Rock

The Qasr al-Farid Tomb resists definition; its form falls between ground and building, its status between found and authored. It is a composite of different ontological orders, merged in a single mass. While the clarity of its image places it in the realm of the iconic, its character is deceptive, duplicitous, and withdrawn.

Translated from Arabic as "The Lonely Castle," Qasr al-Farid is a solitary figure in the barren Arabian Desert. It is an autonomous object, with the blank ground and sky as its only context. The funerary site — just southwest of the city center of Mada'in Saleh — provides no evidence of any neighboring development. Only a few of the surrounding 93 monumental tombs carved by the Nabataeans appear off in the distance.[1] The convex curve of the boulder's base rests on the sandy terrain, implying its independence from the ground. All of this allows its silhouette to remain uninterrupted and highly legible. However, its edges are not as stable as they initially seem.

The tomb presents a dichotomy between nature and architecture, between the found object — a gigantic boulder — and the designed facade, an ornamented frontispiece. Around most of the megalith, the elevations look only to be natural stone surface, but the northwest elevation depicts the elements of an architectural facade. As a true monolith, its builders carved the facade and the interior from a megalith without any need for assembled parts. The process of its creation and its resulting visual effect bears more of a resemblance to a *non-finito*[2] sculpture than to a building. The naturally formed, rusticated surface of the boulder makes for a profile that is too articulated to be imageable, one that is further contradicted by its carving.

Qasr al-Farid's silhouette is weakened not only by the texture of the stone face but also by the profile of its carved portion. An asymmetrical wedge was removed from the face of the boulder. What remains is an exterior corner where the carved face intersects with the rock's untouched striations at the eastern edge of the facade. Conversely, the remaining rock face frames the western side of the rectangular facade within an interior corner. The tomb's "loneliness" is ultimately realized in the withdrawing of its front face. Here, the remaining rock frames the central and symmetrical facade, producing a backdrop for the object within itself. As a result, the tomb has a double silhouette: (1) the rectangular profile of its carved face, backgrounded by the boulder and (2) the irregular profile of the boulder against the blue of the sky. Surreal in its combination, the two faces of the tomb are visually separable and, at the same time, entangled as superimposed figures.

The excised wedge also leaves a shallow chunk of material remaining at the base that acts as an integrated plinth. This plinth further complicates the object's relationship to the ground, forming a new ground that is integral to its mass. Visitors can access to the tomb by crossing a subtly sloping terrain that reaches up toward the merged plinth. The slight difference in level and distinction between the loose sand of the ground and the solid rock of the plinth reasserts the autonomy of the tomb from its site.

Undermining Qasr al-Farid's separation from the ground is the fact that it is a geologic landform. It is much like the Great Pyramid of Giza that was quarried on site, but in this case, the ground is not cut into blocks and piled into a new form. Rather, it is left as is, with only a small area reshaped through carving. As with the Pyramid, the seamless and all-encompassing sandy color of the desert landscape and the tomb merge to produce a monochromatic image. The shared materiality of the two further deteriorates their clear separation.

The carving is of two distinct orders: rigorous manual sculpting and random geologic erosion. Written evidence of labor and ownership are inscribed on the facade, integrating time into its surface.[3] However, it is the pile of sand deposited by the wind around the tomb's base that implies a material ecology, one which exposes both human and geologic labor involved in carving the megalith. In the overlap of boulder and architecture, historic and geologic time detach from the rock and leave a profound ambiguity as to its history.

The rough naturality of the rock face contrasts sharply with the smooth and ornamented facade. The carved portion is recognizable as architecture, borrowing stylistic elements from Assyria, Phoenicia, Egypt, and Hellenistic Alexandria.[4] The smooth carving portrays oversized details, including four disproportionately large pilasters, stepped projections, and a broad entablature. Even with these details, the face is austere and reductive. The result is a defeatured symbol that depicts the constituent components of an architectural facade. These chiseled features merely represent parts, but ones that adhere to the whole as they are carved out of solid rock.

While we could say that there is more detail in the area that was manipulated by tools to procure orthogonal edges and ornamental details, this face is sparse and has far less surface articulation than the naturally formed mass of the boulder. In fact, at the line where they interface, the boulder's texture and the carved features of the facade might even appear to be intertwined. A close reading blurs the distinction between the two, suggesting that the base of the entablature and other horizontals align to the natural striations that circumscribe the boulder. Given the fusion of the two, it is possible to read the natural rock face as being layered in densely packed, fine-grain detail. These conflicting systems produce an uneasy reading of the object's scale in the otherwise scaleless site.

The striations across the rock heighten its relationship to images. This texture appears as "lines of resolution" on a damaged screen or stripes across a printout from a printer that is nearly out of ink. Between this and its juxtaposition that seems more like photo-editing than an extant artifact, the boulder resists easy interpretation. It infiltrates the realm of image production to become an image-object. Qasr al-Farid's image-like qualities allow it to slip between definitions and realities. Its past does not appear tied to truth, unhinging its formal origins from a singular narrative. The monumentality of its form withdraws, allowing it to exist as object and background, figure and ground.

1 Eric A. Powell, "Petra's Sister City," *Archaeology*, Vol. 63, No. 4 (July/August 2010), 21.
2 A sculpting technique meaning "unfinished" in which an artist sculpts only part of the stone block, leaving the figure to appear to be emerging from the unrefined material chunk.
3 Powell, 22.
4 Ibid.

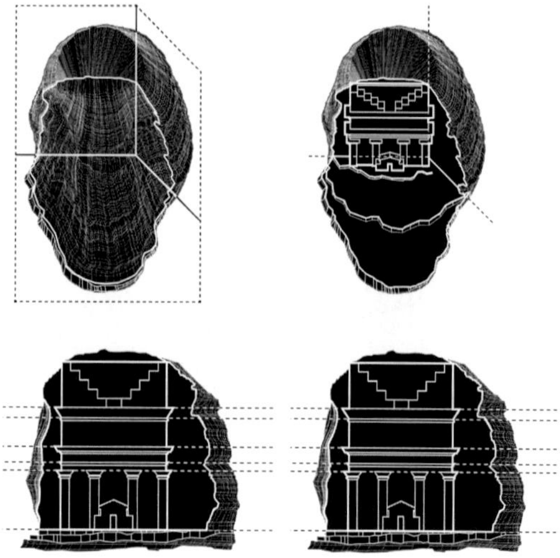

ABOVE: Diagrams

2.02. Qsar al-Farid Tomb

TOP: Plan oblique, oblique elevation, **BOTTOM:** Oblique elevation

ABOVE: Plan oblique

2.03 Quéribus Castle, 13th century

Architect: Unknown Location: Languedoc-Roussillon, Aude, Cucugnan, France
Project Type: Castle Material: Limestone

The Quéribus Castle casts a lone silhouette on the uninterrupted horizon, becoming an image as much as it is a building. The fortress is a visual synonym of the rock and the geologic formation of the mountain on which it precariously rests. Built by France to defend the country's border with Spain, it occupies a defensive overlook on a precipice. An icon of power and military defense, the Castle is a human-made, impenetrable addition to a mountain.

Piled atop a steep site, the Quéribus Castle assumes the scale and verticality of the mountainous terrain on which it sits. The longitudinal axis of the fortress runs parallel with the steep surface of the rock outcropping below and with the Pyrenees Mountain ridgeline further below still. Conflicting definitions of ground and object abound: there is the mountain as ground, the rock outcropping that sits atop the mountain as an object that simultaneously creates a new ground, and the object of the Castle that rests atop the new ground of the outcropping. This deferral of the ground and repetition of the object throws any typical relationship between the two into question.

The terraced form looks to be a large complex descending the slope of the crest when, in fact, it is but a single fortified tower with an adjoining chapel. The other chunks, which make the fortification appear to be much more extensive than it is, are mere foundations put in place to retain the surrounding surfaces that grant access to the tower. The Castle and its walls appear to be embedded — tapering to disappear into the rock's irregular contours — and, at the same time, precariously piled at the edge of a precipice, stacked irregularly and looking to be just moments from collapsing.

Given their visual similarity, the fortress and monolith on which it sits are made equivalent, reinforcing the apparent solidity of the tower. From the exterior, the masonry structure is visually impenetrable and appears to be just as solid as the rock. The rock acts as a natural plinth, with its grey limestone formation matching the facade of the keep and tower above. Even the stain of time is present on the facade and rock alike, with calcite discolorations streaking the limestone, and plants growing in the mortar joints.

But even with their equivalence, at a distance, the rock and fortress remain distinct and contradictory. The fortification is geometrically precise with smooth walls at its center, plain in character and without ornament of any kind. It is only accented by its pock-marked rustication and the rubble walls at its base. The walls' irregular planimetric organization, which responds to the available footprint as the rock falls off more steeply, follows precise lines and curves at the edges. The precision of the smooth stone and orthogonal walls is dichotomous with the rock's rough-hewn faces. The tower projects a megalithic profile that looks like another rock, albeit a geometric version of one.

However, viewed up close and examining the interior, the distinction between rock and building blurs again. In a state of ruin, the once crisp edges of the openings at the Quéribus Castle have dematerialized over time leaving rough edges and violent punctures in the facade. Jambs are broken, leaving open breaches with irregular contours that follow the edge of the rough-hewn stones. In the plan, it is clear that there is a thick stone poché only punctuated by a few passageways, apertures, a chamber, and a spiral staircase. The solidity of the tower and its surrounds is made all the more uncanny due to repairs that have sealed the already narrow arrowslits with the same limestone used for the original masonry work.

With time, the nearly solid building is becoming all the more solid, and its geometric precision is reverting to its rocky origins. The Quéribus Castle is a monolith, mute in its ability to assume the appearance and solidity of its context. And yet it remains detached, an image of its pronounced silhouette that is hybrid of geometry and geology.

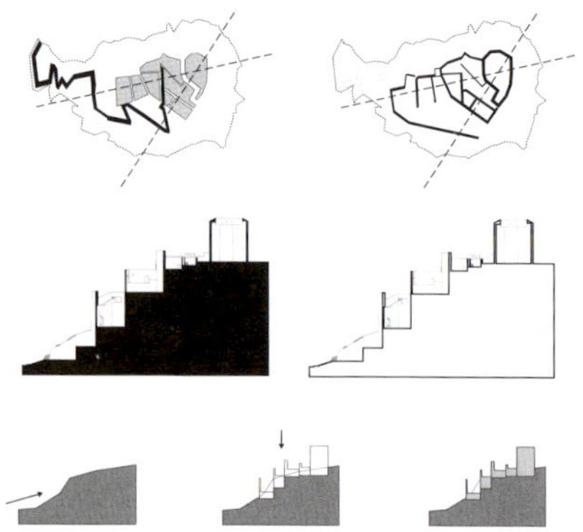

TOP: Diagrams, **BOTTOM:** Elevation close-up

TOP: Worm's-eye isometric, BOTTOM: Elevation

ABOVE: Isometric with context

2.04 Church of St. George, Lalibela, c. 1137–1270 A.D.

Architect: Unknown **Location:** Lalibela, Ethiopia
Project Type: Church **Material:** Carved Stone

The object is the sign — a building that is a cross — at the Church of St. George. But in no other historical case has the cruciform shape been of greater consequence to the architectural icon than in this small, rock-hewn church. The sign, form, and mass are all conflated in one image. The carved, cruciform-rock's roofline is level with the surrounding earth, centered in a cubic void that extends 40 feet below grade. As such, the cruciform figure of the plan becomes the main building facade.

The Church of St. George is both unified with and autonomous from the ground. Its strong relationship with the ground comes from the fact that it is carved directly out of the rock on which it sits and has no discrete tectonic parts. As such, the mass shares the same gritty texture of the rust-colored volcanic rock and is similarly ornamented with chartreuse moss. Situated below the verdant terrain that is punctuated by bedrock, the cruciform's uppermost extent is roughly level with the ground and continues its datum. The flat top surface of the mass is an approximation of the undulating ground that moves up and down to conceal or reveal the mass below.

Conversely, the church's autonomy is clear in that it is an object; it is completely separated from the sides of the excavation. This separation is amplified in the geometric precision and orthogonality of St. George's cruciform figure. There are even engraved cruciform offsets etched into its top face, as well as ornament and aperture that distinguish it in elevation. The void negotiates the orthogonality of the building and the conditions of the site, but it is close to a perfect square and is bluntly cut to clearly define the void's edges. The irregularity of the rolling hill of the ground makes the extruded cruciform shape appear all the more radical in its simplicity.

While historically architecture has been thought of as emerging from the inhabitable datum of the ground, in the case of St. George, the building emerges from underground. At a distance, only the top of the cruciform is visible. The elevations can only be seen from a typical vantage — at the base of the building — after a visitor descends a subterranean labyrinth of grottos and narrow passageways. For a moment, these visitors occupy the surrounding void then reenter the near solid of the building mass. This aspect of spatial and temporal deferral makes the experience of the project all the more earthy as the visitors penetrate the ground's solidity.

Scenes of pilgrims populating the ground at the void's edge and in the excavated areas below are profound. From pedestrian level, the perception of the church hinges on anticipation in light of visual absence. Architecture is both ground and object, monument and space, nature and artifice, everything and nothing. First, you see the building but can't access it. Then, you descend beneath the ground and can no longer see the object in its entirety since you are too close to back away. The building's continuity with the ground creates a strange sense of multiple horizons as the virtual datum is continuously reconstructed by the visitors in their approach. It even eludes a stable relationship to vocabulary and experience by doubling grounds and interiors.

Despite its remote location, the Church of St. George can only be viewed as if in an urban context. It can be seen either from an aerial view — an urban one, as if from the roof of a neighboring building — or seen up close, as if from a constricted urban alley. The object-building is tied to, or seen from within, the frame of its context. Like an inverted plinth, the void separates the built object from its context, but by submerging rather than lifting, the building becomes indelibly tied to the ground that frames it.

The overlap of experience and plan view privilege the iconic image of the project. The solidity of that experience and the tension between ground and object, engagement or independence, increase the project's opacity and unstable status. The Church of St. George's characteristic contradictions overwrite the clarity of its form and perpetually reframe any understanding of it.

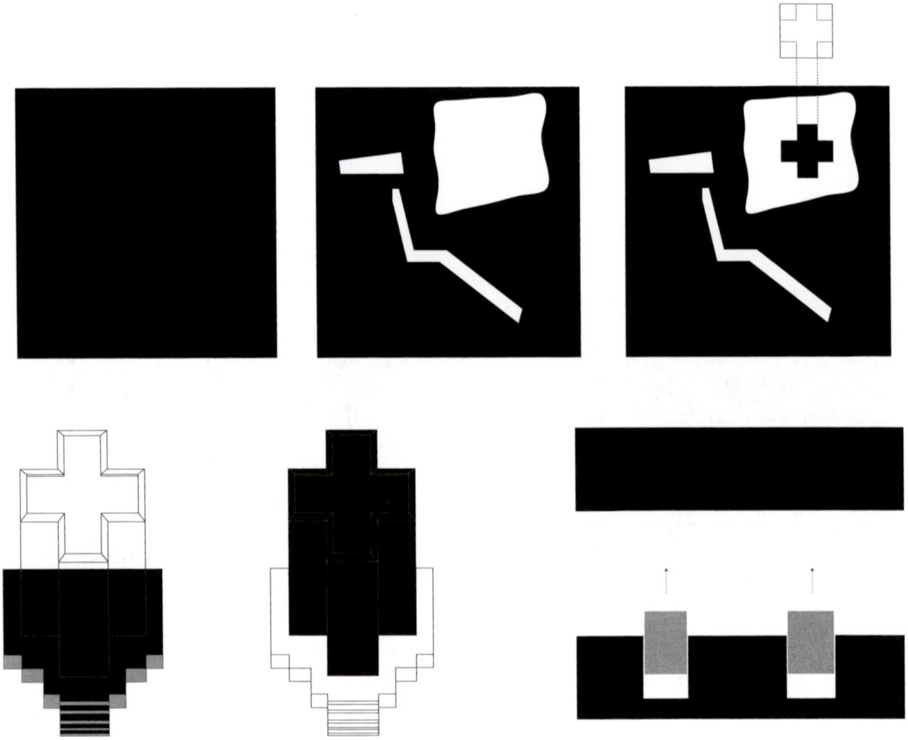

TOP: Plan oblique, **BOTTOM:** Diagrams

TOP: Worm's-eye isometric, **BOTTOM:** Oblique section

2.04. Church of St. George, Lalibela

ABOVE: Plan oblique

2.05 First House of the Lumbermen, 1804

Architect: Claude-Nicolas Ledoux
Location: Chaux, Arc-et-Senans, France
Project Type: Residence Material: Logs and Stone

The iconicity of Claude-Nicolas Ledoux's First House of the Lumbermen resides in its pyramidal silhouette, its relationship to the surrounding forest and nearby city, the set of referential forms it calls into play, and its deliberate relationship to function. Yet each of these is suppressed by a multiplicity of contradictions. The silhouette is singular and a composite of many, the relationship to context is overt and subversive, the form is referential and Platonic, and the visual ties to function are undermined by its strange characteristics.

Like the bulk of Ledoux's ideal city, the First House of the Lumbermen remains unrealized. The house's context was imagined to be the Forest of Chaux, located to the northwest of Ledoux's Royal Saltworks at Arc-et-Senans. Ledoux envisioned the Royal Saltworks expanded into an ideal, self-sufficient city he called Chaux, which was to include labor, residential, government, and punitive buildings and would complete the circumference of the Saltworks' semi-circular form.[1] Each building in the city is depicted in his publication of 1804, *L'architecture considérée sous le rapport de l'art, des moeurs, et de la legislation — Architecture Considered in Terms of Art, Morals, and Legislation*. Among these depictions is a perspectival etching of the First House of the Lumbermen.

In the etching, the house sits at a remove from the dense patches of forest and occupies an opening such that its profile is highly visible. The dwellings for lumbermen were to be set at the intersections of the forest's allées in order to provide access to the city and to use the lumbermen's houses as surveillance at the center of many routes through the forest.[2] But most interesting about the etching is the relationship of the house to the natural surroundings. The house is clearly different from the vegetation, both materially distinct and formally abrupt. However, the vegetation is choreographed into clusters of trees that mirror the pyramidal profile of the house's roofline. This suggests a dichotomy between the house as an autonomous artifice that is distinct from nature and the house as a calculated assembly of nature.

This tension with context extends to the House of the Lumberman's relationship to the city. The organization of the house's interior is similar to the plan organization of the city it serves. The interior has a fireplace, peripheral bedrooms, and four openings that face outward, all laid out around a hollow center. Its cross axes are similar to those of the city, which is also vacant at its center, bounded along its perimeter with buildings that are interrupted by extending, radial paths. As such, the house is both a part of the city and an autonomous replication of it.

The Lumbermen's House is an unsteady figure; while its stark silhouette is a stepped pyramid — a quickly apprehended image — multiple profiles intertwine and compete with its dominant roofline. Composed of a truncated pyramid set atop a cubic structure, the two are formally merged. The cubic base meets the ground, acting as a plinth and lifting the pyramid, thus deferring its relationship with the ground. Compounding their interrelation, the top profile of the cube is not simply cut off by the pyramid but follows an alternate profile created by ramped steps that encircle the cube's perimeter. The composite figure is highly legible, but its shifting between Cartesian and two sets of oblique geometry disrupts this legibility.

This is made explicit in the depiction of the house on its corner, revealing two symmetrical facades. Despite their symmetry, the two sides are inversions of one another. The left is highlighted, revealing the stepping of myriad planes and contrasting with the deep shadows that darken the interior and cause each opening to appear more solid than its exterior. The right side of the etching veils the facade in dark shadow, favoring the singular silhouette. However, where the two meet at the corner, light crosses irregularly into shadow, revealing the three-dimensional intersections of the mass that show the complexity of its composite silhouette.

There is a dualism to the house; cube and pyramid, plinth and hip roof, form a set of contradictions further complicated by material resolution. Following from the etched, horizontal striations of the drawing that cover the sky, ground, and roof, Ledoux's etching depicts a roof composed of horizontal logs, felled from the surrounding forest.[3] The walls on the partial cube below are rendered with vertical lines and imply a base would be smooth, perhaps wood deployed in a planar fashion or plastered brick and mortar. The stark contrast between a horizontally-textured pyramidal shape and smooth, square base creates a powerful and unresolved tension.

Further complicating its figure, the Platonic geometry of the cube and pyramid are juxtaposed with and allude to archetypal elements and forms selected from architecture. The lower, stepped roofline resembles a blank pediment. The symmetrical entry on each face includes a Venetian door framed by square pillars that resemble a triumphal arch. From Egyptian pyramids to Palladian villas, the project is a dense complex of heretofore unrelated references, each of which is easily legible.

The Lumbermen's House is intended to reflect its function but productively depletes this clarity with formal oppositions. Ledoux intended for it to be composed of logs and to be unadorned in order to emphasize its rurality and to clarify the occupation of its inhabitants. In effect, the program is tied to its material and character, making it an icon for its function. As Anthony Vidler notes,

> What had been, since the late seventeenth century, a vague and polite admonition to architects that their buildings should be endowed with a character "suitable to them and to no other," now became an overriding theory and practice of expression... a pictorial rule whereby the entire building must be marked according to its own nature.[4]

However, its role as an icon of its function is undercut. Why should a lumberman live and work in a pyramid? Even its functionality as a house is questionable, given its continuity, lack of overhangs, and limited aperture. Why should a house appear monolithic? The conflation of types is performed seamlessly, and the character is in conflict due to this conflation.

The First House of the Lumbermen is not straightforward. It is a hybridized crossover of form, type, image, and character. These are all productive dualisms that mute the original expression of the pyramid. As a result, the geometry is obscured, not as absolute as a singular Platonic solid, yet equally powerful.

1 Emil Kaufmann, *Three Revolutionary Architects: Boullée Ledoux, and Lequeu* (Philadelphia: Transactions of the American Philosophical Society, Vol. 42, No. 3, 1952), 476.

2 Anthony Vidler, "The Theatre of Production: Claude-Nicolas Ledoux and the Architecture of Social Reform," *AA Files*, No. 1 (Winter 1981–82), 62.

3 Kaufmann, 527, 535.

4 Vidler, 62.

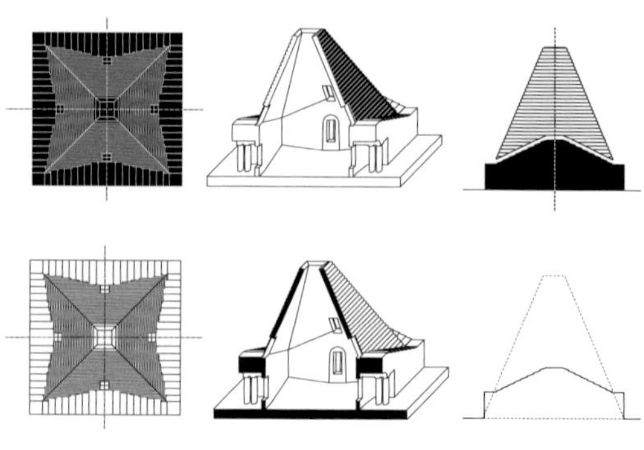

ABOVE: Diagrams

TOP: Isometric close-up, BOTTOM: Worm's-eye isometric

ABOVE: Plan oblique

2.06 Cénotaphe à Newton, 1784

Architect: Étienne-Louis Boullée Location: France
Project Type: Monument Material: Stone

The iconicity of Boullée's unbuilt Cenotaph is connected to its spherical shape and enormous scale. The funerary monument, dedicated to Sir Isaac Newton, is depicted in a set of rendered drawings that emphasize the play of light and shadow. The representation flickers back and forth between light and shadow, solid and void, iconic and mute, abstraction and realism, where these categories are not simple dualisms but a cluster of oscillating contradictions.

The sphericity of the project is omnipresent, repeated in the cylindrical plinths, the cutaway of the plinth that traces the continuity of the sphere's edge below its midline, and even the spherical entrance that leads into an arched tunnel. Everything echoes the curvilinear. Boullée praises the sphere as "the image of perfection"[1] due to its geometric properties:

> Every point on its surface is equidistant from its centre. The result of this unique advantage is that from whatever angle we look at it, no optical effect can ever spoil the magnificent beauty of its shape which, to our eyes, will always be perfect.... It has the simplest possible form, the beauty of which derives from its uninterrupted surface.[2]

Boullée's emphasis on sphericality privileges analytical thought and geometric order, but to the ends of aesthetic effect. Spheres have no orientation; they imply an equality in the equidistance of all surfaces from the center. Boullée's choice of the sphere is a deeply political one and suggests the potential of mute icons to subvert existing hierarchies.

The Cenotaph's enormity makes it all the more iconic, breaking down a clear reading of scale. What appears to be the ground is, in fact, a large, square plinth surrounded by cypress trees. In the elevation, stairs are cut into this platform, clarifying that it is raised at least 10 feet off the ground. Set atop the first plinth are three terraced cylinders, the first two lined with cypress trees and a third cylinder hidden behind the trees, all of which encircle the 500-foot sphere. The sphere is fully embedded in these layers. If the cylindrical podiums were removed, the sphere would meet with the square plinth, touching at only one point. In effect, the supersized square podium nullifies the spherical curvature of the Earth's surface and sites Boullée's sphere in pure geometry. And it is not only the one new ground but the hybrid object-ground cylinders that overtake and completely eliminate the terrestrial ground in the drawings — there's simply no room for it on the page.

Issues of scale are raised not only in the project's implied scale but also in its representation. Boullée lavished the rendered drawings with so much detail that they behave differently when viewed at a remove or in close range. At a distance, the image only depicts the large features of its mass and outline, privileging the austerity of its Platonic forms. When viewed close up, a finer grain is revealed; material units, vegetation, and human figures populate the image, indicating its monumental scale. Given their stark contrast, the representations suggest that architecture should hide rather than show. Seeing the project up close, or even entering would mean something completely different than seeing it from afar. Layering atmosphere on geometry, the form of the Cenotaph is a hybrid object melded with its shadows.

In the portion of his text *Architecture, Essay on Art* entitled "Character," Boullée describes architecture as the art of combining volumes "in such a way that there is a great deal of play among them" in their part-to-whole relationships.[3] And character, Boullée argued, comes out of "producing no other sensations than those related to the subject."[4] While interested in ancient models like the Egyptian pyramids, Boullée's primary fixation was in the combinations of Platonic geometry and the apprehension of these through optical effect. The character of these forms in combination is decidedly austere, echoed in the chiaroscuro renderings. Both form and shadow calibrate the Cenotaph's muteness. Mute in its opacity, the project appears solid despite its hollow interior.

Importantly the scalar indicators that can be seen up close are not the product of surface decoration. Instead, the powerful effect of shadow across the Platonic form is emphasized. Herein, shadows supplant ornament, silencing its attributes and ornamenting it in unknowability. This "architecture of shadows"[5] is deeply sublime, simultaneously powerful, somber, and sinister. The drama of these images is tied to Picturesque aspects that misalign with Boullée's rational tendencies.[6] This effort to "reconcile the irreconcilable"[7] in combining the theatricality of the Picturesque and the purity of geometry[8] — two aesthetic regimes typically confined to separate worlds — makes an outcome that is entirely other.

Characteristic of the edgeless surfaces, diffuse shadows obscure the form of the Cenotaph, contradicting its clear profile and singularity. The one-point, elevational perspective shows an eerie luminous presence projected on the cutaway of the plinth. The shadow that frames it is mysterious; its edge matches that of the solid sphere above, producing an uncanny duplication of the circular profile on the face of the plinth. However, it is not clear what is shadowing the sphere. Perhaps the most likely answer is that this shadow's cast implies that the Cenotaph is so large that the profile of the sun can be read across its surface with clearly delineated edges. In this interpretation, the sun's eclipsing projection is a perfect equal to the sphere's size.

In fact, the Cenotaph has an unstable relationship with the sun on its interior. Through its haunting images, the project inverts day and night. During the day, the dome's interior surface is covered in stars, with the section revealing these as simulated by pinholes piercing through the thick shell of the sphere. At night, the interior is washed in light, as the sarcophagus and stars disappear and are replaced by a glowing armillary sphere suspended at the geometric center of the void. The armillary sphere appears to contain a second sun, operating on exact opposite schedule of the one that governs the world outside the Cenotaph. This creates an inversion of time within the discrete world of the Cenotaph; when it is day outside, it is night inside, and vice versa. We can see this as a response to Diderot's challenge: "I defy the most daring of our artists to suspend the sun or moon in the middle of his composition.... I defy him to give us a sky like nature's, sprinkled with glittering stars as is might be on the clearest night."[9] What is made clear in the enaction of light in the renderings is that the project does not favor purity or realism — which would seem to rule these representations at first glance — as much as it does the capacity of shadow and light to alter the reading of form, space, atmosphere, and time.

At the center of Boullée's project is a scalar conundrum related to this same tension with reality. The Cenotaph's interior is in excess of its exterior. The small sarcophagus within the vast sphere is a nested architectural situation, one with its own clouds, its own sun, and its own cosmic array of stars. It would seem that the interior relies on magic. A temporal mirror that follows the spherical boundary of the building envelope, flipping the behavior of time and refracting the universe across its centerline produces the illusion of an artificial universe, a duplicated infinity. Architecture is the horizon between two oppositional twin realities, that of the interior and that of the exterior.

Between geometry and effect, light and shadow, interior and exterior, the Cenotaph foregrounds contradiction. Emil Kaufmann defines this radical potential of Boullée's work: "... no longer is there that balance of power which was essential to Classic and Baroque architecture, unifying and harmonizing the dominant and

TOP: Oblique elevation, BOTTOM: Section

the subordinate parts. Here we have the irreconcilable contrasts of the small and the large, the finite and the infinite, the mortal and the immortal."[10] It is the interior that is deeply theatrical, with hanging objects and atmospheric effects, supplying a strong counterpoint to the withdrawn exterior. The section exploits the possibilities of poché, asserting the experiential and psychological power of extreme contrast between interior and exterior, solid and void. From interior to exterior there is a form of experiential delay that asserts the project's otherworldliness.

1 Etienne Louis Boullée, ed. Helen Rosenau, trans. Sheila De. Vallée, *Architecture, Essay on Art* (London: Academy Editions, 1976), 86.
2 Ibid.
3 Ibid., 89.
4 Ibid.
5 Ibid., 90.
6 Emil Kaufmann, *Three Revolutionary Architects: Boullée, Ledoux, and Lequeu* (Philadelphia: American Philosophical Society, 1960), 469.
7 Ibid., 473.
8 Ibid.
9 Jean-Claude Lemagny, *Visionary Architects: Boullee, Ledoux, Lequeu* (New York: S.W. Swan Services, 1968), 31.
10 Kaufmann, 469.

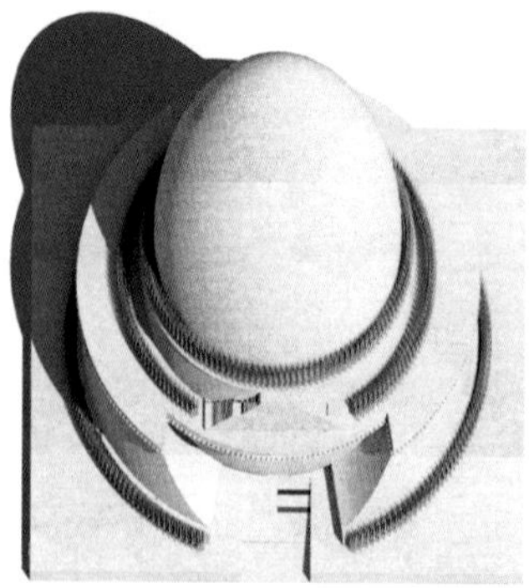

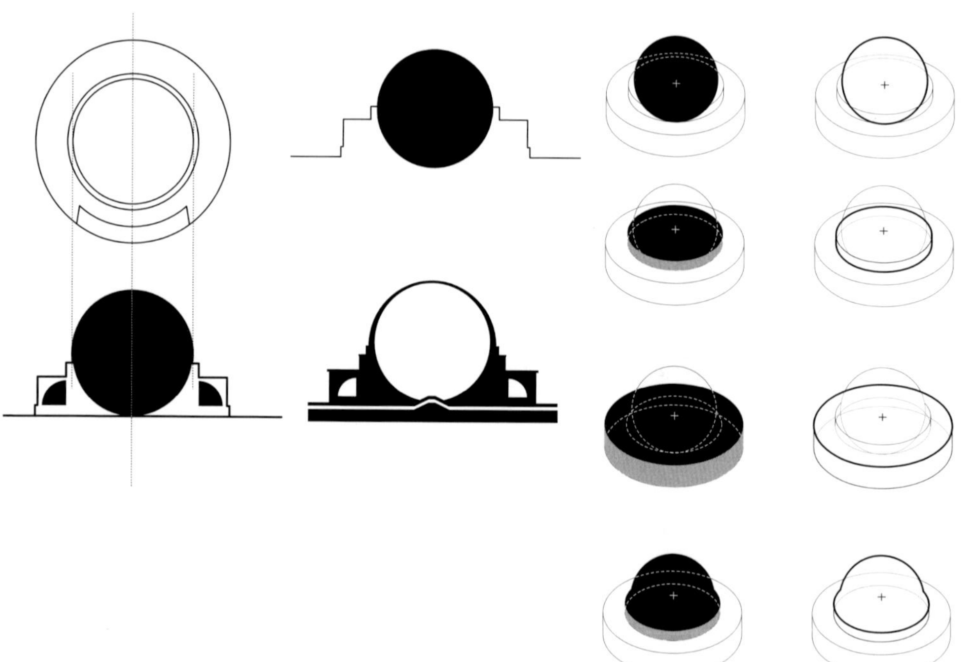

TOP: Plan oblique, **BOTTOM:** Diagrams

TOP: Worm's-eye isometric, BOTTOM: Oblique elevation

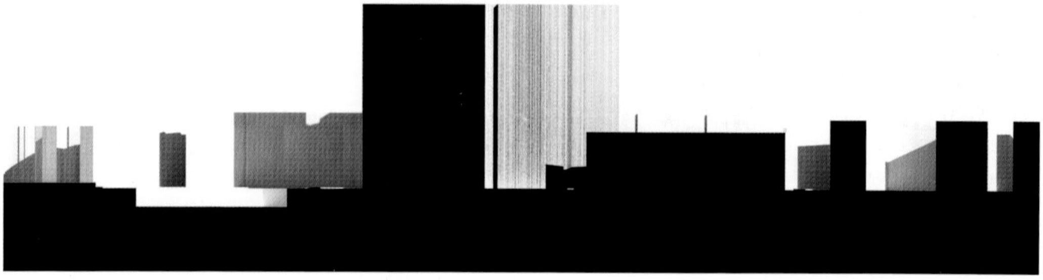

TOP: Worm's-eye isometric, **BOTTOM:** Oblique section

2.07 Friedrichstrasse Skyscraper, 1921

Architect: Ludwig Mies van der Rohe
Location: Berlin, Germany
Project Type: Office **Material:** Glass Curtain Wall

Mies van der Rohe's unbuilt Freidrichstrasse Skyscraper competition entry was as a radical proposal, one that was unprecedented and unrealizable in its time. It was the first skyscraper to be envisioned as a monumental hollow crystal, a steel skeleton clad entirely in glass without a structural or decorative masonry frame. But what makes the project relevant to the mute icon is not found in the typical descriptions of its historical significance. Rather, it is the set of drawings as a whole that illuminates the project's peculiar paradox; its representations present inconstant material effects and aesthetic qualities.

The iconicity of the plan is found in its vegetal or geologic profile. The shape implies natural or ancient history, and yet would have required the most sophisticated construction technology imaginable at the time to realize it as a built form. The volumetric envelope is inscribed in the triangle of the site, bounded by the busy shopping street Friedrichstrasse, the Spree River, and the Spree Train Station. The volume splinters along its edges as it draws back to expose the core located at the center of its three-pronged mass. Given the depth of the concavities between its parts, each could be mistaken for an independent building when depicted in perspective. However, given the interconnected nature of the parts, the project is entirely monolithic in elevation; it is capped at the same height, thereby muting any form of difference that might emanate from the plan.

The most well-known among the drawings Mies produced for and after the competition is a photomontage perspective. In this drawing, a darkened photograph of Friedrichstrasse is lined with stone facades, doubly concealing their interiors in shadowed opacity. The tower stands in luminous opposition, its stacked plates barely concealed behind a transparent layer of glass. Mies' descriptions of the glass curtain wall hover between a desire for invisibility — initially wishing to propose an unenclosed framework "open to the air"[1] without any cladding — and a profoundly new kind of visibility. To the latter point, in the architect's own description, "the important thing [with a glass envelope] is the play of reflections and not the effect of light and shadow as in ordinary buildings."[2] Mies' intent was to render glass in its reflectivity, as surfaces under constant transformation. Both transparency and reflection are present in the drawings as a set, existing in duplicitous tension and depleting its static imageability across the set.

But this translucent photomontage with horizontal floor plates — the version code-named "Honeycomb" — is not the only perspective that Mies produced. There are a number of alternate versions of this perspective. One, in particular, shows vertical striations on an opaque facade that obscures its floor plates. When articulated as such, the project appears more monumental, and its true size is unclear. While it's likely that Mies simply revised the project's representation in favor of the "Honeycomb," it is the unsettling difference between these images that increases the project's intrigue. Imbued with two entirely different natures, the very inconstancy of the representation destabilizes the image of the project.

Even more interesting than the opaque perspective is the largely uncelebrated charcoal elevation. It portrays a monolithic and textured square on a blank page. Neither the horizontal nor the vertical fully supplant one another as they do in the various versions of the perspective; rather, there is a lightly traced grid that favors the vertical. Most confounding to its other visual descriptions, the "hovering lightness"[3] of its glass surfaces appears to have been traded in for a darkened weight. We might consider its solidity to be the optical illusion of reflection and refraction, but there is little evidence in the drawing of either luminous effect glinting across smooth surfaces. Instead, its surfaces look to be textured and under the play of light and shadow — that very stuff of the past that Mies claimed to reject.

The facade moves in and out of shadow to demarcate volumetric depth; the deeper the concave corner in the facade, the darker the blackening of the surface. Dappled with a thick atmosphere of texture, the materiality and scale of the Friedrichstrasse Skyscraper are thrown entirely into question. Instead of the glass tower with legible floor-to-floor heights, the facade veils its interior under what looks to be any of a number of things: a textured stone surface, the fluted chunk of doric columns, or the drapery lines of curtains just behind a curtain wall screen.

Paired with the other drawings in the set, the elevation is able to hover ambivalently between transparency and opacity. It's worth noting that the old stone facades — which figured prominently in the photomontage perspective and are even modeled in the later Curvilinear Glass Skyscraper's model photos — are conspicuously absent in this drawing. The elevation doesn't need to depict the opposition between glossy abstraction and brutal realism because it is enacted as an internalized binary across the set of depictions. The context has become internal to the facade, visually superimposed onto it and suppressing its sheen of near immateriality. But, despite its ties to its context, the character of the elevation is clearly different from that which surrounds it. Undecorated and without any significant material differentiation to punctuate the facade, Mies' skyscraper remains anomalous to 1921 Berlin. Through its duplicitous renditions, the tower becomes both strange and familiar to the surrounding city fabric.

The stone mirage that can be seen in the elevation shares some affinities — albeit fictional — with the skeletal frame. Both versions of the project are in a state of becoming: the composing of a frame under construction, and the decomposing of a rusticated stone facade as time wears it into an ancient ruin. The ruin and the glass tower as one coincident project can be characterized in Mario Gooden's terms as "the ultimate erotic object caught between sensuality and rationalism, revealing both the 'traces of reason' and the 'sensual experience of space.'"[4] The tower is a geometrical rationalization crossed with a material object under the influence of phenomena. Read as such, the Freidrichstrasse Skyscraper is an enigma to either rational or sensual realms, thereby transcending traditional categorization.

All this said, it is impossible to discount Mies' articulation of his clear preference for the invisible envelope: "In the course of their construction... skyscrapers show their bold, structural character.... [W]hen the facades are later covered with masonry this impression is destroyed and the constructive character denied."[5] Considering this preference, perhaps the solid appearance is a trick played on the jury to convince them to build the tower, or it mirrors the stony reality of its context, or it is a glass wall in front of curtains; regardless of its imagined reality, it brings to light Deitrich Neumann's observation that the project isn't based in the rational revelation of structure. Mies' interests lie in "the display of load-bearing structure for the creation of magical effects, optical illusions, and poetry."[6] Simultaneously eluding and subsuming its context through the magic of optical effects, the tower masks its material and structural properties in mystery. The Friedrichstrasse Skyscraper's mirrored surfaces are just as readily an uncanny stone wallpaper.

TOP: Plan oblique, **BOTTOM:** Diagrams

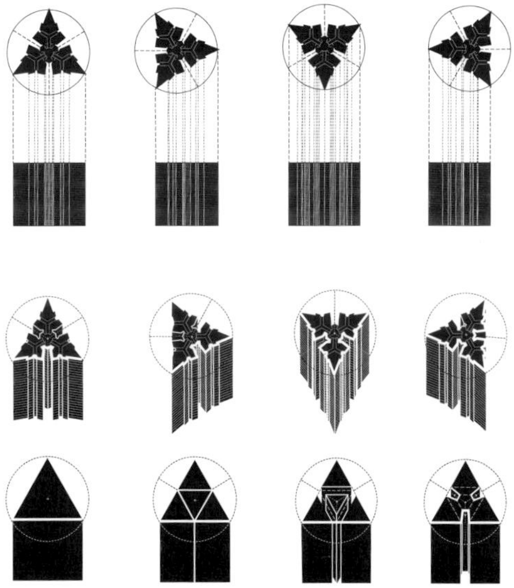

1 Ludwig Mies van der Rohe, in archival footage of an interview that took place in the 1960s, in the film *Mies* (New York: Michael Blackwood Productions, 2005); quoted in Detlef Mertins, *Mies* (London: Phaidon, 2014), 68.
2 Quoted in Kenneth Frampton, "Modernism and Tradition in the Work of Mies van der Rohe, 1920–1968," in *Mies Reconsidered: His Career, Legacy, and Disciples*, eds. Francesco Dal Co and John Zukowsky (Chicago: Rizzoli and Art Institute of Chicago, 1986), 162.
3 Quoted in Ludwig Hilberseimer, "Konstruktion und Form," *G Materialien zur elementaren Gestaltung*, No. 3 (June 1924), 24.
4 Gooden makes this observation about Bernard Tschumi's *Advertisements for Architecture* of Le Corbusier's Villa Savoye shown in a "decaying state." Mario Gooden, "_orm is a Four-letter Word (that Starts with 'F')," *Perspecta*, Vol. 43: *Taboo* (Cambridge, Mass.: The MIT Press, 2010), 102–3. The author cites Bernard Tschumi, "Architecture and Transgression," *Oppositions*, No. 7 (Winter 1976–77), 56.
5 Dietrich Neumann, "Three Early Designs by Mies van der Rohe," *Perspecta*, Vol. 27 (Cambridge, MA: The MIT Press, 1992), 81.
6 Ibid., 97.

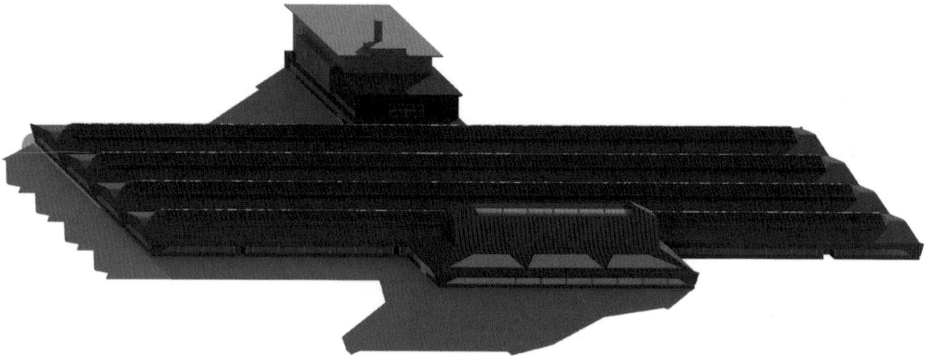

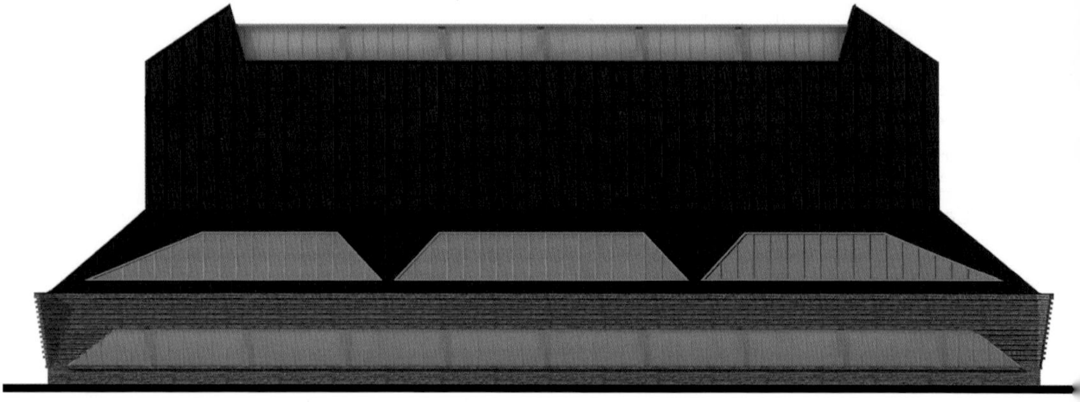

TOP: Plan oblique, **BOTTOM:** Elevation

2.08 Steinberg Hat Factory Dyeing Hall, 1923

Architect: Erich Mendelsohn
Location: Luckenwalde, Germany
Project Type: Factory
Material: Brick and Composite Roof

The unexpected and obscure form of the Steinberg Hat Factory is obscure within the history of architecture. The one-story building consists of four longitudinal production halls that are relatively mundane and repetitive. But the generic portion of the mass is stitched together with an unusual exception; the markedly different fifth hall, the dyeing hall, adjoins this mass and is crowned by a strange roof. One-third the length of the production halls, the dyeing hall projects as an appendage from the plan, while its steep roof pitch projects in elevation. The roof can be seen as a pronounced image of the factory's internal function, but it is so decisively reductive and mute that it almost seems to be a common roof type. Between these two, it might be imagined to be a found object selected from context or function, but upon closer investigation, it is clear that it is highly composed and upsets the normalcy of the whole.

Linked materially, formally, and by the datum at its base with the production hall, the expressive roofline contradicts the mute homogeneity of the linear buildings. Affixed atop the longitudinal shed, the dyeing hall's combination hip roof is deformed into a prismatic chimney, acting as a fume hood and allowing for natural ventilation that funnels the toxic fumes out its chute. The roof of the hall has a low pitch at its base and meets at a concave beltline with the steeply angled stack above. In the short elevation, the stack slopes out to overhang the low roof below and slopes in once more at its top to create a convex corner just a few feet from the top. In the long elevation, a portion in the middle is removed, allowing for light and air to enter, and further degrading the Platonic clarity it would otherwise espouse or the generic type it might resemble. Each strip of the adjacent production halls has its own pitched roof, creating a rhythmic continuity with the roof of the dyeing hall, its shaped roof is of an undeniably different nature.

While concerns about the ventilation of the interior contribute to the form of the dyeing hall's roofline, it plays another role beyond functionality, but relating to this formal conceit. The roof resembles a strange hat, its prominent shape dominating the entire composition. It's a hat, in the most literal sense; the formal and aesthetic distinction between the mute, corduroy brick box below and that of the angular, smooth black surfaces above make the roof completely foreign to the volume it covers. Whether or not this was meant as a signifier — a hat factory should look like a hat — it articulates an interest in the iconic expression of character. While its character is tied to its program through its resemblance to a hat, it is also tied to its context; the roof is a weird form of vernacular, reminiscent of German sheds and industrial barns. Despite its resemblance, it is radically dissimilar from any roof or hat that has been seen before. The black protrusion of the roof is so powerful in its estrangement of the lower volume of the hall that the entire composition is altered.

The dyeing hall, as the most significant component of the project, must be read in interaction with the production halls. Located on an industrial road with clusters of other factories, the production halls block out any adjacent buildings beyond and become the background of the dyeing hall. While the dyeing hall projects out from the rest of the building, and can thus be read as a discrete object, it is fully attached on one of its long faces to the production halls. In fact, its base is the same height as the adjacent halls and the same beige corduroy brick striations cover the entirety of the building, indelibly linking the dyeing hall with its background. However, at the same time, the roof's color and formal distinction cause it to stand out from this ground. The building would be entirely mute were it not for the tension present in the dyeing hall's form.

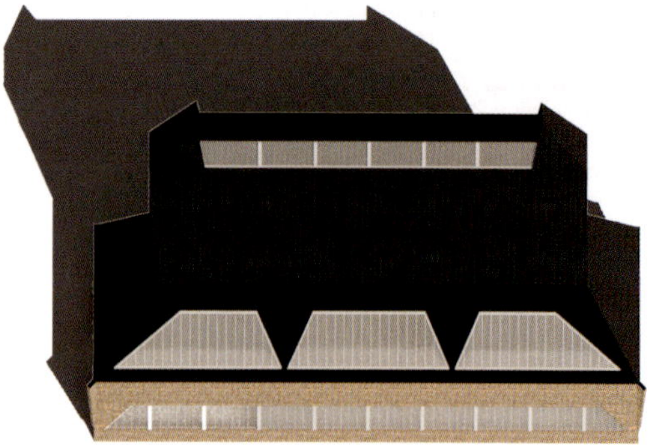

The relationship between the dyeing hall and the production halls is further complicated in their details. The long ribbon windows braced with steel supports turn the interior corner where the two meet and imply a continuity between the volumes. As such, the alien mass of the dyeing hall is once again bonded to that of the production halls. At the exterior corner of the dyeing hall, a thin surface of stacked bricks projects outward to cantilever three feet from the corner of the foundation.

While the material continuity of the corduroy brick is reinforced, the visual continuity of the elevations is disrupted, and the ribbon window is prevented from turning the corner. This once again breaks the mass of the dyeing hall apart from the production halls. The ribbon windows on all the halls end on a 45-degree angle, following the lowest pitch of the dyeing hall roof and, in effect, projecting the elevational silhouette of the roof across the entirety of the generic volumes below. Despite its apparent objecthood, the dyeing hall is inseparable from the production halls, caught in an ongoing play of part-to-whole relationships.

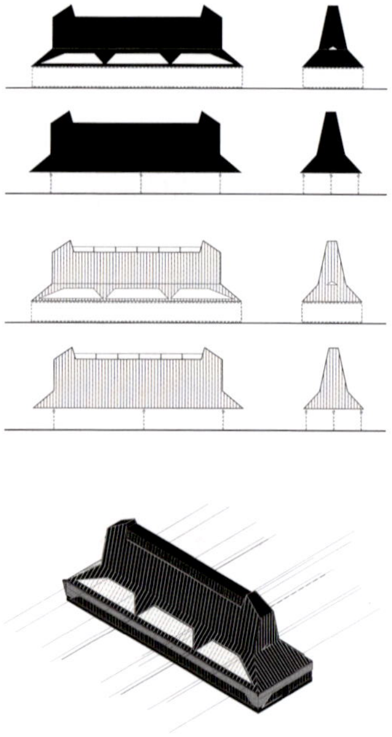

The odd yet coherent combination of two very different types — that of a rectilinear, modern volume and that of the strangely shaped hat above — situates the project between muteness and iconicity. It's an image of its function and context, a study in character, but one that is nearly Platonic and almost neutral in its abstraction. Its alien roof repeatedly reiterates the project, suggesting multiple readings.

TOP: Plan oblique, **BOTTOM:** Diagrams

2.08. Steinberg Hat Factory Dyeing Hall

TOP: Worm's-eye isometric close-up, **BOTTOM:** Worm's-eye isometric

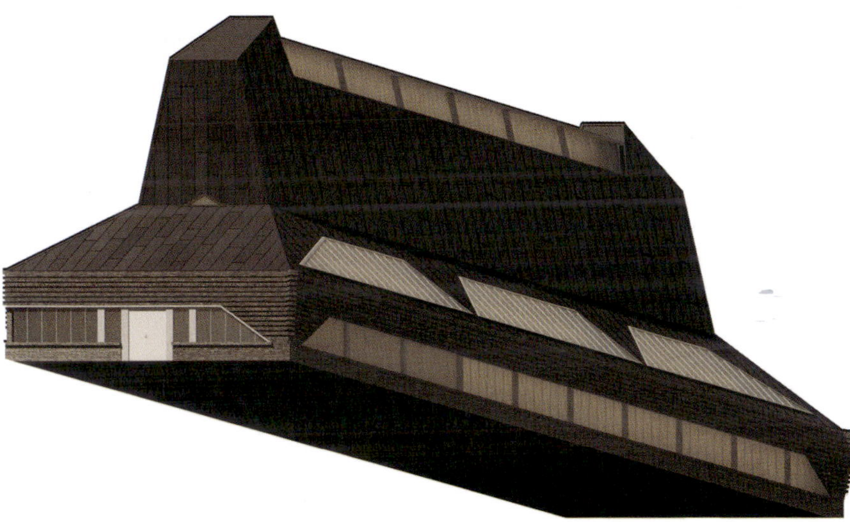

TOP: Worm's-eye isometric, **BOTTOM:** Elevation

2.09 Ennis House, 1924

Architect: Frank Lloyd Wright
Location: Los Angeles, CA, USA
Project Type: Residence
Material: Pre-cast Concrete Blocks

Part of Wright's Textile Block Houses, the Ennis House is not only the largest but the most monumental and enigmatic of the set. Its monumentality is driven by its otherness, the fractal intensity of its details, its relationship to its physical and cultural context, and its ability to swallow that context whole so as to increase its own magnitude. But the Ennis House is not so large as it projects, nor so foreign. And what's more, disguised by ruination, its form and its relationship to time are obscured.

Built atop a ridge of the Santa Monica Mountains in Los Angeles' Hollywood Hills, the house's interlocking volumes are lifted on a monumentally scaled podium that retains the hill and constructs a new datum. The walls of its base and volumes are constructed of textured concrete blocks that taper, and step-like fortress batters exaggerate the structure's height. The architecturalization of the hill — earth turned object — conceals interior and solid earth alike behind a concrete envelope, making the house appear far larger than it is. Given the steep slope of the road winding up around its walled perimeter, the Ennis House has the effect of being a displaced city block, a foreign entity that has landed amidst the suburban scattering of homes. Near the driveway, the house is an unassuming one-story structure, but approaching from downhill, it looks to be at least four stories tall. It towers above the city from its constructed hilltop as a sinister and looming presence.

But its context isn't only the Hollywood Hills; the Ennis House's true site is one of fiction and fantasy. It has appeared in film and television productions, many of which envision dark futures. Its facade was featured as the eerie haunted mansion in the horror B-movie, *House on Haunted Hill* (1959) and, most famously, it appeared as an interior in Ridley Scott's neo-noir sci-fi film *Blade Runner* (1982) set in a dystopian future Los Angeles.[1] It is telling that for the span of its existence it has been cast in the role of the frightening and foreboding menace. The stark primary forms with ornate patterning lend the house to many possible interpretations that aesthetically bridge a ruinous past with an extravagant future.

Contrary to many projects in this book, the composition of the massing is neither strictly monolithic nor repetitive. Making it even more of an outlier, the order of the Ennis House's formal composition is not top down — it does not follow a traditional design methodology of beginning with mass and then adding fenestration — but seems to have considered mass and aperture in parallel. The aperture is either centered on a face and seemingly generating that face around it, or is placed at the corners and accentuated by an irregular figural frame of protruding concrete block that distorts the reading of the mass. The fenestration has a menacing and mysterious muteness that may be dispelled or, more likely, amplified by venturing inside.

At close proximity, the tectonic "textile" units take precedence, situating the project between ruin and baroque fantasy. The abrupt Platonic massing and varied relief ornamentation on its textile blocks are, by Wright's admission, inspired by the massing and symmetrical reliefs of Mayan temples.[2] The stack bond grid of square blocks is infilled with one of the following varieties: standard concrete blocks, blocks with an etched texture, blocks with cut pores, and absent blocks that create gaps in the masonry and turn the wall into a screen. These concrete blocks distribute an irregular, rusticated texture of reliefs and incisions, covering the envelope in a hatching of shadows.

The detail on the masonry unit implies another tectonic logic altogether, one that is linear

20.9. Ennis House

rather than massive. Regardless of material composition, the hieroglyphic texture in Wright's *Gesamtkunstwerk*, or total work of art, is pervasive; it repeats on the walls, metal gates, doors, stained glass windows, and even some of the furniture. Rather than being tied to a material logic, this texture creates an atmosphere and gives rise to scalar misreadings. Akin to the Death Star's greebles,[3] the immense amount of detailing increases complexity and consequently the perceived size of the house. So dense is the packing of textures that it is as if an entire world has been compacted on the surfaces of the Ennis House. The aesthetic produced by this density imparts a psychological effect, a sense that continuously zooming in on the house would reveal infinitely increasing detail.

In the perspective renderings of the Ennis House, the texture is depicted along with draped vegetation creeping across the architectural surfaces. Both work to imply a constructed state of ruination. Ruination is typically understood as the degrading of a material object, deterioration of its geometric precision, and erosion of its original qualities. In the case of the Ennis House, this is inverted; ruination is built into the DNA of the architecture as its genetic code, precisely eroding its iconic figure. The rough surfaces of the concrete block aesthetically accept unsolicited deterioration over time. Without aiming to make an irresponsible judgment about the recent, problematic condition of the house,[4] it is possible to speculate that existing as a ruin is the most natural state of this architecture. The Ennis House is not timeless, but it never belongs to the present. It is a futurist archeology, forever trapped between the ancient past and distant future.

Frank Lloyd Wright saw an opportunity in employing concrete block, writing in his autobiography, "It was the cheapest (and ugliest) thing in the building world. It lived mostly in the architectural gutter as an imitation of rock-faced stone. Why not see what could be done with that gutter rat?"[5] His question implies an interest in how the mundane, banal, generic, standardized, industrial, cheap, imitative, and ugly material can be repositioned to supersede its inherent qualities to become "permanent, noble, and beautiful."[6] The provocation is a good one, but mostly because he missed the mark of his original intent. The Ennis House is not "beautiful," certainly not by any conventional measures. It operates in a different aesthetic category that has made it the perfect backdrop to science fiction, action, fantasy, and horror genres, where its flirtation with ugliness, eeriness, and austerity is a virtue.

The Ennis House falls into the category of the *unheimlich*, the uncanny or creepy, that Anthony Vidler describes in *The Architectural Uncanny*. Vidler elucidates the qualities of the *unheimlich*: "Walls were blank and almost literally 'faceless,' the windows, 'eye-like' but without life — 'vacant.'"[7] But perhaps even more pertinent is Mark Cousins' series of texts on the ugly.[8] Removed from beauty's obligation to truth, "The ugly object is an object which is experienced both as being there and as something that should not be there. That is, the ugly object is one which is in the wrong place."[9] And, "Rather than a lack (of beauty), [the ugly object] has an excess"[10] or even in a "lack" of features.[11] We can see these in Wright's house, in its excessive scale and packed detail, its absence of traditional house features, its unusual character relative to its surroundings, and its starkness and opacity. The Ennis House is an unhomely visage, an obscure and ugly object.

TOP: Plan oblique, **BOTTOM:** Diagrams

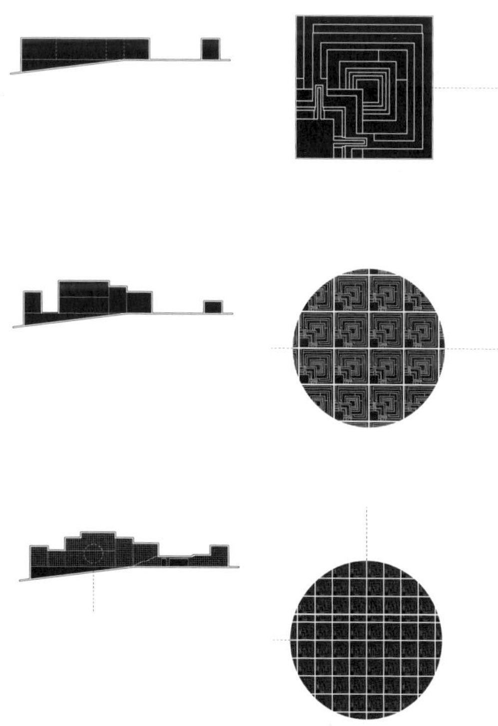

1 The list goes on to include *The Day of the Locust* (1975), a surreal film featuring a destructive riot; action thrillers *Black Rain* (1989), *The Glimmer Man* (1996), and *Rush Hour* (1998); sci-fi crime thriller *The Thirteenth Floor* (1999); David Lynch's mystery horror drama *Twin Peaks* (1990–91), fantasy drama *Game of Thrones* (2011–2019), and Jonathan Nolan's science fiction western *Westworld* (2016–present).

2 "Frank Lloyd Wright," *Frank Lloyd Wright: An Autobiography*, (Petaluma, CA: Pomegranate, 2005), 191.

3 In popular lore, the term "greeble" was first used by Industrial Light & Magic, Lucas' special effects company.

4 Until the completion of its restoration in 2018, the house was in a state of decay.

5 "Frank Lloyd Wright," 234.

6 Ibid., 235.

7 Anthony Vidler, "The Architecture of the Uncanny: The Unhomely Houses of the Romantic Sublime," *Assemblage*, No. 3 (Cambridge, MA: MIT Press, July 1987), 8.

8 Cousins doesn't regard ugliness as an aesthetic category, but rather as an offshoot of "the interesting." Mark Cousins, "The Ugly (Part 3)," *AA Files*, No. 30 (Architectural Association School of Architecture: Autumn 1995), 68.

9 Mark Cousins, "The Ugly (Part 1)," *AA Files*, No. 28 (Architectural Association School of Architecture: Autumn 1994), 63.

10 Mark Cousins, "The Ugly (Part 2)," *AA Files*, No. 29 (Architectural Association School of Architecture: Summer 1995), 3.

11 Ibid., 5.

ABOVE: Oblique elevation close-up

2.10 The Metropolis of Tomorrow (Evolution of the Step-back Building), 1929

Architect: Hugh Ferriss Location: New York, USA
Project Type: Tower Material: Charcoal Drawing

Among the most significant drawings in the development of New York City's high-density, vertical built environment is the first in the series "Evolution of the Step-back Building" by architectural delineator Hugh Ferriss. It is an unquestionably iconic image in the history of architecture. Striking in its monumentality, the rendering portrays an icon, but it is one that is not expressive. It is austere mass controlled by legal parameters. The character of its severity and its withdrawn nature result from its dark aesthetic, the chiaroscuro of Ferriss' shadows concealing the form in a black veil. It is withdrawn in its darkness and severe in its monolithic impenetrability.

It is a mute envelope by its very definition, an image of legal limitations. This rendering is one in a four-part perspective series that demonstrates the architectural consequences of the 1916 Zoning Resolution in New York City. In the first rendering of the series, Ferriss envisioned the possibilities of a new skyline produced by responding to the mandated setbacks. Ferriss described it as "a neutral solid," saying further, "It must be understood that the mass thus delineated is not an architect's design; it is simply a form which results from legal specifications.... It is a crude form which [the architect] has to model."[1] That is, the drawing at hand is not of a building, per se, but rather a representation of the maximum mass allowed by law to be built on one city block.

He described the results of these limits to the city, "... towers will rise from the center of the masses that they dominate. Terrific verticals will no longer spring from nothing but a sidewalk.... Summits will have the composition of mountain ranges."[2] The skyscraper — in attending to the mathematical ruleset of zoning — is not contextual but is bound to produce context, to cast enormous shadows and to act as a mountain range forming the backdrop of the city. As such, this rendering is situated between an abstract diagram that responds primarily to mathematical rules, and an atmospheric image imbued with aesthetic character.

Materiality and elements that would serve to indicate scale are utterly denied in the drawing. If anything, it is simply "crude clay for architects."[3] But more than that, the reductiveness of its form is not simply awaiting features. As Ferriss described, "The very simplicity of such forms, the very absence of adornment, is itself a recommendation.... a certain starkness and even nakedness — those qualities which are, indeed, the norm for all newly arisen forms."[4] The dark, featureless tower is steeped in drama. It bears two subtly protruding stripes and sits precariously atop a steep, gabled structure with a smaller, echoing set of four crossing gables. It is framed on either side by two pyramidal forms, each toothed by two more sloped gables. There are no windows or doors; it is a true monolithic solid. It is depicted not frontally, but from the corner, in two-point perspective, with the vanishing points outside the limits of the page. What's more, the tower's pinnacle extends off the top of the page, fading into the foggy atmosphere of its altitude, implying potentially infinite height to which the pyramids point.

The ordinance implies pyramidal forms, and Ferriss argues the superiority of the pyramid to a cube, comparing this new mass to an "Assyrian ziggurat"[5] that "incites the return of the third dimension."[6] Both the isolation of the massing on its plot and the pyramidal forms inscribing the zoning envelope expose the faces of the form, preserving its individuality from its context and making it indelibly an object, a singular icon. Were it submerged in a city, many of its faces would be visible, rather than the cube's single visible facade with the rest buried in a continuous series of the same.

The conte crayon renders a subtle range of blacks and dark grays on a nearly white page; any surrounding context that might be nearby is absent. The effects of this work are not to be discounted; while Ferris agreed with Louis Sullivan's "form follows function," he said, "The axiom is not weakened by the further realization that Effect follows Form."[7] The tower's dark monumentality comes through the chiaroscuro of the drawing, with the darkened parts of the figure falling into one another as the distinction between each face is muted. The form appears to be sharply backlit, casting a wide shadow on the ground as if drawn in the late afternoon. Like the images of DC's Gotham City that it later inspired, it is menacing. While Ferriss' interest in "effect" is certainly referring to the effects of tall buildings on the city in a pragmatic sense — providing access to light and air — the effects of monumentality, iconicity, and sublimity so present in the drawing are even more critical.

In its starkness, severity, and featurelessness, the image argues for radical muteness. It relies on the legal formula's implications on volume and transforms this into an aesthetic atmosphere of light and shadow through its representation. Baring its stripped faces, it reveals nothing of its material, scale, or context. These drawings continue to incite the imagination of architects — as powerful images of desire found in the intersection of form and code.

1 Hugh Ferriss, *The Metropolis of Tomorrow* (New York, NY: Ives Washburn, 1929), 74.
2 Hugh Ferriss, "The New Architecture: Evolution of a City Building Under the Zoning Law," *New York Times*, March 19,1922.
3 Hugh Ferriss, *The Metropolis of Tomorrow*, 83.
4 Ibid., 80.
5 Ibid., 98.
6 Ibid., 78.
7 Ibid., 60.

ABOVE: Worm's-eye isometric

2.10. The Metropolis of Tomorrow (Evolution of the Step-back Building)

TOP: Plan oblique with context, **BOTTOM:** Diagrams

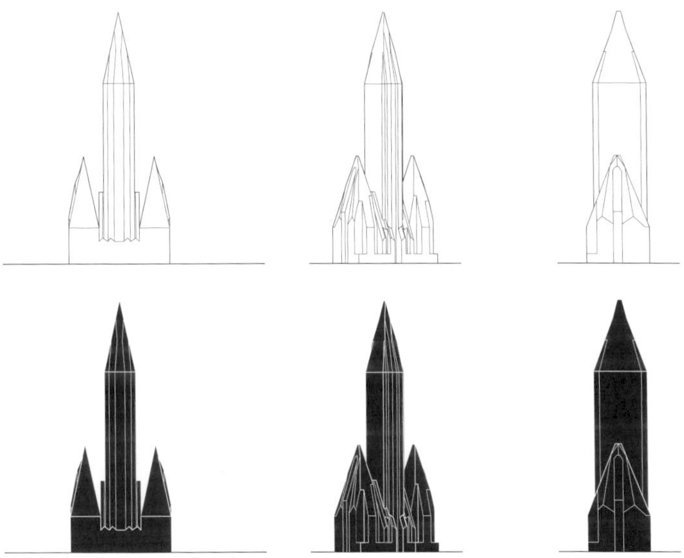

ABOVE: Oblique elevation close-up

2.11 Palazzo della Civiltà Italiana, 1935

Architect: Giovanni Guerrini, Ernesto Bruno La Padula, and Mario Romano
Location: Rome, Italy
Project Type: Museum **Material:** Travertine Marble

The Palazzo della Civiltà Italiana is a reductive image. Nicknamed the Square Colosseum for its square plan and resemblance to its ancient Roman namesake, it creates a low-resolution image of its predecessor. Apparently generic, it is mute in its neutrality, yet it remains an icon of Benito Mussolini's Fascist regime. The project is deeply fraught, falling between the bankrupt ambition of nationalist propaganda writ large and a blankness onto which anything can be projected.

Its vertically elongated volume is perforated by six stories of stacked loggias, with nine arches across the width of each facade. The pattern of the loggia repeats on a loop, becoming a texture rather than punched openings. The marble's continuous vertical striations and invisible joints conceal its panelization and thickness. These disguised panels cover the underlying concrete structure, making the building appear as if it is solid marble. Featureless and flat, the Square Colosseum's facade is unornamented and entirely clad in travertine marble that is made to look solid.

But what appears to be flat is actually thickened; the building has a double-layered facade composed of two offset envelopes. Inset by the depth of one bay, a glass enclosure behind the Square Colosseum's outer facade delimits the interior spaces from the loggias on the perimeter. Groin vaults line the ceiling of the space between, reflecting the facade's geometry back into its deep facade. When viewed up close, the arches reflect in the glass layer beyond or step back to repeat nine layers of vaults on the building's open corners, creating an impression that these arches repeat infinitely.

Echoing the endlessness of its repetitions is the mirrored uniformity and vastness of the surrounding district, the Esposizione Universale Roma (EUR), which was commissioned by Mussolini to illustrate a new monumental center for Rome. The Square Colosseum is elevated on a podium that can be accessed by two staircases located on opposite sides of the cube, perpendicular to Viale della Civiltà. It bookends the symmetrical axes of Viale della Civiltà with the Palazzo dei Congressi punctuating the boulevard's opposite end. Giuseppe Pagano criticized the EUR for the "false traditions" and "monumental obsessions"[1] it carried forward. We can recognize the district's dependence on these through its rigid orthogonality that evokes the idealized organization of ancient Roman imperial towns. The entire district is under the spell of its pervasive set of regulating lines, echoing its gridded repetitions and covered in a uniform wash of cream marble. What is compelling about the severity of this system is that the entire site's authority is bestowed upon the Square Colosseum; it has given the Square Colosseum the iconic weight and monumental effect of the entire district.

The Square Colosseum was constructed for the 1942 World's Fair in Rome, also referred to as *The Esposizione Universale di Roma* or E42, but the exhibition was canceled with the start of World War II and fell into disuse after the fall of Mussolini's regime. Left to remain an empty husk for the first decade after its completion, the Square Colosseum was for all intents and purposes not as much a building as it was an image of one.

The vacuousness of its programmatic past is repeated in the incipient emptiness of its monumental facade — reminiscent in its eerie blankness of Giorgio de Chirico's metaphysical cityscapes, complete with an empty plaza and arcade, and with a facade full of absence. A one-point perspective of its elevation, rendered by Ernesto Bruno La Padula, is backgrounded by a green atmosphere. Its arched openings frame the same greenish hue, causing the facade to look like a perforated screen, open to the sky beyond. A reflecting pool in front of the building mirrors its facade and the green sky, replicating its horizontal axis of symmetry and creating an overturned vertical double. This rendered hollowness is visible in built form; the sky is framed by the open, peripheral bays and reflected, or even seen through the glass when viewed from a height and distance where the bays at the front and back of the building are aligned. But up close, the arches frame a different kind of emptiness, that of the stark black of deep shadows cast by the thick outer shell and deep-set interior layer beyond. Its flatness and hollowness invert its monolithic qualities in favor of its reading as a stage set, a thin ghost of a facade.

As it were, the Square Colosseum has acted as a ready-made set in multiple films. In many cases it has been borrowed in order to convey its qualities as the "ever more anonymous, alone, excluded, incapable of communicating"[2] that "supplants the role of the film's human characters, becoming 'a lonely and uneasy protagonist with nothing to say for itself.'"[3] Its mute character is radically silent under the repetitive stamped system of its facade and its radically unarticulated form. In Federico Fellini's 1962 film *Le tentazioni del Dottor Antonio*, part of the anthology *Boccaccio '70*, a dream sequence centers on the plaza in front of the building. The shots are cut so that the character having the dream can be recorded in the streets while the woman he dreams about is filmed in a 1:6 scale reproduction so as to look six times her size.[4] What is most striking is the seamlessness of the scaled set piece and the building. The Square Colosseum is so reductive and without scalar cues that it's interchangeable with a model.

It would be difficult to argue that this project isn't a problematic icon, given its association with a fascist regime. But the films that have co-opted its image and the Italian fashion house Fendi, for which it is now the headquarters, have shifted its cultural potential. The Square Colosseum can be a harbinger of generic social orders, conservatism, and militarism that points to the risks of iconicity when it is charged with meaning. But it also speaks to the value of the mute icon's mutability. Impressed in its surfaces is a new cultural legacy; the misappropriation of its image allows its history to be fluid and aggregative. Taking cues from the work of Aldo Rossi — from his San Cataldo Cemetery in Modena and many of his projects that reflect the memories of Italian fascist architecture — the Square Colosseum can be translated into a mute signifier, available for perpetual redefinition.

1 Giuseppe Pagano, *Casabella*, No. 122 (February 1938), 20–21; quoted in Borden W. Painter Jr., *Mussolini's Rome: Rebuilding the Eternal City* (New York: Basingstoke, 2007), 127.
2 G.B. Cavallaro, "L'eclisse," *Bianco e nero*, Vol. XXIII, No. 5 (1962), 59–60; quoted in John David Rhodes, "The Eclipse of Place: Rome's EUR from Rossellini to Antonioni," in *Taking Place: Location and the Moving Image*, eds. John David Rhodes and Elena Gorfinkel (Minneapolis: University of Minnesota Press, 2011), 43.
3 David Bass, "Insiders and Outsiders: Latent Urban Thinking in Movies and Modern Rome," in *Cinema and Architecture: Melies, Mallet-Stevens, Multimedia*, eds. François Penz and Maureen Thomas (London: BFI, 1997), 92; quoted in Rhodes, 43.
4 Alberto Zambenedetti, "Filming in Stone: Palazzo della Civiltà Italiana and Fascist Signification in Cinema," in Flaminio di Biagi, *Il cinema a Roma: Guida alla storia e ai luoghi del cinema nella capitale* (Roma: Palombe editori, 2003), 5.

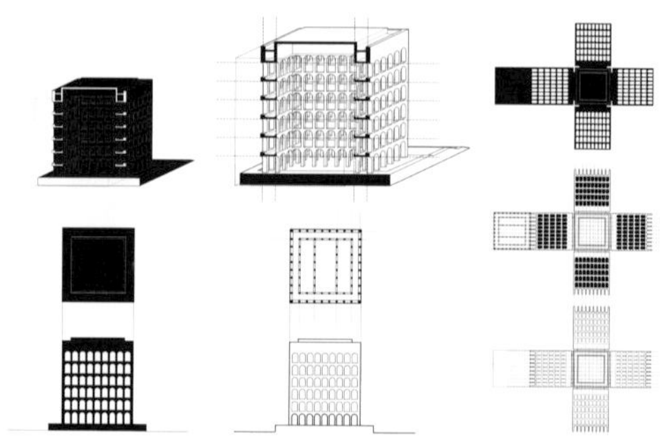

ABOVE: Diagrams

2.11. Palazzo della Civiltà Italiana

TOP: Plan oblique, BOTTOM: Oblique elevation, Worm's-eye isometric

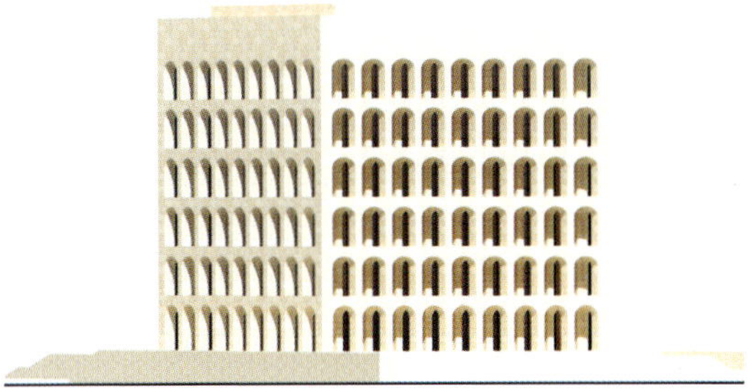

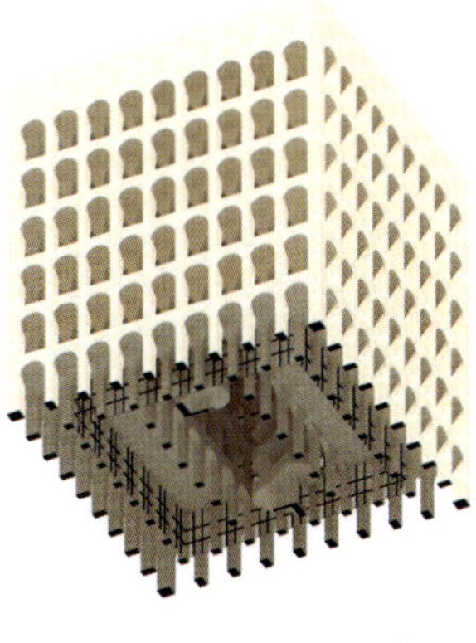

ABOVE: Worm's-eye isometric

2.12 Karola Bunker, 1948

Architect: Documented by Paul Virilio
Location: Ars-en-Ré, France
Project Type: Fortification Material: Concrete

Designed to go unnoticed and intended to communicate nothing, the Karola bunker is devoid of social functionality. Not required to attract or engage, its instrumentality is to deter, defend, and destroy. But, even with its intended austerity, this iconic structure's evasive outline is strangely alluring. Karola numbers among the 15,000 Nazi bunkers of the Atlantic Wall, built during World War II along the coastline of France.[1] Like its counterparts, it is a defensive structure, placed in a strategic site to catch incoming Allied forces unaware. Paul Virilio's *Bunker Archaeology* introduced these engineered structures to architectural discourse. Karola features on the cover, notable among the collected set within the book for its particular formal complexity and iconic quality.

Virilio suggested that the strange nature of these concrete structures resulted from the uncanny collaboration between highly advanced French construction companies specializing in reinforced concrete and the all-too-powerful German war machine.[2] This instrumental partnership led to bunkers designed to operate much like vehicles or monocoque construction so that when struck by enemy fire, they would simply tilt rather than break or fracture.[3] That is, although constructed of concrete, many of the Atlantic Wall bunkers were erected without piles or footings. Many photographs taken after the war show the bunkers tilted, either as a product of battle, erosion, or decay, but still intact as quasi-solid masses laying on the ground. The simple constructive fact that the bunkers are without foundations emphasizes their autonomy, literally separating the building from terra firma and detaching the bunker from much of architecture's historical relationship to the ground, in which foundations constitute the basis of construction.

Karola's unique autonomy from the ground can be identified in the contextual cues that deny its terrestrial tethering. Its privileging of verticality rejects the ground. The tower structure is lifted above the earth on a partially submerged podium with edge fillets at its top. It appears only to be a shallow pedestal given its low height. This slightly embedded mass is, in fact, pressed into the ground, hiding that it contains an occupiable interior. The pedestal resists any further acknowledgment of the ground and, most importantly, makes it so the predominant mass is disengaged from the earth.

Despite its disassociation from the ground, Karola looks like a geological formation and is almost entirely monolithic. Karola is a withdrawn building that resists social engagement. It has only a few portholes and entryways, all of which are to the northeast and tucked fully below the terrain. With its rough finished concrete and steel reinforcement laid bare, Karola precedes and predicts the aesthetics of béton brut. During wartime, the roughness and neutrality of the exterior was further exaggerated; netting was used to cover it with suspended brush and further mask its mute form under a false canopy. In these ways, the conventions of context are completely done away with, as there is no need for promenade or sensitivity to the surroundings. Entry and access are completely hidden, and their exact placement is driven by defensive views and strategies to camouflage the structure.

The articulations of Karola are calibrated at two distances — close-up and far away — embedding two different scales in the bunker. The lower portion covers the nearby grounds, defending the bunker from incoming enemy fire, and distant territories are viewed from the upper deck, allowing soldiers to foresee an approaching invasion. The mass atop the plinth merges disparate parts to form an unsteady composite figure that shifts between smooth curvature and blunt cuts. This tower is dominated by an inset rectangular prism that has edge fillets and remains uninterrupted for the first three-fifths of its height. After this point, a semi-circular balcony projects to the southwest, sliced by a horizontal embrasure. Stepping in from the projection, there is an upper deck that is a compound geometry still continuous with the lower prism on the southeast and northwest. Set atop this is a further recessed small cube on the southwest with a single firing slit, a projecting rectangular platform to the northeast, and a truncated cone at the center that was originally capped by a hemispherical piece of heavy artillery. The southwest and northeast facades are highly articulated, complex intersections of forms. On the remaining two facades, no surfaces project, emphasizing the shape of the silhouette. Every feature shifts in size, orientation, and form, scaled to near and far.

As precise as the above description of this structure might be, it doesn't begin to convey the drama of its image. One is left wondering why so much compositional dexterity and plastic synthesis was put forth in the construction of this defensive machine. Karola's form must be the manifest of some kind of excess, divined from a more mysterious set of operations. The design is too composed to be driven exclusively by a strictly performative logic; the controls are so strangely tuned that the specifics of its formation remain obscure. Virilio suggests that in the absence of an architectural image or tradition, bunkers take on the qualities of small military objects, resembling helmets, projectiles, and bullets. All of these objects belong to the military genre and are designed based on directionality and projection, not unlike the bunker.[4] In the synthesis of its figure and similarity to a helmet, Karola resembles a head with a mouth but no eyes, a strange totemic character, or a menacing giant that sits defiantly in the landscape.

In light of all its negative cultural, social, and moral connotations, it's hard to argue to the general public the importance of acknowledging bunkers in architectural history. But the history of architecture can supply no equal that might challenge its profoundly paradoxical nature. While Karola is tasked to defend, enclose, and maintain its autonomy, it cannot escape its alluring nature that communicates, engages, and attracts.

1 Paul Virilio, trans. George Collins, *Bunker Archeology* (New York: Princeton Architectural Press, 1994), 82.

2 Ibid., 41.

3 Ibid., 37.

4 Ibid., 47.

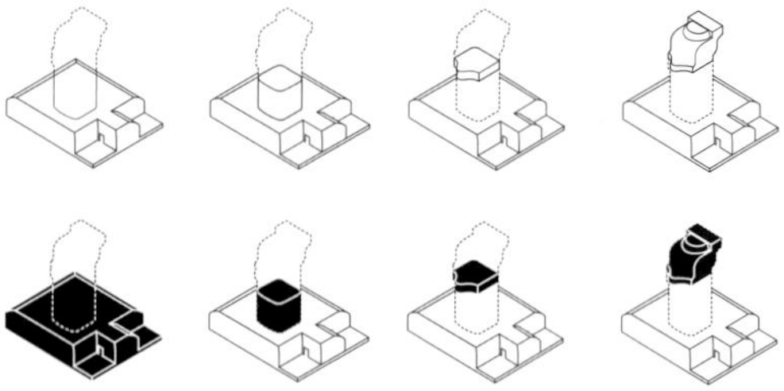

TOP: Diagrams, **BOTTOM:** Elevation

TOP: Plan oblique, BOTTOM: Oblique elevation

ABOVE: Worm's-eye isometric

2.13 Tower of Shadows,

1950–1965, built mid-1980s

Architect: Le Corbusier
Location: Chandigarh, India
Project Type: Pavilion **Material:** Concrete

An exercise in geometric precision, The Tower of Shadows — also known as the Tower of Four Horizons — is tuned on each of its four facades so as to respond to the sun's angle of incidence. The project is a monument with no specific function; it is programmed by shadows. Its frame is a legible, open structure, but it is closed by the oblique orientation of its brise soleil to create a mass out of the repetition of light and shadows. Corbusier privileges cubes, cones, spheres, cylinders, or pyramids, as "light and shade reveal... the great primary forms" with distinctness, tangibility, and lack of ambiguity.[1] And yet the clarity of the near cubic tower is depleted by its irregular faces and eaten by shadows.

The Tower of Shadows was created as part of Le Corbusier's commissioned master plan for Chandigarh, the capital of the two neighboring states and one of the early planned cities in post-independence India, and included as part of his design of all the buildings in its Capitol Complex. Sited just to the southwest of the monumental esplanade that connects the Palace of the Assembly to the north and the Palace of Justice to the south, the Tower of Shadows is decidedly off axis. The only other structure in the complex oriented just like the Tower of Shadows is a small pyramid on the roof of the Palace of the Assembly. Along with the pyramid, the tower is distinguished from its surroundings, perfectly orienting not to the other buildings, but to the cardinal directions.

Even with its orientation that separates it from its context, the Tower of Shadows exists in a tense unity with the Capitol Complex. On the interior and embedded in the brise soleil, there are nine round columns that define a four-square grid. These columns and the top tier of the tower are rotated 45 degrees from the bulk of the structure, carrying the grid of the Palace of the Assembly into the form. This secondary connection contradicts the Tower of Shadows' partial independence and ties it to the larger complex.

A similar link to the surrounding buildings can be found in the vista to the north; from this view, Le Corbusier intended for the Tower of Shadows to interrupt only the Secretariat — located further north beyond the Palace of the Assembly.[2] Seen transposed on the Secretariat that forms its background, the Tower of Shadows looks like a ruin or well-preserved fragment of the larger building beyond. Both buildings are made to look all the more ruinous, given their béton brut aesthetic of rough, unfinished concrete. With the Secretariat forming its backdrop, the Tower of Shadows falls into this ground, resisting it through its unique orientation.

Contrary to nearly every other building by Le Corbusier, the Tower of Shadows appears at first glance to lack volume or mass. It is an empty frame inside without any floors or walls and has no enclosing or continuous surfaces in elevation. In his "Three Reminders to Architects," Le Corbusier complained about frame construction, claiming that, as a work of engineering and not architecture, it lacked a sense of aesthetic expression and spatial mystery.[3] But, Detlef Mertins points out, Le Corbusier's interests are in dealing with the necessary interruptions to mass. That is, "For architecture to remain 'the masterly, correct, and magnificent play of masses brought together in light,' '... the architect is to vitalize the surfaces which clothe the masses [...] [H]oles and transparencies that were 'often the destruction of form...[had to] be made an accentuation of form.'"[4] Introducing aperture or transparency to a given mass presents a problem. At the Tower of Shadows, everything is an aperture, but aperture that describes mass.

Despite its permeability, the Tower of Shadows' mass is implied in the composite of surfaces coming together to imbue it with visual opacity, as seen in specific drawings and vantage points. That is, the structure's physical attributes don't match its representations or the experience of it. The hollowness or solidity of the pavilion depends on the angle of view. It only appears hollow on the south and north elevations or when viewed obliquely from the southeast or southwest on the east and west elevations. A frontal view or elevation drawings of the east and west indicate an impenetrable solid. While aimed to capitalize on the effects of the solar incidence over a physical structure, the project is also a speculation on oblique geometry and optical effects.

This optical density is due to the accumulation of crisscrossing brise soleil surfaces that cover the form on every elevation except the north. The system that controls this mechanism involves a series of vertical wall segments, set at angles to provide solar protection in the morning and late afternoon, and horizontals that block the sun for the remainder of the day. The structure says so little about its interior that it's hard not to think there is a complete building inside with floors and walls. It even appears to be larger than it is, given its proportion and number of vertical subdivisions. This scalar misreading is echoed in its very name; it is called a "tower" even though it isn't particularly tall.

The problem of shadow, central to Le Corbusier's most spatial and humanist definition of architecture, is here the very substance of mass and volume. Rather than physical mass and volume, shadow emphasizes the voided interior. Both the shading in the elevation drawings and in the shadows in situ paint the interior void a deep black, creating a hollow solidity that can be read as a black mass. That negative space is loosely trapped within the deep hollow shell, a shell which is so full of oblique shadows that it is impossible to see straight through it. The contrasting angles of shadow and form and its shifting proportions make the Tower of Shadows decidedly ambiguous.

1 Le Corbusier, "Three Reminders to Architects, First Reminder: Mass," *Towards a New Architecture* (Eastford, Conn.: Martino Publishing, 2014), 29.
2 Le Corbusier and Pierre Jeanneret, *Œuvre Complète*, eds. W. Boesiger and O. Stonorov (London: Thames & Hudson, 1964), 110.
3 Ibid., 29; quoted in Detlef Mertins, "Open Contours and Other Autonomies," *Monolithic Architecture*, eds. Rodolfo Machado and Rodolphe el-Khoury (Munich: Prestel, 1995), 28.
4 Mertins, 28.

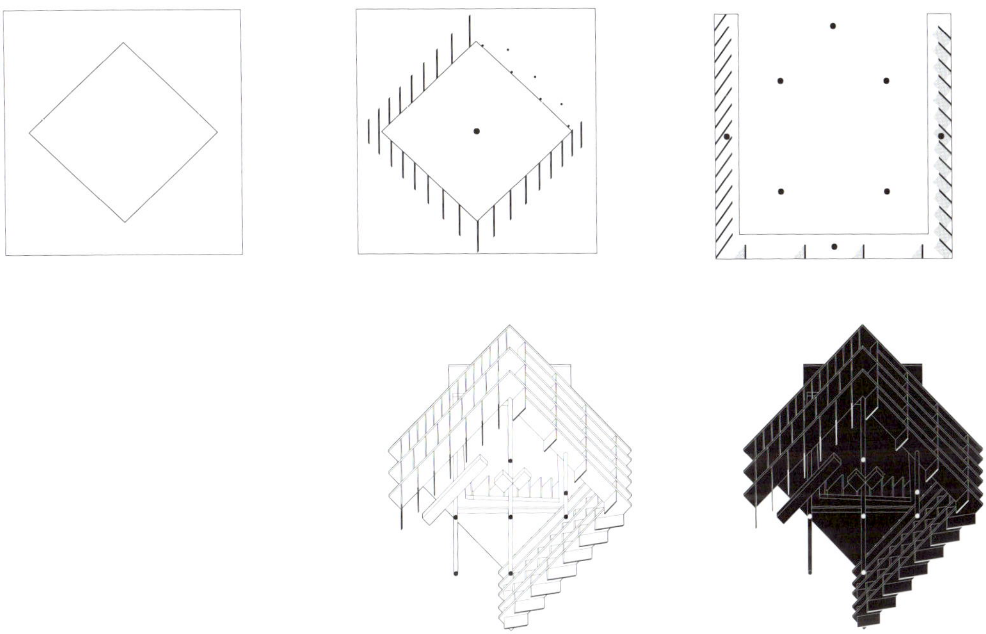

TOP: Diagrams, **BOTTOM:** Oblique elevation

ABOVE: Worm's-eye isometric

2.14 The Met Breuer, 1964–1966
(formerly the Whitney Museum of American Art)

Architect: Marcel Breuer
Location: New York, NY, USA
Project Type: Museum Material: Granite

The former Whitney Museum of American Art — now the Met Breuer — is an aggregative monolith. Formally analogous to a fortress,[1] the museum protects the cultural artifacts it houses. To enter this "cultural fortress," visitors must first disengage from the pedestrian world and its grounded reality. In this project, we find that the ground has shifted and fallen out from beneath the massive sarsen.

Carrying the fortress analogy forward, the museum stands decidedly apart from its context. It is disengaged from the surrounding city by a sunken court that acts as a moat, a literal gap introduced between the street and its entrance. Only a covered drawbridge-like entry connects the city's sidewalk to the building's interior. Similarly demarcating its literal separation, the Met Breuer's party wall falls in behind it to the south as a backdrop. Breuer goes so far as to build the disengaged party wall as tall as the building's mass, guaranteeing control over the adjacent context by providing a background on which the silhouette of the building may be read.[2] These formal moves isolate the building from its surroundings and make it an object in a tight, urban site.

The museum's dissociation is also a result of formal and material qualities that reference the existing context, only to depart from it. The surrounding residential and commercial buildings on Manhattan's Upper East Side are strict extrusions that reveal their scale and structural composition on limestone and brick facades. The Met Breuer too is rectilinear and falls within a muted masonry palette, but the material application does not offer a clear reading of its scale, and the receding mass directs the building toward a contextual ambivalence. The northwest facade, on Madison Avenue, is characterized by stepped massing that overhangs progressively further out as it moves upward. This front facade, as compared with the flatness of the side facade on 75th Street, reveals that these two different regimes of legibility are at play. This evasive strangeness extends to the building's massing and can be read as both pile and monolith, inverted ziggurat and solid rock.

The stacking order of the northwest facade is not completely clear, at least not at first glance. Starting from the basement level, the proportional vertical order is A, A, A, B, wherein B = 2A. However, when including the height of the concrete guardrail that surrounds the sunken plaza, the ratio of the vertical steps changes into A, B, B, C, wherein C = 2B and B= 2A. This recursive multiplication of the height, and depth undermines perceptual foreshortening, causing the building to appear even more top-heavy and imposing from the street. Furthermore, these proportional changes and the opaque facade defy any clear reading of the building, offering no simple clue as to how many levels it has or how high these levels may be. The only curtain wall glazing on the facade extends from the first basement to the ceiling of the ground floor, tucked mostly below grade. Where it is visible, the glazing's position under the cantilever above veils it in shadows, reinforcing Breuer's intention to make the building both literally and phenomenally opaque.

The northeast facade on 75th Street is a flat and left nearly blank, privileging the building's stepped silhouette. It is only disrupted by six thick-framed, irregular-trapezoidal windows. The frames and panes of these sit proud of its flat surface, projecting obliquely to orient toward the intersection of Madison Avenue and 75th Street. The random placement and variable size of these windows add to the foreign nature of the building, not only from the surrounding context but also within itself.

Rather than keeping with the brutalist credo and leaving the concrete exposed, Breuer sheathed the entire facade in grey granite. Nowhere on this facade does the thickness of the stone become apparent, instead, the envelope's hermeticism produces a reading of complete solidity. From afar, the horizontal alignment of the panels resembles the lines of the formwork in cast-in-place concrete, while their irregular vertical patterning resembles the textural grain of concrete. Up close these lines reveal themselves to be the clean joints between the stone panels. This creates a visual conceit and a material duplicity, a building that looks rough from afar but refined up close.

At night, when illuminated from the sunken garden, the building casts shadows over itself in a profoundly unnatural way. The shadows project upwards instead of following the typical downward trajectory of building shadows that respond to the sun's rays. The flat elevation facing 75th Street receives no artificial illumination; its surface remains hidden in pure darkness. The mysterious light source, in combination with the window centered on the illuminated facade in the upper module, suggests the sinister figure of a one-eyed monster,[3] a giant cyclopean being with a single distorted eye.

The estrangement of the interior from the outside world works in the interior as a form of denial. The building offers a continuous internal realm with only a few rifts that expose the external urban reality. The bridge cantilevers toward the interior, passing over the moat and ending at the lobby's threshold. It is held off by reveals with nothing touching the glass surface; a seam at the floor announces the physical separation of outside and inside.

Crossing the threshold of the interior, the ceiling of the lobby is a luminous field, filled with an endless grid of disc reflectors housing half-silvered lamps. These lamps supplant the inverted light source on the exterior and replace it with an internal homogeneous diffusion. There are no piers or beams that would interrupt the effect that the looming mass above is suspended by nothing more than these rays of light. The interior galleries vary in height from 12'-9" to 17'-6," but there is no evidence of this shift in floor-to-floor height on the facade. The interior further blurs the material reality of the building; bush-hammered concrete surfaces, bluestone, and granite accents all occupy a range from grey to earthy-green that bring to light the conflation of material on the building's exterior. The Met Breuer's interior world is reflected back out upon the city; its presence reshapes its context and presents Manhattan anew.

Beloved or hated by the public, Breuer's museum endures history without being a crowd pleaser. It is a paradigmatic example of the mute icon. An actual aesthetic and cultural irritant, it is distinct both from the city and within architectural history.

1 Jeffrey Kipnis, lecture, A. Alfred Taubman College of Architecture and Urban Planning, University of Michigan, Ann Arbor, November 12, 2010.
2 In what may seem as an anticipated denial of any form of contextualism, it is also important to remember that few of the now adjacent buildings were in place when the museum was originally built.
3 The building has been dubbed "the monster of Madison Avenue" by New Yorkers. Andrea K. Scott, "Inside the Breuer Building, After the Whitney and Before the Met," *The New Yorker* (March 12, 2016).

ABOVE: Elevation close-up

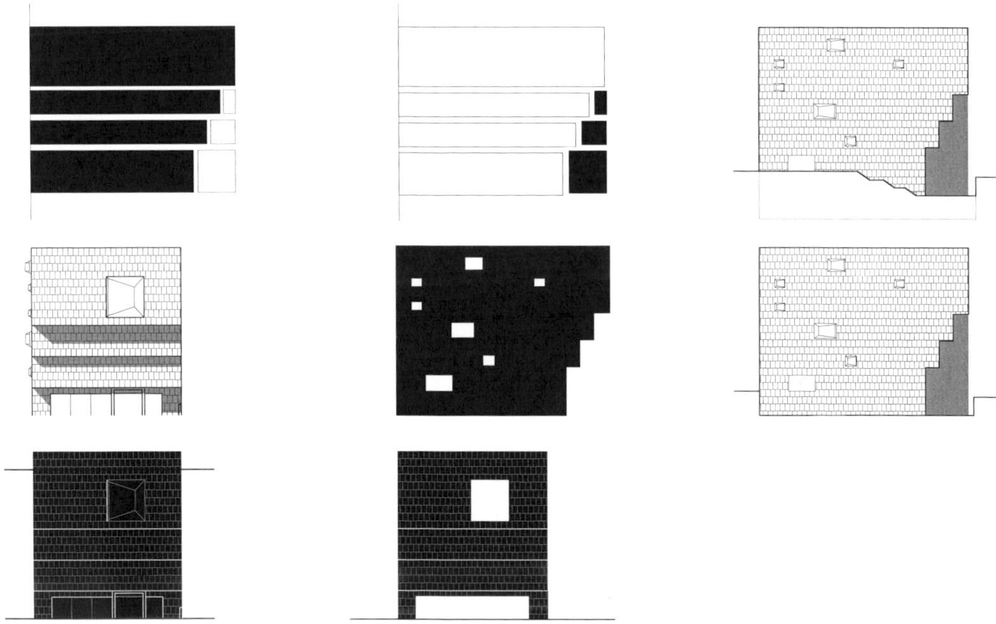

TOP: Diagrams, **BOTTOM:** Oblique elevation

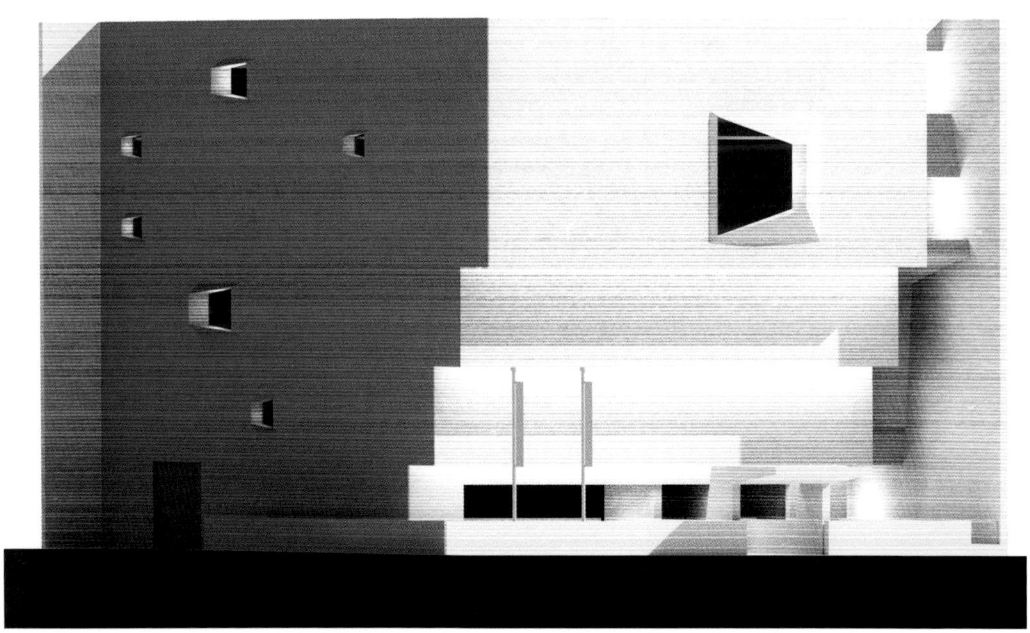

2.14. The Met Breuer (formerly the Whitney Museum of American Art)

ABOVE: Isometric close-up with context

2.15 Pilgrimage Church of Mary, Queen of Peace, 1968–1972

Architect: Gottfried Böhm
Location: Velbert-Neviges, Germany
Project Type: Church
Material: Cast-in-Place Concrete

An uncanny image of a mountain, Gottfried Böhm's Pilgrimage Church is architecture recast as a monolith. It is evasive in its solidity and overtly expressive in its form, utterly confounding communication. Set amidst a Franciscan Monastery, the Church is a pilgrimage site, home to the miraculous icon of the "Immaculata." The competition jury selected to represent the Archdiocese of Cologne feared that in Böhm's design "residents and beholders would be forced into an artificial world"[1] due to its extreme otherness. Their fears were not incorrect, only misplaced. The estrangement they perceived in its design is realized in its execution. It is a rock from a different planet, one that displaces our understanding of the world around it.

An eccentric likeness to its surroundings, the Pilgrimage Church is a reductive geological formation set at the highest point of the gently sloping monastery site. There are no right angles and almost no two surfaces the same. The crystalline figure is highly differentiated, with irregular polygonal cells interpenetrating in the plan to produce its multiform perimeter. The roof emerges from this irregular plan extrusion, introducing the oblique surfaces that define the peaks and valleys of its roof. Despite the incongruity and complex intersections, the surfaces read as a continuous, monolithic mass. Inverting foreground and background and upsetting perceived distance, the building as a solid mountain appears in front of the rolling hills beyond.

The roof has yet another strange but familiar relation to the context. The Pilgrimage Church is radically different from the historic German village around it, but its roof bears a resemblance to the irregularly clustered, pitched slate roofs of the half-timbered houses. In the section or elevation drawings, Böhm draws the church in context, almost always showing the pitched roofs of the surrounding monastery or adjacent houses beyond. Viewed in the chiaroscuro of the rendered elevation, in strong shadow with a pronounced silhouette, the church could be mistaken for a group of houses that are collapsed into a single profile.

Monastery buildings are nearly always shown as cut through, and in other sketches, he includes the pitched roofs of the adjacent houses beyond.

The silhouette — the way the project meets the sky — is crucial to its power. It is useful to note that both in its placement in the site and depiction in the drawings, the Pilgrimage Church is not an entirely isolated object. With the exception of the clear view of its facade in the stepped entrance piazza, the lower portion of the facade is partially obscured by the adjacent monastery and the buildings that cluster together to form the village of Neviges. Being taller than the surrounding buildings, its animated roofline is always visible on the horizon, collapsing the distance to the hills beyond. With this, its supporting vertical walls are hidden, and its silhouette appears all the more mountainous. Böhm's drawings also dispense with the building's lower half and emphasize the silhouette of its upper portion. In the elevation, the form is made to disappear at ground level, with the charcoal of the drawing fading out to the white of the page. It is this roof profile that reifies the image of the mountain dropped amidst the town.

The effects of the drawing are further entangled with the building, sharing aesthetic qualities with its material surfaces. On the building, the sand-blasted, site-poured concrete walls and roof have a grainy, rough texture imprinted by the wood formwork. The charcoal strokes on the sections and elevations sweep across a toothed page to imply a brutalist effect that is even more charged than the material surfaces of the building. Both drawing and built work create a fuzzy texture, a low-resolution version of geologic surface articulations.

Its image lies; the aggregate and chunky nature of the Pilgrimage Church's prismatic roof offers a silhouette that could easily be mistaken for a bundle of pitched roof houses or a mountain. Its texture is drawn from its representation, appearing as if it were sampled from a blurry image of its context. Yet the church remains autonomous from its context, the opacity of its monolithic envelope and its reductive form imbue it with an otherworldliness.

1 Monastery Archive Neviges, *Omnibus Volume* (Konvolut, 1963), 552.

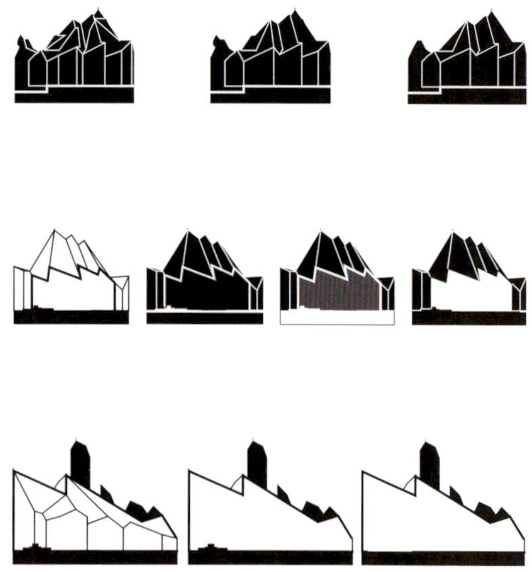

TOP: Diagram, **BOTTOM:** Plan oblique with context

ABOVE: Elevation close-up, BELOW: Oblique elevation

ABOVE: Plan oblique

2.16 San Cataldo Cemetery, 1971

Architect: Aldo Rossi (with Gianni Braghieri)
Location: Modena, Italy Project Type: Cemetery
Material: Plaster/Concrete

The San Cataldo Cemetery is an eerily defeatured twin of the neighboring cemetery by Cesare Costa, with the remarkable exception of its central cubic volume. Referred to as the ossuary or sanctuary, the ruddy cube is covered in deep-set, punched openings arranged in a grid of squares. Conceived as a generic house or tomb — a house of the dead — its prosaic form is as anonymous in its ordinary features as it is iconically identifiable in its unambiguous shape.

The thickened frame is as deep as a concrete bunker, with wide divisions between each opening. From vantage points where the front and back facades misalign, these openings are backed by a dark black layer of shadow resulting from their extreme depth and obscuring any view of the interior when seen on the oblique. The cube's solidity is enhanced by its material continuity; the exterior is a single color: the reddish hue of the clay brick. All of this contributes to the cube's reading as a monolithic solid. But, when the windows do align, an uncanny lack of solidity becomes apparent. The building, in fact, has no roof and no windowpanes; it is just a thick shell. The blue of the sky, seen through the windows when they align to those on the back or the absent ceiling, reveals the cube's hollow depth.

Oppressive in their repetition like a constant mechanical pulse, there are nine openings across and eight down each facade. These behave less like openings and more like a large-scale texture. But, read as an ocular reference, the facade returns a blank stare into its heavily shadowed interior or of occasional glimpses of the sky when its windows expose the absent roof and vacant interior. This ossuary resembles the paintings of Giorgio de Chirico in its relentless repetition, blackened windows, and geometric simplicity. Situated next to long colonnades on the northeast and southwest, the cube appears especially flat and surreal. The external solidity of the cube is completely refuted; its volumetric, shadow-heavy punctuation reveals an empty carcass.

There is nothing that alludes to its scale beyond the window and door openings, and these reveal little, as there is no detail, tectonic, or material seam that would link them to a human proportion. Furthermore, the length, width, or depth of these openings are not regulated by any standard dimension. The impression given off is that one may be looking at a paper model or stage set, which would naturally lack details or parts that would reveal its scale.

The interior is an empty husk that is a flattened sign of a building. The interior shifts in character, covered in a pallet of grey and white that is maintained in the niches and window openings, the latter of which is only subtly inflected by the red glow of the exterior. The interior side of these thick walls consists of multi-layered, delaminated grids. The attenuated interior colonnade supports a stair on the north and south, bounded on both sides by rows of columns and a continuous band of catwalks. The depth of the facade is revealed to be not solid but a series of hollow cells disrupted only by the window and door openings. Each compartment of the columbarium is individually numbered, articulating the bureaucratic aspects of death; it looks as much like a generic office building on its exterior, as it does a series of ganged filing cabinets on its interior.

The repetition of the facade speaks to Rossi's investment in the "unfinalizability" of a project, which would allow the viewer to join the architect in effectively co-authoring the work. According to Rossi, this concept aimed not for a state of incompleteness from an unprepared response or lack of response, but instead, a state of perceivable completeness that remains open-ended and inexhaustible.[1] In his words,

"But always this possibility of conclusion has escaped me."[2] Ultimately, in so doing he realizes a profound muteness, a character that is perceptible but not assertive. In the repetition of elements or building units, those perceiving the building develop its identity and individualize its repetition.

The fact that this project is decidedly withdrawn does not rest in simple muteness. The silence advocated by Rossi is not that of a building disabled from speaking, but one that is quietly restrained.[3] Dramatic and deeply theatrical, the cemetery is neither completely mute nor utterly generic. If iconicity is commonly associated with extroversion, the cemetery is so absolute in its introversion that it is pronounced and inescapable, creating an architecture of irritation. It is in this articulated evenness and aesthetic monotony that the project forms the capacity for social irritation. Rossi saw the possibility of stimulating individual identity and, therefore, true difference.

1 Val K. Warke, "Type — Silence — Genre," *Log*, No. 5: *Postcriticality* (Spring/Summer 2005), 124.

2 Aldo Rossi, *A Scientific Autobiography* (Cambridge, MA.: MIT Press, 2010).

3 Warke, 124.

ABOVE: Oblique section, **BELOW:** Plan oblique

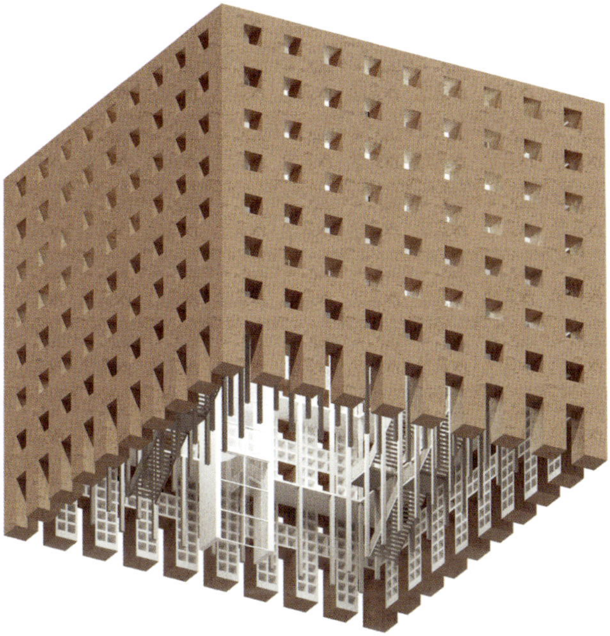

TOP: Worm's-eye isometric, BOTTOM: Diagrams

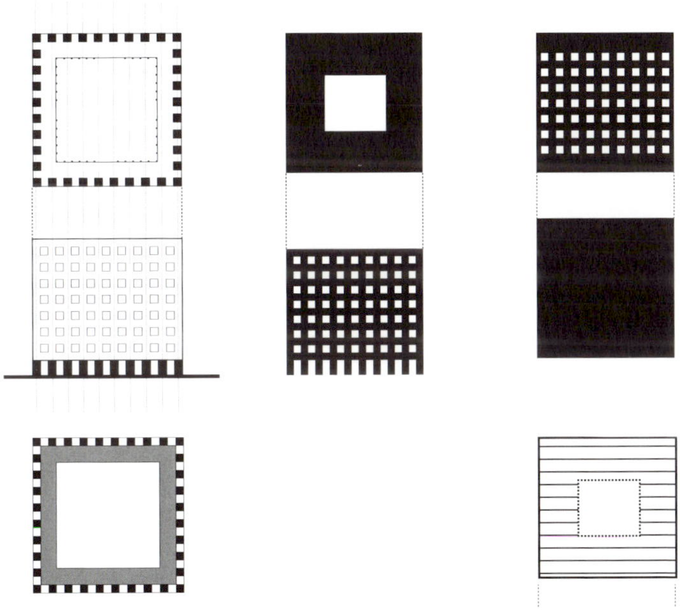

ABOVE: Worm's-eye isometric close-up

2.17 Palmas 555, 1975

Architect: Juan Sordo Madaleno
Location: Mexico City, Mexico Project Type: Office
Material: Dark Aluminum/Bronze Sheating

Palmas 555 is unmistakably iconic in its monumentality and stepped silhouette. And yet it exhibits a repetitiveness that equates to a kind of blankness, and a dark mysteriousness as to its function, size, and material composition. An oddity among many more monolithic and mass-driven projects in this book, this office building demonstrates a massiveness of an entirely different order.

Situated among the normative high-rises that line Paseo de las Palmas, the nine-story office tower consists of a series of stacked, thick masses, set atop a two-story plinth used for the commercial program. The stack of masses shifts horizontally at each level creating a reading of instability. But the stack of plates is responsible for a much stranger reading. More than an office tower, it bears a striking resemblance to a variety of Mexican vernacular architecture: the building looks like a totem in its vertical stacking, a ruin in the irregularity of its massing and striations, and a ziggurat in its stepped displacement — albeit one that need not respond to gravity. The stacked opacity and darkness of Palmas 555 conceals its functionality as a corporate building behind a pseudo-historical figure.

While Palmas 555 masks its program, it also provokes a scalar misreading of its form. The tower seems to be much larger than it is due to its monumental presence. This is controlled by the relationship of the masses to the gaps that alternate between them. All of the masses and gaps are the same height. Set back in the gap, far behind the face of the mass, is a ribbon of storefront glazing that, were it visible, would undermine its monolithic quality. It might initially seem that each opaque mass is too solid to be occupiable and that there is an extremely megalithic slab suspended between the glazed levels. At the same time, the stacked masses appear to be large enough to be entire floor levels in their equivalence to the glazing.

It is useful to note that while there is a significant amount of glass in the building, most photos of the project suggest otherwise. Those photos in question are captured from the street, looking up. From that point, the glass is mostly hidden behind black chiaroscuro shadows. These shadows deny the very presence of the glass and replace its ephemeral materiality with a black solid that is akin to the textural solidity of the masses.

In section, it becomes apparent that each mass is actually a balcony surrounded by a guardrail with the glass continuing behind it. So, both possible readings produce a perceived doubling in height, where one level is read as two. The guardrail is covered in darkly colored, vertical striations that lack visible seams, all pointing to an expected materiality. The immediate assumption is that we are looking at a Brutalist building made of board-formed concrete that has stained with age. But, in fact, the project is clad in dark aluminum panels. The image of the building is controlled, manipulated to hide its reality.

Every thin steel plate that forms the rail of the balcony implies the stepped masses described above through tricks that are disguised in elevation and exposed in section. The thinness of the metal layer is never seen; each rail is folded back to have a flat top — making an L-shape in the section — such that they look at least half a meter thick from the exterior. In cases where a plate projects out beyond the one above it, a thick poché is introduced to the guardrail. Visually disguised as a massive structure, Palmas 555 is actually incredibly thin.

The building section sheds light not only on the height of each level and the thinness of its construction, but it also reveals the relationship between that periphery and the core of the building. The core is set back as far as possible from Paseo de las Palmas to the south and still inset several meters from the north facade in order that the building's stepped silhouette can be maintained. Also visible in section, but not apparent in photographs, is the regularity of the horizontal shifts of each plate. A pattern of offsets is repeated every four floors, balancing the apparent randomness of the staggered composition with a necessary redundancy.

The deep facade, resulting from the displacement of the plates and recessing of the windows, allows interior views to be detached from the street and maintains a sense of mystery around the structure. It allows for the crucial effect of strong shadows that impede the reading of depth of each level. Despite being orthogonal, the articulation of the facade shifts the order of things. The oblique, deep shadows displace the building from the office high-rise typology significantly, rendering it in a character that is entirely other.

There is an overall unsettling effect, not only based on the apparent instability of the project but also in the visual juxtaposition of the opposing stacked horizontal masses and vertical surface striations. The vertical texture appears to be interrupted, almost cut off by the shadowy voids in between every volume. In this, the texture appears far more vertically continuous, making the volume seem not to be stacked but rather subtracted and displaced.

Palmas 555 is deeply duplicitous. Through a series of calculated tricks, the building disguises its typology and structure and falsifies its verticality and materiality. It deals in mystery, concealing its true nature and constructing lies.

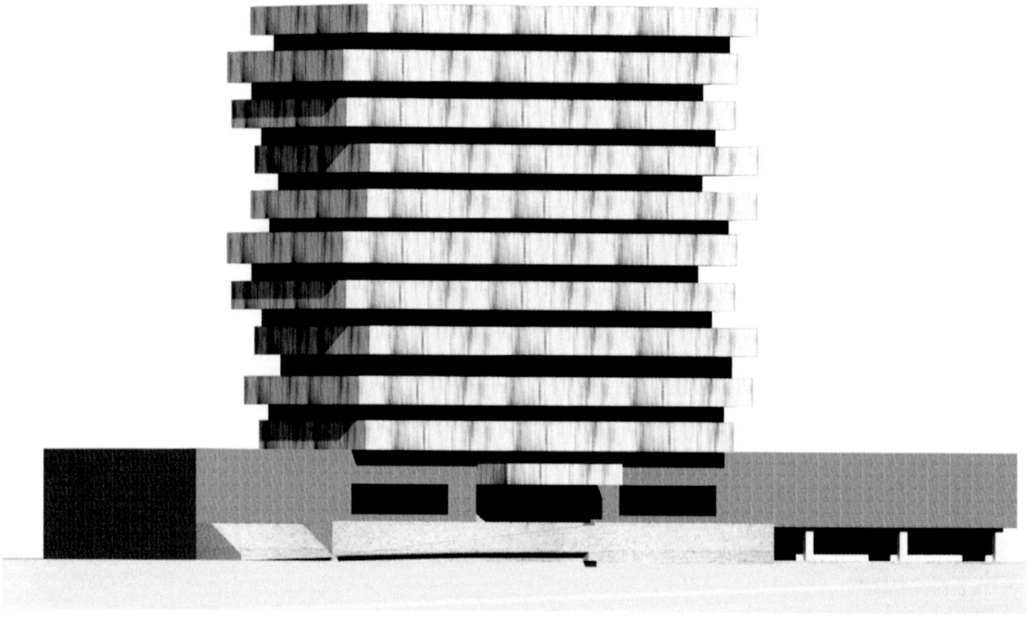

ABOVE: Elevation

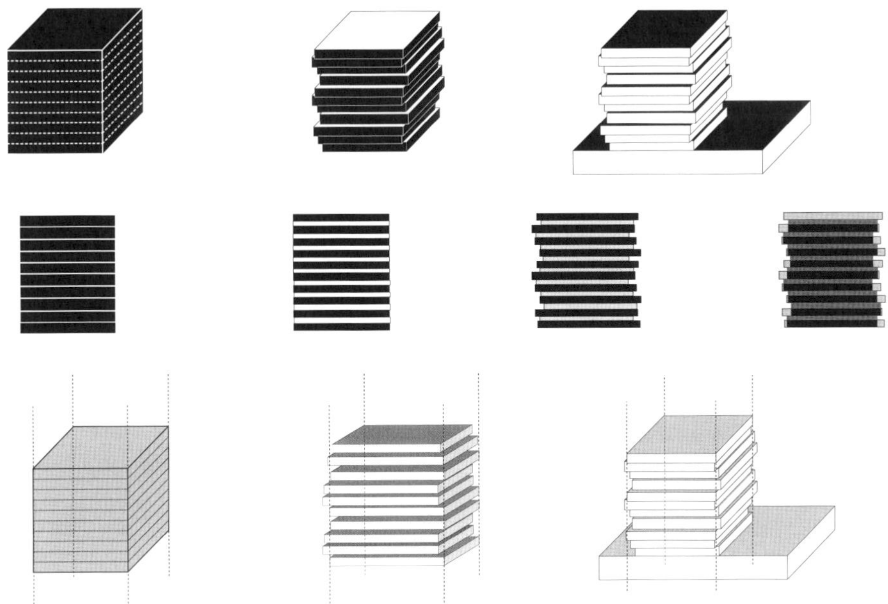

TOP: Diagrams, **BOTTOM:** Oblique section with context

ABOVE: Elevation

2.18 Death Star II,

A long time ago / 1983

Architect: Geonosians / Industrial Light & Magic (Concept Colin Cantwell and Ralph McQuarrie)
Location: A galaxy far, far away / Van Nuys, CA, USA Project Type: Battle Station
Material: Model prop

While it may initially seem odd to find the Death Star in the context of architectural history, its aesthetic and formal qualities are embedded in the collective imagination, and it has transformed culture, much in the way significant works of architecture have. While it is a pop cultural icon, it is also deeply iconic in a formal sense. It is a dichotomous object, singular in its spherical monolithicity and multiple in its dematerialization.

Featured in George Lucas' space opera, *Star Wars*, the Death Star is, by its very nature, a multiplicity. It is both a fictional structure and is constituted of myriad physical props and sets. Internal to the fiction, it is a planet-sized, orbital battle station with superlasers, which enables its operators to destroy entire planets and inspire fear through its power. But, this machine with its hollowed-out interior is disguised by its enormous scale and spherical form to masquerade as a planetary solid — a dead star, a planetoid, or a moon. Despite its lack of solidity, its massiveness is implied by its own artificially produced gravity. Gravitational force is directed towards its center on the outer surface and directed to the south on the inner, stacked decks.[1] As a result, it is a double; a building nested inside a planet, with the physics of both left intact.

The Death Star also evades a singular reading of its temporal status. It is unclear whether it is a futuristic construction or an ancient ruin. The Death Star has some of the luster of advanced technology, but it has lost its sheen. Lucas' story pairs with his photorealistic documentary fantasy aesthetic that depicts a gritty version of the future.[2] In his words, "The trouble with the future in most futurist movies is that it always looks new and clean and shiny… [when] what is required for true credibility is a used future."[3] The Death Star exists in this "used future" of a once-shiny world that has tarnished, shifting between states of construction and destruction that upset any clear relationship to time and leave its state of being tenuous. The iteration most relevant to the mute icon is the Death Star II — also known as "The Incomplete Death Star" — a disfigured sphere, covered in a flurry of scaffolds. In a perpetual state of becoming while still being built, it also appears to be eroding, decaying, decomposing. However, it is designed for this in-between state as a perfectly incomplete object.

Adding to the intrigue of its enormity and strange temporality is its ominous sphericity. The Death Star II appears smooth when viewed from far away, viewed from the right angle, or viewed against the blackness of outer space. Given the matte gray of its exterior, when looking at the concave cone embedded in its shell to form the superlaser cannon well, the darkness of its right side reflects no light, and the left side looks as if it may only be obscured in shadow. However, when seen up close, at the correct angle, or in front of another planet, it becomes apparent that the obscurity is internal to its deeply eerie, disfigured sphere.

The Death Star II produces a radical contrast between monolithic spheroid and frayed edge. The sphere is the planetary antecedent, the ideal archetype to play against. In opposition to this, the synthetic, circuit-like gridding of surfaces and volumes suggests accumulation and assembly or dissolution and decomposition. Cascading Cartesian gridded frames and stacked slabs imply thousands of scaffolds that complete its spherical boundary. Imagined to be made of steel plates, even the relatively smooth face of the station's outer hull is roughly textured, covered in city blocks that extrude from its several-kilometers thick, habitable crust.

The Piranesian horror vacui of the frayed volume extends in low-relief across the sphere's surface. But for all the information packed into its surfaces in nested intricacies, the reticulated patterns are actually ornament that artfully fake their usefulness. No purpose was assigned to any of its articulations during their invention. They are covered in what came to be known as "greebles,"[4] a dense collection of finite surfaces details that included a variety of Platonic geometries or more complex tectonic figures. The intricate tectonic elements were often sampled from shop-bought model kits using a technique known as "kitbashing."[5] At times, the intricate parts were manufactured for the model; for example, the Death Star II's grid of miniature scaffolds are made from thousands of acid etched brass sheets organized into stacked plates.[6] All of this detailed intensity causes the Death Star to appear incredibly complex and convinces the audience that it is, actually, of an immense scale.

The immensity of the Death Star II is echoed in the quantity and scale of the models produced to depict it. The full spherical model is 5.5 feet in diameter and packed with tiny components, the detail model of the meridian trench ran for 60 feet and included 10,000 windows painted on by hand, each requiring dedicated teams of set builders.[7] Models that were the size of small buildings were large enough that they required airplane hangars to be built around them. Importantly, when the smaller models were scaled up, every detail of the miniature was recreated, even including the visible thickness of styrene surface edges or the indentation of the meridian trench that was introduced to alleviate the imperfect connection of two polystyrene hemispheres.[8] These mega models, which register the material thickness of smaller models, work to convincingly superimpose one scale on the other. The composited density of a 60-foot model on one that is 5.5 foot creates the impression of a fractal increase in detail.

The Death Star's scale is implied through its texture. The austerity of its form disguises it as a planet. It is sublime not only by virtue of its scale, but in the density that covers the model and detail models. The resulting object is one that is, by definition, incomplete and an entity that is as aesthetically fascinating as it is physically implausible. It is precisely in that gap, in the strong speculative nature of this constructed, fictional planet, where the architectural content lies — in its capacity to be real even if it is a fiction.

1 "Death Star I," *Wookieepedia: The Star Wars Wiki*, starwars.wikia.com/wiki/DS-I_Orbital_Battle_Station (accessed June 14, 2018).
2 Julie A. Turnock, *Plastic Reality: Special Effects, Technology, and the Emergence of 1970s Blockbuster Aesthetics* (New York: Columbia University Press, 2015), 149.
3 Ibid., 171–2.
4 In popular lore, the term "greeble" was first used by Industrial Light & Magic, Lucas' special effects company.
5 Colin Cantwell used this technique to create the Death Star I.
6 "*Star Wars* Episode VI: Death Star II Under Construction Model Featurette," *YouTube*, youtube.com/watch?v=4yRnfFVZSoA (accessed June 14, 2018).
7 "*Star Wars* 40th Anniversary," *Empire Movies*, empireonline.com/movies/features/star-wars-behind-scenes/ (accessed June 14, 2018).
8 Colin Cantwell, "Death Star: and How the Death Star Got Its Trench," colincantwell.com/death-star/ (accessed June 14, 2018).

TOP: Elevation close-up, BOTTOM: Diagrams

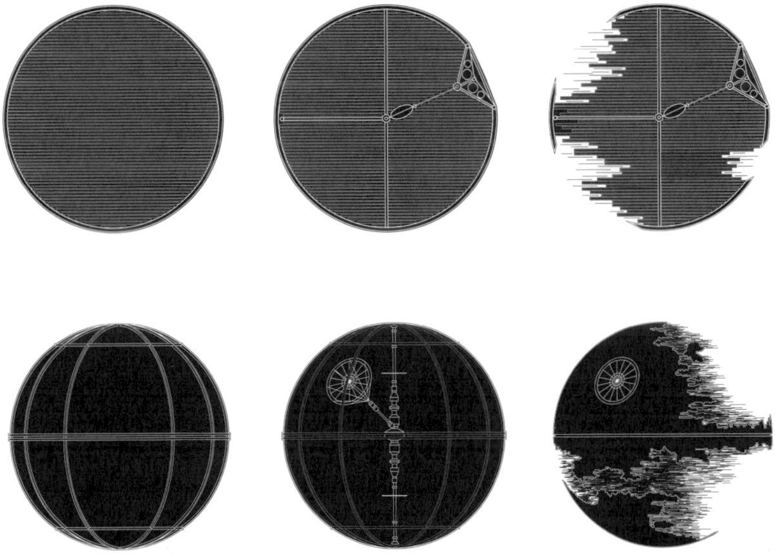

2.18. Death Star II

ABOVE: Worm's-eye view isometric close-up

2.19 SESC Pompéia Sports Complex, 1986

Architect: Lina Bo Bardi
Location: São Paulo, Brazil
Project Type: Mixed Use
Material: Board Formed Concrete

Part bunker, part fortress, and part infrastructure, SESC Pompéia ends up being a bloated building and a small urbanity unto itself. In fact, Bo Bardi referred to the project as a "citadel and cidadela," walled city and fortress, and dubbed the wider of the two buildings that compose its sports complex the "bunker" based on Brazilian military forts that served as a precedent.[1] The project is uniquely strange given the severing of its form; the sports complex is split into two parts, with the negative space between these two functioning as a public promenade.

Located in a neglected industrial zone, the buildings take on the aesthetic of the surrounding factories. The complex is composed of former factory buildings and three vertical masses: the large rectangular prism of the recreation hall, the smaller pentagonal form with circulation and service program, and the tallest of these, a cylindrical water tower. The separation between these programmatic chunks and their architectural parts is highly defined. SESC Pompéia resists wholeness in its form but regains it through its uniform brutal aesthetic.

The exterior is raw, rough, and unpolished. Bo Bardi's aesthetic interests lie in producing "poor architecture " — "poor," as in humble and undecorated, rather than destitute.[2] Further describing her aesthetic intentions, Bo Bardi said, "SESC is an homage to the common people, to the forgotten, to the losers, to the 'ugly' and is a critique of a world that punishes weakness."[3] The effects of this ambition can be seen in the heavily textured, béton brut surfaces of the blunt masses. This undecorated ugliness advocates for a new standard of aesthetic judgment, one that is inclusive and conveys the social and political potential of mute icons.

Playing into the analogy to the fortress, both masses of the sports complex have few apertures, making it so the concrete shell conceals the interior and gives away very little about the building's interior organization. Beams project from its parapet like the machicolations of medieval fortifications, a structural detail that reinforces the reading of the building as a castle. The square punched openings of the pentagonal building are all misaligned from each other, acting to obscure the interior levels. The large, prismatic gymnasium is covered with regularly gridded amoebic windows chiseled away from a solid mass. It is unclear whether they are in a partial state of completion or are the product of ruination. Carved out rather than designed, these windows further suggest the project's monolithicity. The windows, masked by red metal grates, neither glazed nor framed, are simply holes into a prehistoric or ruined structure.

The project's dualistic nature resides in the contradictions between its parts that produce an unstable and evasive quality in its multiplicity. The two concrete masses that form the sports complex are bound together by a set of obliquely forking footbridges. These figural bridging elements are the source of the project's iconicity, whereas the masses are its silent background. As a result of the tense unity between massing and bridging elements, SESC Pompéia can be read as a pair of buildings, or as a single building with its masses stitched together. Their connection to one another fluctuates between that of Siamese twins and a bonded pair of figures, inextricable and separable at the same time.

Devoid of any walls, the larger building contains only five floors of multi-purpose sports halls in its near hollow interior. There are no bathrooms or changing rooms within its shell, no fixed benches for spectators, and most unusual, no staircases. Despite being largely hollow it behaves monolithically; the gymnasium is literally inaccessible without its slender counterpart. The adjacent, thinner building is 11 floors tall and includes all of the amenity spaces for the gymnasia, two elevators, a red metal spiral staircase, and external emergency stairs. If wishing to access one of the gymnasia, a visitor must enter the slender building, wind up the stair, and cross through one of the four bifurcated footbridges.

In an apparent cyclopean inversion, what should programmatically be one appears to be two; each mass rejects the other in having its own orientation and distinct aperture. And yet the profoundly connected pair share the blotchy complexion of their board-formed concrete and are entangled by their footbridges, both formally and programmatically. While there is symmetry in the chunky massing, the symmetry of the whole is disturbed by the rotation of one building and one bridge. SESC Pompéia's irregularities compete with its iconic verticality and entwined profile.

1 Olivia de Oliveira, *Subtle Substances: The Architecture of Lina Bo Bardi* (Barcelona: Editorial Gustavo Gili, 2006), 201.

2 Ibid., 228.

3 Ibid., 203.

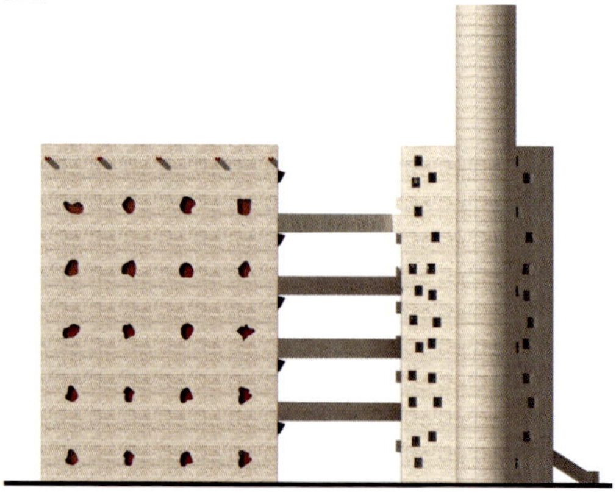

TOP: Elevation, **BOTTOM:** Plan oblique

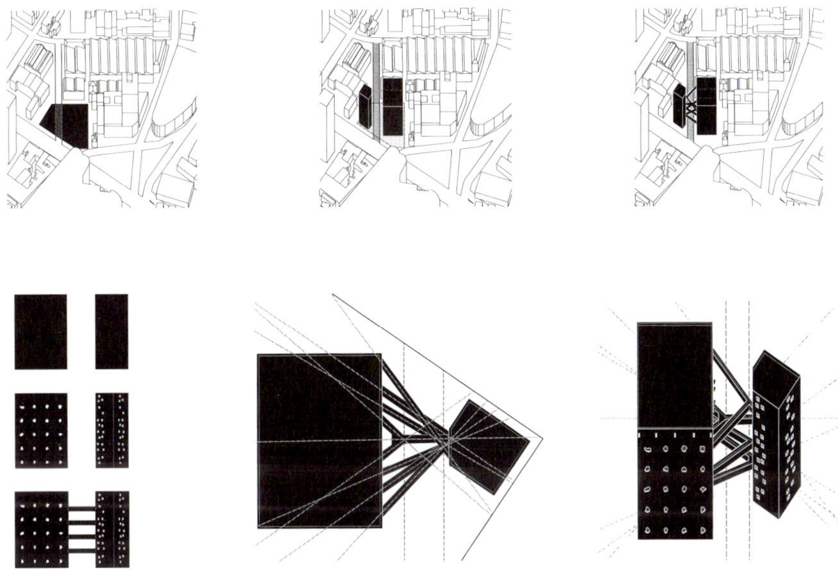

TOP: Diagrams, BOTTOM: Plan oblique with context

2.19. SESC Pompéia Sports Complex

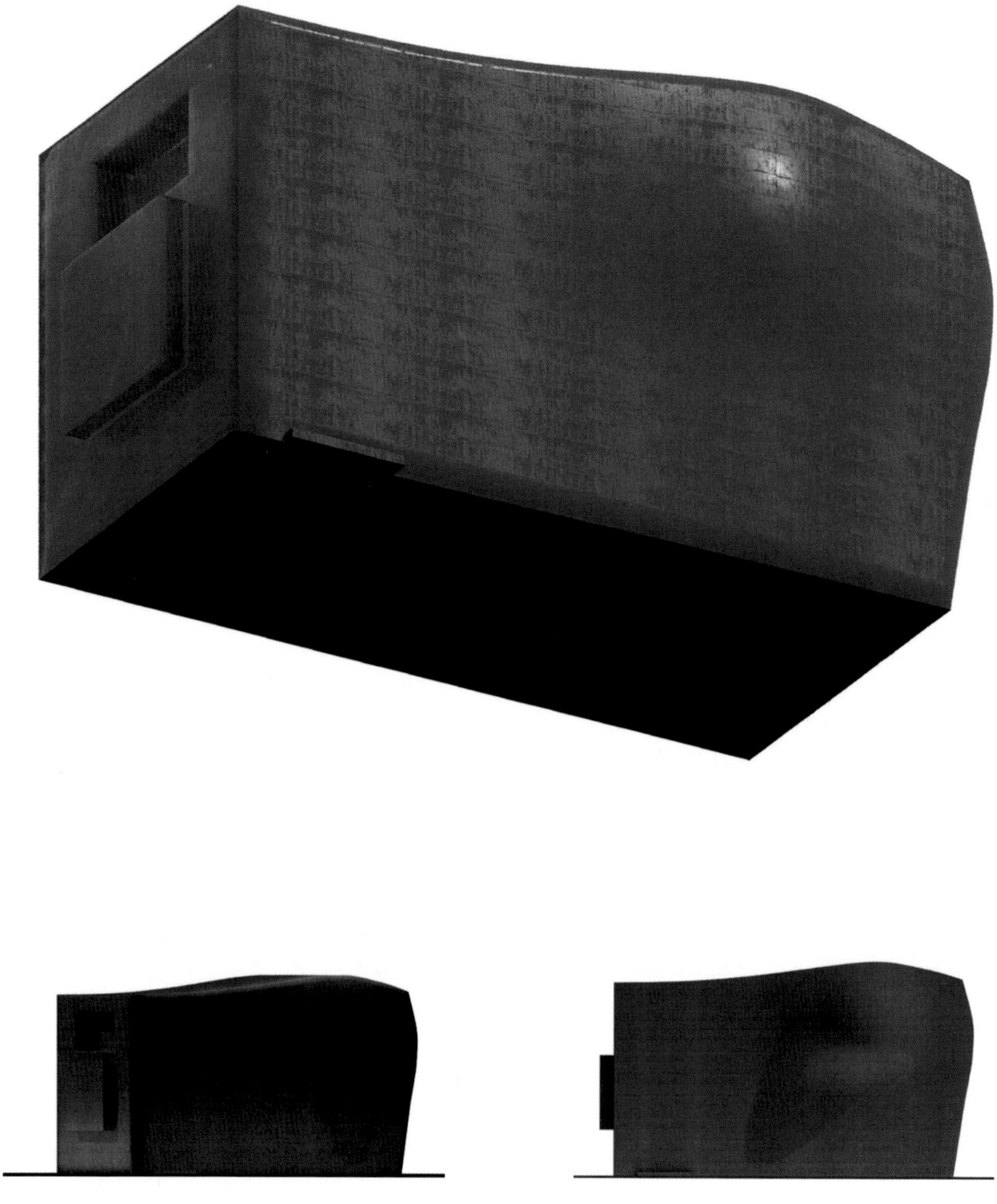

TOP: Worm's-eye isometric, BOTTOM: Oblique elevation, elevation

2.20 Tokyo Opera House, 1986

Architect: Jean Nouvel & Philippe Starck
Location: Tokyo, Japan
Project Type: Performance Space
Material: Black Stone

No project better relates the idea of the mute icon than the Tokyo Opera House. In its sectional intricacy, it represents a shift in the disciplinary approach to architectural interiority and interstitiality. While unbuilt, the project has gained iconic status in architectural circles as the cover image of Rodolfo Machado and Rodolphe el-Khoury's *Monolithic Architecture*. As quoted in Detlef Mertins' essay for the book, Jean Nouvel described his unbuilt Tokyo Opera House as "… a monolith of polished black granite that contains three precious objects. A great shining stone that acts as a mirror for the sky, the city, and the people. A building that 'shows'… or 'conceals' the mystery it contains, thus recognizing itself as a magic box."[1] Its image is subdued by its monolithic qualities, muted in the static of its reflections, and veiled in obscurity.

The carbon pencil renderings sketch a mysterious picture of the project. In the perspective rendering, its pure, rectangular facade blends into the prototypical mid-rise buildings of the background. Its shape is generic, its envelope mundane, it fulfills what is expected for a theater typology. But on the adjacent face, a slightly convex outline can be seen: a bulge that distorts its geometry and hides the angles that define the box and separate one surface from the next. Curiosity is piqued by the inexplicable inflection of curvature. The smoothness of the facade and the smoothness of the bulge's geometry harmonize to deplete the building's clarity. But it always maintains its sharp edges, even as they take on the pressure from the interior and begin to curve. The outline never quite matches the flatness we might expect from its hard edges.

The stone facade looks as if it is a stretched, thick silicone or fleshy material. It is as if the physical properties of stone have changed to render its surfaces elastic. In Philippe Starck's description, "It's a strange object which has come from somewhere else, it's the whale that swallowed Mecca."[2] It is as if its cubic figure has been misshapen by something hidden within it, the building having swallowed something larger than its body. Only one volume projects from the enveloping bubble, a protruding cuboid sticks out and a small impression is inset on the only flat facade. Looking something like a handle, it provokes additional curiosity about the interior, begging us to crack it open.

In the elevation, the background context is dropped and replaced by a desaturated fog of medium gray. In the absence of context, the so-called black "mirror" reflects one, but it is one which is not there. Mountains and diffuse clouds are mapped onto the facade, estranging the concert hall from its urban surroundings. These mountains are not visible in the perspective rendering, nor are they nearby in the physical site; there are mountains to be sure, but they are a great distance away — 40 miles to the west and 60 miles to the north — their visage likely blocked by the buildings that shape the skyline of Tokyo. The representation of some remote real is layered onto an abstraction; a fine grid is just barely visible on top of the image. The two layers drawn onto the facade share historical roles as backgrounds: the grid as a background of a constructed drawing and the mountains as a backdrop to a landscape painting. In their presence on the facade, the consummate object overtakes and becomes the background.

The model is a uniform black solid. When photographed frontally, it looks entirely flat, only punctuated by highlights on its subtly curving edges and a small rectangular projection at its center. It is a black vacuum that eats light. When photographed obliquely, the glossy sheen of the black plastic reflects the white walls of the room in which it is captured. The model depicts a true monolith with no gridded subdivision of parts and no projected image, unlike the elevation. So, what would seem to be a reflection in the elevation must be a mirage imagined in the refractions of light. Wrapped in the ambiguity of an atmospheric illusion, the bulging object flirts with formlessness.

The massive scale of the Tokyo Opera House is first implied by those mountains seen on its facade in the elevation. Starck speaks of it as, "Object and non-building, huge dimensions, formidable weight, you'd say it was made of solid marble: the weight of a black hole" and suggests that those who would come in contact with it would "... experience a certain dimension, a weight, almost an anxiety — standing in front of a huge object, beyond comprehension."[3] Zooming in, tiny figures can be seen at the base of the elevation drawing. Mere dots on the page, the figures are located in an entry portal that is less than one-fiftieth of the building's overall height.

Returning to the model, it can be opened to reveal the section. The unassuming exterior has been hiding three polished golden objects lodged in its thick shell. The container is partially fitted to these precious objects, swelling as they push against its walls. The geometry of the golden volumes is pulled taught unlike that of the exterior, but instead of hard edges, these have corner fillets. It is clear that the gold pieces within are not only a different material and color but follow an independent logic. Rather, it is the container that is formed in part by the nested objects; it is a box made to loosely conform to them. Detlef Mertins describes the relationship between container and contained:

> Like the case of a musical instrument, the membrane of an organ, or the protective shell of a machine, Nouvel's solidity is hollow, but not empty. Or perhaps the hollowness of its Piranesian interior marks an indeterminacy and splendor that lighten the weight of civil society, opening up its worldly pomp and spectacle to unnerving winds from alien places.[4]

Both the black exterior and gold interior objects — case and instruments — have unique silhouettes that are only seen simultaneously in section. These sectional objects[5] are not isomorphic; instead, they are loosely fitted in relation to the box. A portion of the black monolith's core has been hollowed out, creating an interstitial space bracketed between the black and gold objects. The analogy to the instrument is not what is interesting. Rather, it is that the color and material palette is chosen not by any conventional means, but in relation to the objects the building organizes: the instruments that play in its halls. The concert hall becomes an enlarged image of that which it stores.

Visitors are granted entry through its low, wide door into a long passageway, as the section drawing reveals. In this passageway, the same kind of bulge present on the envelope can be seen in the ceiling, just below one of the golden volumes, consequently wrapping the mystery of the envelope into the broad corridor. The hall breaks open to the massive interior, over 165 feet high, lined in the same black polished granite with an understated grid tracing its surfaces. The three golden volumes protrude in this room. Its sublime characteristics — its magnitude, the way the figures of people are drawn into these representations, and even the procession in section through a low passageway into a vast interior — are strikingly similar to Étienne-Louis Boullée's Cenotaph for Newton.

What looks like a skyline forms beyond the golden volumes. The back wall of the section is broken into many gridded surfaces. It would seem that the interior is big enough to contain an entire trapped city, as if the context of Tokyo's skyline has been reproduced in the immense interior, creating a city within a city. Stairs crisscross in this mega-atrium leading to the different theaters, backgrounded by a huge operable window, thirty meters high. Visually — and even literally, when open — it connects interior and exterior urbanities. There are almost no openings in the facade, just this one, leaving its interior opaque, closed so as to hide its inner world.

As Mertins observes, "Bounded but boundless, familiar yet tense, whole and fragment, enigmatic and unassimilable, the building visibly eludes itself, failing to hold its shape as it enters an expanded field of correspondences with other things, known and unknowable."[6] In its strange relationship to its context, the visual cues to its magnitude, and its inconceivable interiority, it is intractably an unspeaking icon. Both a black hole and a world unto itself, the project resides in absolute contradiction.

1 Jean Nouvel, "The Crucible," *La Obra Reciente 1987–1990 / His Recent Works 1987–1990* (Barcelona: Quaderns Monografies, 1990), 64; quoted in Detlef Mertins, "Open Contours and Other Autonomies," *Monolithic Architecture*, eds. Rodolfo Machado and Rodolphe el-Khoury (Munich: Prestel, 1995), 38.

2 Franco Bertoni, *The Architecture of Philippe Starck* (London: Academy Editions, 1994), 76; quoted in Mertins, 38.

3 Bertoni, 76; quoted in Mertins, 38.

4 Mertins, 38.

5 Jeffrey Kipnis, "Towards a New Architecture," *Architectural Design 102: Folding in Architecture* (Hoboken, NJ: John Wiley and Sons Ltd., 1993), 56–65.

6 Mertins, 38.

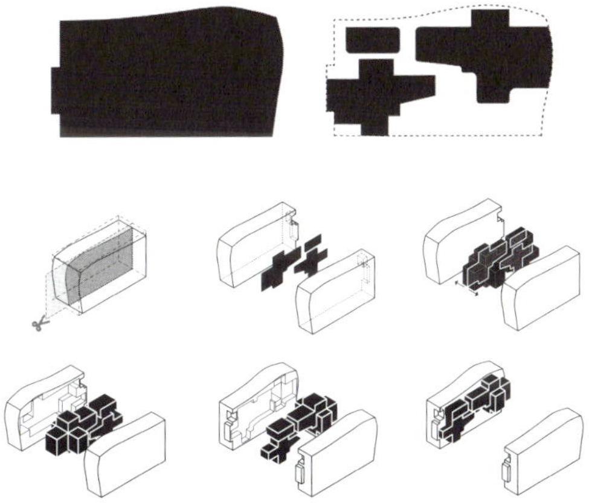

2.20. Tokyo Opera House

TOP: Diagrams, **BOTTOM:** Section

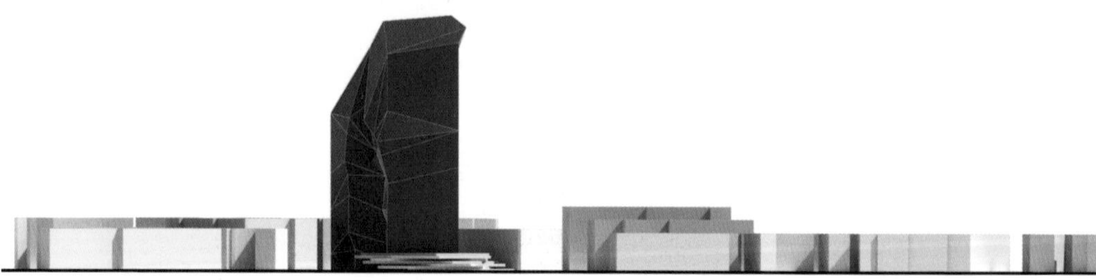

TOP: Elevation, BOTTOM: Elevation with context

2.21 Max Reinhardt Haus, 1992

Architect: Peter Eisenman Location: Berlin, Germany
Project Type: Mixed Use Material: Glass Curtain Wall

Peter Eisenman's unbuilt Max Reinhardt Haus is an unwilling icon and an unspeaking edifice that holds within it a protean universe. Due to the diversity of the program it houses and the magnitude of its scale, the project internalizes an urbanity within a single iconic envelope. But the envelope is not singular, nor is the form it enwraps. The wrapper is folded and faceted so as to trace multiple partial figures. The tower looks to be one, then two, then utterly infinite.

Conceived just one year after the demolition of the Berlin Wall was completed, the project was to be part of a major rebuilding effort in what had been an area of East Berlin. The site was to be located at the major cross-axis of Unter den Linden and Friedrichstrasse in the former location of Hans Poelzig's Grosses Schauspielhaus that had been designed for the theatre director and impresario Max Reinhardt. Situated on the north bank of the Spree River, just across from the site of Mies van der Rohe's unbuilt Freidrichstrasse skyscraper, Eisenman's proposal is as radical as its absent predecessor in its attitude toward its context. The drawings and models describe the project as simultaneously strangely connected and detached.

Densely packed low-rise buildings surround the proposal on three sides to create a virtual podium for the 34-story towering figure. In the model, Eisenman maintains the project's separation from the ground as an autonomous object, setting it atop a raised plaza that is fragmented as if by a geometric earthquake. Its form is based on a Möbius strip, a geometry that is by definition self-contained as an infinite three-dimensional loop made of a single surface.

The project slips into looking like a simple prismatic tower, squared off by a rectangular boundary in plan and elevation. In one model of the project, the tower even completes its loop at the subterranean level to connect across the two sides at its base. Considering the continuity of the Möbius shape in this model and the facets that shape the decaying boundary framing the void, the project reads as one form with a hole through its center. However, viewed from another angle, the Möbius loop can be seen, splitting the form quite nearly into two figures. The prismatic boundary and the void create a tension between singularity and duality. The form turns in on itself so that one leg produces a backdrop for the other. Framing a void in its center, the project creates an interior in the city, a void that ruptures its continuity. A larger-than-life icon, the Max Reinhardt Haus backgrounds an image of itself and frames an image of the city.

In spite of its autonomy and otherness, it is entangled in affiliations with the city both formally and conceptually. The city plays a role in its formation, albeit "artificially," as Alejandro Zaera Polo points out, "through the encoding of accidental qualities of the site and programme as indexical traces."[1] The process includes elements of Berlin's architectural past, inserting cubic volumes that reference Karl Friedrich Schinkel.[2] While the process of the project's creation is tied to the city, the product is where the inflection of city is interesting to the mute icon.

More than a proposal for a building, the complexity and intricacy of the urban terrain is folded up in the interior and enmeshed as a tornado of colliding prismatic forms. The program is a multifarious collection that includes the Max Reinhardt Center for theatre with auditoria and archive, a hotel, a conference center, a media center, a fitness club, offices, restaurants, a vertical mall, a sports center, and press agencies. Its heterogeneity becomes apparent in section with the large auditoria interjecting and disrupting the floor plates and smaller atriums carved out as public voids. Its internal and external interstitially makes it a simulacrum of the city.

The layered relationships of interior and exterior cross conventional boundaries. This is in part due to its conception as a Möbius strip, which is a surface with only one side, with no hierarchy of interior to exterior, and which can't be oriented. In effect, the void is an interior on the exterior of the building. The territory of what might be understood as the interior is shaped by the tumbling cubes that cut through the floor plates to create a multiplicity of voids. Like a city subdivided by blocks and interrupted by public squares, the interior's monotonous floor plates are interrupted by the large-scale cubic volumes that produce a nested interior. From its interior urbanity to its urban interior, in every way it undermines a dialectic of city to building, inside to outside, public to private. It confounds language in its ambiguous complication of terms; its muteness comes in part from its ability to silence.

Multiple models have been built of the project, some white or light gray, some in reflective dark grey with a grid across all of its surfaces — what is shown to be glass that is rendered bright blue in the sections and elevations — but the most striking model is a black solid. It has an imposing presence in its darkness. Its attributes add up to its being a monument, a landmark, an icon, albeit a strange and enigmatic one.

To call this project iconic is somewhat contentious. Charles Jencks identified architectural meaning as taking place when a building looks like something else, like the "ducks" Robert Venturi describes. Peter Eisenman argued in favor of an architecture that refers to nothing other than itself and directly opposed to icons or images in favor of text, index, and process.[3] Jencks critiques Eisenman's resistance to the icon saying, "... Eisenman certainly designs [iconic buildings]. His early white buildings were Terragni ducks... [T]he Max Reinhardt Haus and the Memorial to the Murdered Jews of Europe were each volumetric ducks. The Reinhardt Haus is an icon of folding and an arch."[4] Jencks' argument is a fair one; the Max Reinhardt Haus is undeniably iconic. But while it definitely looks like something — folding, an arch, a Möbius strip, or a cube — that something is a generic, near-Platonic abstraction. And it isn't clearly any of those; you can't put your finger on what exactly it is, and it is difficult to remember its outline precisely. It is identifiable but indefinable, changing on every elevation drawing, around all 360 degrees, and in every plan and section cut. It is at once a formal diagram and a formless entity that is vague in its complexity.

However, what makes the Max Reinhardt Haus stand out most of all is that which is not there: the absence at its center. A black hole in the sky and wormhole through the city, the project sucks in everything in its wake. It is muted by its darkness, emptiness, inconstancy, ambiguity, and unknowability.

ABOVE: Plan oblique

1 Alejandro Zaera Polo, "Eisenman's Machine of Infinite Resistance," *El Croquis*, No. 83, (1997), 57.
2 Terence Riley and Guy Nordenson, *Tall Buildings* (New York: Museum of Modern Art, 2003), 42.
3 Mario Carpo, "The Duck's Swan Song" from "Letters to Log," *Log*, No. 9 (Winter/Spring 2007), 7.
4 Charles Jencks, "Eisenman Ducks" from "Letters to Log," *Log*, No. 9 (Winter/Spring 2007), 10.

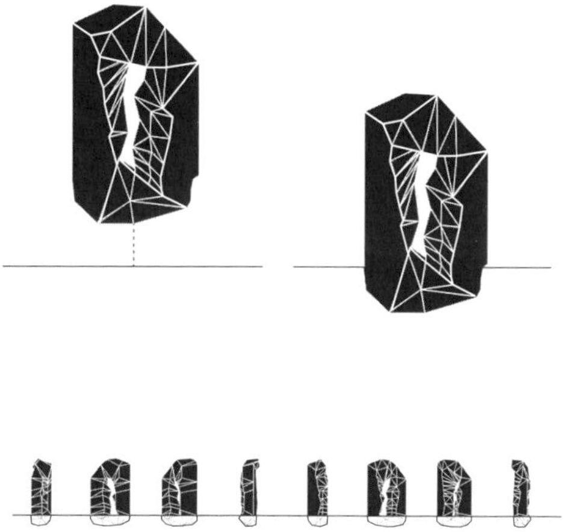

TOP: Diagrams, **BOTTOM:** Elevation

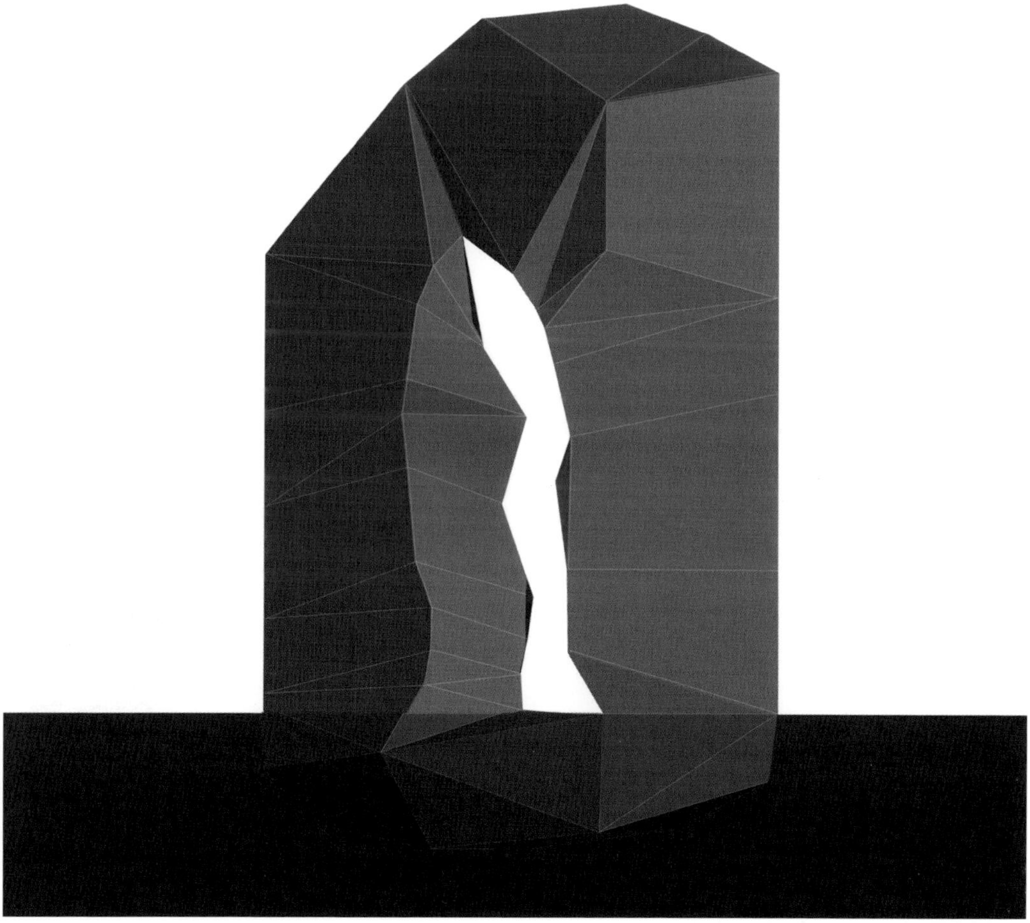

2.21. Max Reinhardt Haus

TOP: Worm's-eye isometric close-up

2.22 Bruges Concert Hall, 1999

Architect: Neutelings Riedijk
Location: Bruges, Belgium
Project Type: Performance Space

Designed to be a venue for performance, Neutelings Riedijk's unbuilt concert hall itself performs in equal measure, taking on a figural posture and projecting an icon over the city of Bruges. Prepared in response to the city's competition — which also included Peter Eisenman, Kisho Korokawa, and the winning team Robbrecht en Daem — Neutelings Riedijk's entry is a powerful architectural provocation. Even with its cartoonish extroverted character, it is strangely mute, posturing an open legibility with a multitude of readings that cancel out any singular image of the project.

The large mass is intended to cantilever over its small, square footprint, with the bulk of its mass elevated to avoid intermingling with the underlying infrastructure, which includes a demolished train station, underground parking, a sunken motorway tunnel, and King Albert I Boulevard. The project is designed to avoid interactions, withdrawing to maintain its autonomy. Its massing faces all directions, seemingly indifferent to its surroundings. But its relationship to the ground and city is strangely tailored. Its short facades are oriented to the medieval town to relate with a weak, squarish silhouette. Its long facades are perpendicular to the boulevard, a pronounced sign to passing motorists with a strong silhouette — its large hull overhanging cars as they descend below the Het Zand Plaza to the west, and its stern embedded in the treed King Albert I Park at its rear.

Appearing like a strange ancient tool or vessel, the project looks too top heavy to rest on the earth and suggests that its natural milieu is not a contemporary city or even a firm ground. The architects describe the project as a "monumental volume with a minimal footprint" and a "distinctive totem sculpture that inscribes itself in the medieval skyline with its belfry tower and church spires as a high-powered symbol of Bruges' new elan."[1] The project is totemic in its figurality and faciality due to its large windows and stacked parts. The elevation of the dominant mass appears like the profile of a ship, lifted above much of the city so that the surrounding buildings of the site model appear as an invisible sea on which the project floats. The site model was photographed as if it was a night shot, with the entire city bathed in blue light and the concert hall illuminated in bright yellow light, reifying its profile as an icon, and making it look all the more like a ship at sea. The project presents a strong image, albeit a restless one. It is always suggesting something other, but what exactly is not clear. The major achievement of this project hovers between multiple images.

The central portion holds the fly tower, with the two performance halls cantilevering out from the core. These programmatic appendages produce the elongated volume that is tilted on one side and curved upward on the other — both beautiful and clumsy features. In the model, the curved appendage is nearly filled with a looming red-orange orb that represents the great hall as a nested object. Between the envelope and the hall, the model is covered in pins and lights, a stand-in for an occupiable girder space with a multilevel stair. The lights cast a reddish hue on the amber interior face of the shell, creating a deeply atmospheric, occupiable poché.

Paradoxically, the heterogeneity of this assembly is made into a difficult whole by draping the parts in a uniform cladding. An embossed vegetal filigree of reddish-brown scallops and flora on a yellowed background — resembling intricate stone masonry of the surrounding context — is wrapped onto the project as a thin sheet of paper. The patterning is out of scale relative to any typical ornament or patterning, with a single petal easily being 10 to 20 feet tall. At a distance, the massive scale of the project might be misunderstood due to the oversized graphics. Stamped across the surfaces in horizontal stripes that are indifferent to the form, the figurative texture masks corners and volumetric juxtapositions. Bob Somol describes Bruges Concert Hall as a "logo," "enact[ing] a hybrid state of figural decoration by overcoming previous alternatives (e.g., of duck and shed), largely through intensifying the incongruence of mass and surface, and condensing them into a 'saturated shape.'"[2] The project is an iconic shape, one that is in tension with the decorative image mapped on it.

The central tower is the only part that rests on the ground while the others seem to be tacked, plugged, or glued onto it. And while the program seems to be tied to these parts, they all step partially into the central tower, crossing over their figural boundaries. The relationship of this massing to the wrapper fits well with Rodolfo Machado and Rodolphe el-Khoury's description of "the composite monolith" in *Monolithic Architecture*. Composite monoliths are:

> assembled from discrete architectural elements, but they sometimes contain contrasting programmatic units that are distinguished by different geometries.... [T]his disparity is only reconciled on the surface, in a unified and continuous envelope that only occasionally yields glimpses into the spatial complexity of the interior.[3]

While it is made from various parts, the individuality, origin, or meaning of those parts is lost. The central tower is not so stable and can be pulled into a relationship with its appendages, composing multiple wholes in various recombinations.

The Bruges Concert Hall creates a potent dichotomy between an assembly of distinct parts and the continuous skin that blurs the boundary between separate elements. Many different combinations of parts are latent in the figure's polyvalence. While the project can be read as a single mass, it multiplies possible formal readings exponentially by erasing the inner boundaries of the intervening parts while keeping their outer projections.

1 Jan Willem Neutelings and Michiel Riedijk, *At Work: Neutelings Riedijk Architects* (Rotterdam: 010 Publishers, 2005), 21.

2 R.E. Somol, "Green Dots 101," *Hunch*, No. 11 (2007), 33.

3 Rodolfo Machado, Rodolphe el-Khoury, *Monolithic Architecture*, (Munich: Prestel, 1995), 15.

TOP: Oblique elevation

2.22. Bruges Concert Hall

TOP: Plan oblique, BOTTOM: Diagrams

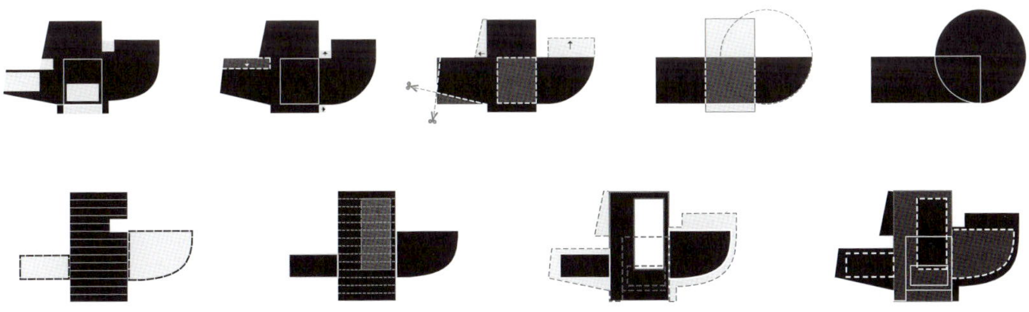

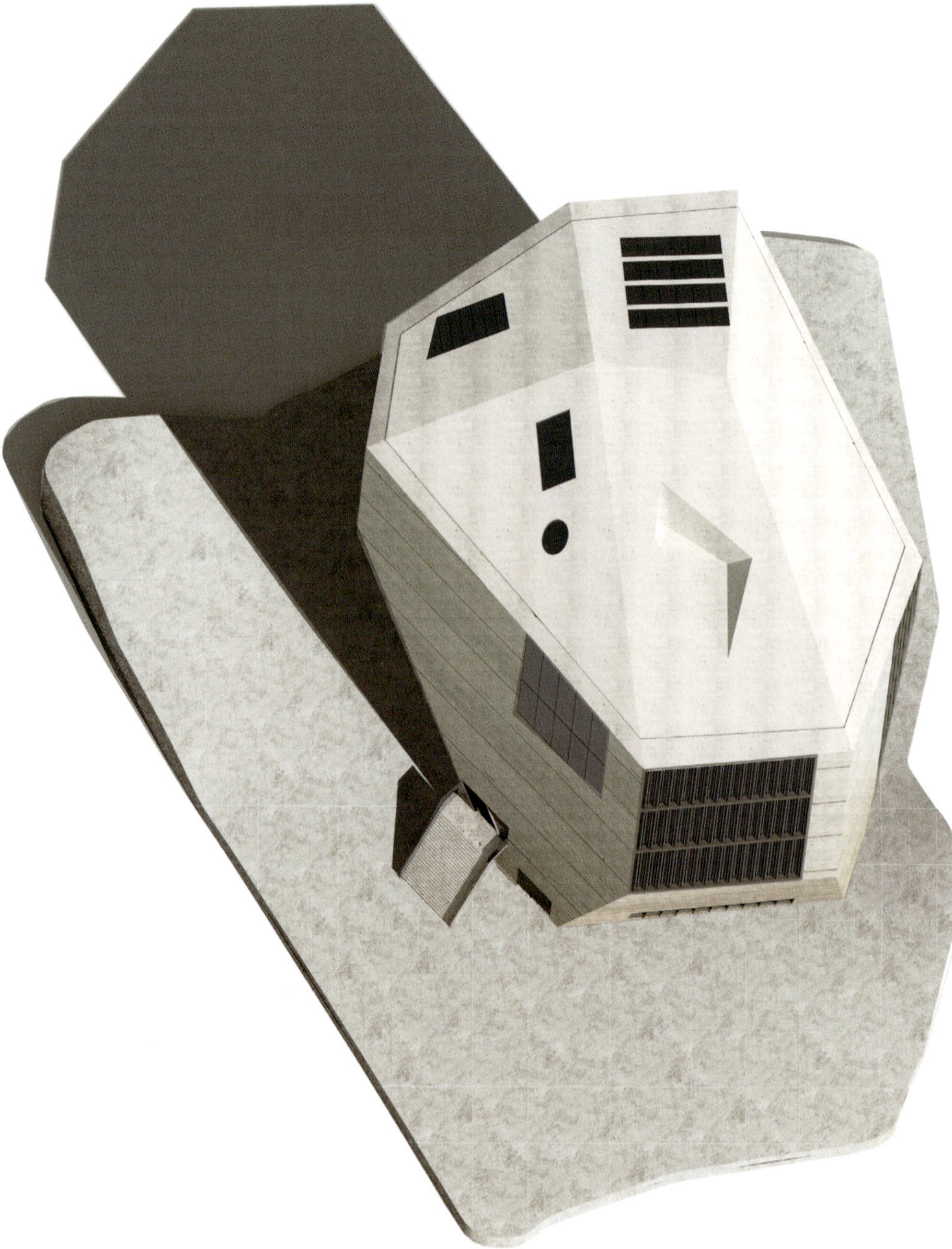

TOP: Plan oblique

2.23 Casa da Música, 2005

Architect: Rem Koolhaas, OMA
Location: Porto, Portugal
Project Type: Performance Space (Concert Hall)
Material: Cast-in-Place Concrete [White Cement]

Casa da Música stands as a singularity within its physical context and in the context of cultural production. The project is an alien, one that incorporates vernacular features that appear unfamiliar in their re-composition. Even the Portuguese tradition of whiteness, concrete, and silence, pioneered by Álvaro Siza, is restaged. Its image is memorable despite its mutability. It is a monolith in a structural sense and in the apparent solidity of its compact, angular mass and unarticulated facades. Rem Koolhaas himself identifies the mass as "stupid and simple."[1] One of the projects best matching this book's definition of a mute icon, this building is not stupid and simple in its layered complexities, rather it is so in the sense that it is loud, but it does not speak.

The elevation of the building is barely articulated with just 16 surfaces despite its immense size. Casa da Música is profoundly iconic, so much so that it is used as a graphic representation for the performance space within its walls, whereby its multiple elevations of its obscure figure act as a variable logo for the concert hall.[2] Casa da Música is identifiable in its crude polyhedral shape; even though it never orients to one particular elevation, it avoids solidifying into a single figure.

Enigmatic not only in its form, the project displays a similar inscrutability in its relationship to context. The building site is bounded along the southeast by Rotunda da Boavista, a park in the center of a roundabout at the intersection of several radiating boulevards. Casa da Música stands on a new travertine-paved public square, a counterpoint to the existing circular park. Within the continuously dense city fabric — otherwise disrupted only by the roundabout and a vacant site to the north that OMA conspicuously fills in their site model collage— the building is framed in a strange void. The concert hall is detached from and framed by that density, an icon with its silhouette clearly displayed. Rather than orienting to the park, the new plaza and object within it de-centers the primacy of the circle. This creates a duality between the void surrounded by urban development and the autonomous object surrounded by a void.

The building's geometry is strangely reminiscent of pitched roofs, but with an all-over treatment that disorients these roofs to cover the whole project and blows them up to ten times their size.[3] Neighboring the Casa da Música to the northeast and the southwest are a dense swath of residential buildings, with low-pitched Spanish tile hip roofs, ceramic tile facades, and Juliette balconies. The mass takes on a vernacular attitude by assuming the angles of the residential roofs. At the same time, it imparts its own balconies that are impressed into the mass of the building and clad in ceramic tile.

On the resulting irregular polyhedra, each elevation is different from the next, but in a few remarkable ways it remains constant: the mass of the building narrows as it approaches the ground, at no vantage does it appear to rest easily on the ground, nor does its posture look static. Its surfaces all cant in at the base, giving the building a small footprint that barely rests on the plaza below. The building is an autonomous object that rejects the ground. It is a giant boulder that has tumbled to the earth and sits on the face on which it happened to land. The entrance reveals that what was perceived as a solid rock actually has a 1'-3" thickness. As Jeffrey Kipnis points out, the entrance stair folds out of the facade to reveal a porthole-like opening, similar to those entrances depicted on spaceships, flatly announcing its foreign nature to Porto.[4] Its risers even illuminate at night, extending out from the glowing entrance, making it all the more a strange vessel.

Underneath the Casa da Música, there is a travertine plaza that forms a new ground.[5] The plaza bubbles up to produce small hills with impressed benches in its surface and a vomitorium that allow pedestrians to pass through as it rises vertically. The plaza lifts above grade to reveal its thinness and artificiality at the southwest and northeast corners of the site, making way for vehicles to descend to the underground parking. At the edge of the site facing the park, the plaza is flush with the grade and seamlessly meets the basalt-paved sidewalk as well as bluntly meeting the street everywhere else where no sidewalks exist. The plaza is leveled and associated with the ground as a thin carpet, but clearly other in its material and formal separation.

The exterior is rough, white concrete, a strange contextual nod to the "shades of cloud"[6] deployed by Álvaro Siza in Porto. The expansion joints and formwork seams are nearly imperceptible at a distance, reinforcing its monolithic appearance. From close up, it can be seen that a grid pattern wraps the object, turning the corners of the building in absolute contradiction to the Modernist bar buildings that provide an orthogonally gridded backdrop to the northwest. It is as if the formwork panels, or the Modernist facades, were wrapped around the building, thrown into various oblique directions to follow the angled surfaces of the exterior. We see a mass that is solid, but one that also hints at a flattened, unrolled version of its surfaces. In spite of the building's monolithicity, the formwork pattern makes us see it as a series of flat images enwrapping its three-dimensional form.

For all the eccentricity of its formwork, Casa da Música's curtain wall grids remain normal to a cartesian axis. This aperture is defined by the large internal voids associated with the theaters, patios, and public spaces. Many of the glazed openings of the building are large, at times nearly consuming an entire surface, while others are smaller strips. The openings are applied with indifference: one is placed at a corner and made to fold around its edge, another conforms to the surface's irregularly angled edges, and others are orthogonal and vary between alignment to an edge or seemingly random placement in the center of a surface. The only shared property is that they are all flush with the concrete surface, flattened to the envelope, with the exception of the two corrugated glass panels. These speak to the opacity of the mass, never clearly providing an internal legibility and never revealing a clear index of its making. Its contents are only revealed in part, without didactic clarity.

The interior is composed of nested boxes, creating ruptures of public space in the gap between their regular forms and the irregular shell. In a diagrammatic model, chunks of blue foam associated with the public interiors can be removed to reveal their volumes and replaced to complete the exterior surfaces. Only the main theater passes the whole way through, acoustically isolated in its separation from the rest of the structure as a box within a box. The theater is autonomous from the shell, a box inside a spaceship that only provides blurred views of the city through the corrugated glass. A continuous public route is fitted between the envelope and internal programmatic volumes, connecting the spaces around the Grand Auditorium with stairs, platforms, and escalators. The precipitous cascade of razor-sharp aluminum steps moves down the concrete shell in a dizzying and disorienting wash of solid and perforated aluminum panels backlit by fluorescent tubes. The blunt mass and boxy interiors become estranged in the space of their overlap, fragmented along this continuum.

Every interior enveloped within the concert hall has a discrete material palette: azulejos (hand-painted tiles), color patterned geometric tiles, green texture resembling acoustic insulation, and a padded purple room. The variety of claddings that coat the interiors hint again to the surfaces that compose the mass of the exterior shell. Investigating the interior of the Grand Auditorium, the walls are clad in plywood that is painted with an enlarged, pixelated, gold wood grain. It is an image of plywood mapped onto plywood. This golden icon becomes an oversized gold filigree that breaks down any clear reading of scale and materiality.

Casa da Música is, both outside and in, an unstable image. An otherworldly entity, it challenges and simultaneously enfolds its surroundings. Its silence resonates in a controlled cacophony of formal oddities and syntheses, contextual disruptions and typological referents, spatial overlaps and figural immutabilities.

1 Roberto Gargiani, *Rem Koolhaas, OMA: The Construction of Merveilles* (Lausanne: EPFL Press, 2008), 272.
2 The logo was designed for the Music Hall by Sagmeister & Walsh creative agency in New York. There is even a logo generator that will transform its colors and a different patterning for each musical organization that performs there.
3 It is well recognized that Casa da Música bears a strong resemblance to OMA's earlier unbuilt Y2K House, designed for the suburbs of Rotterdam, so it is likely that this a typological reference to generic pitched roofs that is not specific to Portugal.
4 Jeffrey Kipnis has stated this reading in several lectures, recently at The Ohio State University's Wexner Center for the Arts lecture entitled, "Sherman and Koolhaas, or how to see through a mirror clearly, face to face," November 8, 2017.
5 Ibid.
6 Deyan Sudjic, "Wrong about Rem," *Log*, No. 6, (Fall 2005), 124.

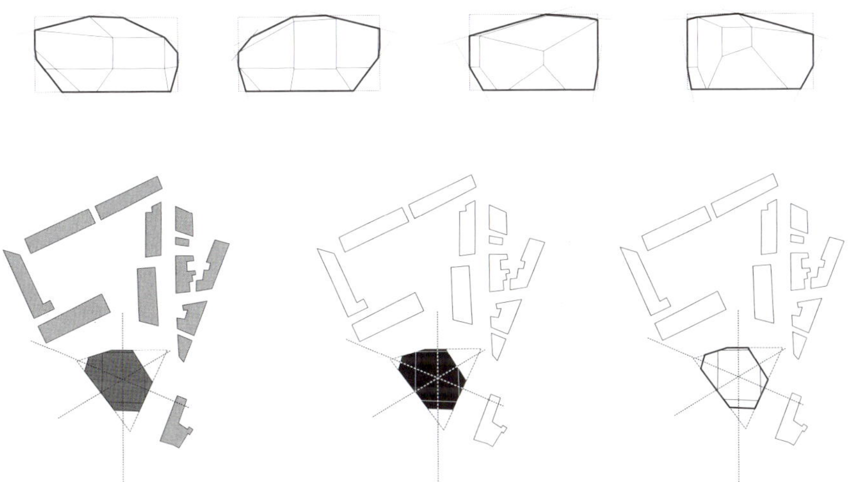

2.23. Casa da Música

TOP: Diagrams, **BOTTOM:** Oblique elevations

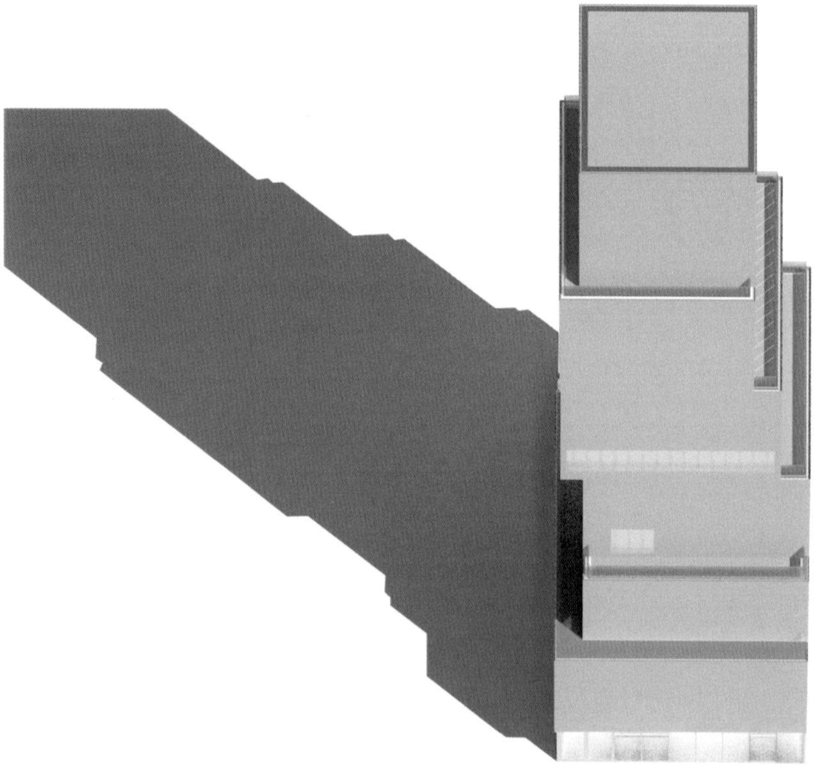

TOP: Plan oblique view, **BOTTOM:** Oblique elevation with context

2.24 New Museum of Contemporary Art, 2007

Architect: SANAA, Kazuyo Sejima and Ryue Nishizawa **Location:** New York, NY, USA
Project Type: Museum
Material: White Expanded Aluminum Mesh

The New Museum is a stacked whole, seven rectilinear boxes orthogonally piled and shifted to conform to a new, unstable body. The tension between part and whole in the tower is a product of the casual displacement of volumes, staggered in relation to the confines of the zoning envelope and central steel core, but uniformly clad in a shimmering veil. The stacking creates a fragility, a precarious state of balance both physically and mereologically.

Set amidst a cluster of relatively small buildings in Manhattan's Bowery neighborhood, the New Museum almost appears as if it was composed out of several context buildings that were defeatured, blanched, and stacked atop one another. From the front elevation, the first volume is the broadest and looks like adequate support for the upper volumes. But upon closer inspection, the entire building appears to hover above the ground, set atop the 15-foot tall plane of clear plate glass that designates the public entrance and loading dock. The next two volumes shift in on the left in relation to the one below, still aligning to one another in the front elevation, but each box steps back from the street. The resulting form is an off-kilter ziggurat like a pile of children's blocks that carries on stepping, offsetting, and overhanging to its top.

Tracing from one elevation to the next, it becomes clear that the seven boxes align to one another in different groupings on each elevation. As such, they create a complex, interdependent set of relationships that shift the reading of the parts on each face. As soon as you think you might be able to group two aligned faces as one, an edge misaligns and pronounces the two surfaces discrete.

Clad in a perforated membrane, the building looks utterly flat. A layer of anodized expanded aluminum mesh gives the impression of paper or fabric in its thin translucency. The metal mesh is suspended just two inches from the opaque surfaces behind it by nearly-invisible welded connections, so that the perforated and opaque surfaces meld and read as one, the corners barely revealing the subtle offset of the wrapper. This conflation of translucent and opaque, milky surfaces visually flattens the volumes, causing their outlines to delicately flicker, enveloping the building in atmosphere.

The New Museum's color cannot be pinned down. It looks to be white on white, a pristine abstraction. With light variably reflecting off the aluminum and the panels beyond, the building shimmers and even appears to glow. This is amplified by the Bowery's "gritty"[1] quality, making the building look all the more elegant, light, and white by comparison. But over the course of the day, the envelope fluctuates between grays, silvers, and whites. In the right light conditions, the silver of the expanded metal can be seen, and the rift between this layer and the white panels behind it is filled with subtle cast shadows, shading the facade with graphite tones. The figure of the shadows is not visible but results in a lack of shadow, of shadow's effects being erased by an all-over diffused cloud of gray.

The shifting of the mass allows the roof planes to break open into skylights, reducing the need for wall aperture to only a few ribbon windows. These ribbons split the volumes and imbue them with strange, new seams that fall behind the seamless screen. The screen simultaneously dematerializes views of the building and those seen out through its windows. When the interior is illuminated at night, the glazing strips glow beneath the screen and light pours upward out of the skylights, driving home the counter-gravity effect of the cantilevers and thin aesthetic.

It is not the actual building components that are seen; these are masked behind the wrapper to highlight the part to whole relationships of the massing and cause the building to look more monolithic. Aperture, balustrades, floor plates, and the massive diagonal bracing of the structural steel frame are all hidden behind the veiled shell that obscures their location and, with it, many scalar cues. Similarly, glass curtain walls are set into the floor in order to mask their frames. The hidden floor plates are partially untethered from the exterior massing, with different heights at each level and eccentric pockets of space interjected at irregular points, further dissolving their relationship to the exterior. The apparent thinness of the exterior looks more like an edited image or a gauzy model than a rough metal building, and its large cantilevers contradict our expectations of physics. Perhaps the only injection of scale can be found on the terraces created by the shifting boxes where people and artworks can be seen from the street. Looking all the more abstract, the building is an alien and neutral backdrop to mundane reality's polychromy.

Situated at the origin of Prince Street on Houston, the New Museum's exposed position and verticality allow the building to be seen from a considerable distance as an iconic silhouette on the skyline. Few towers in the middle of a city are afforded a site that allows the entire front face to be seen uninterrupted from the ground up from several streets away. This long-range visibility exposes an uncanny effect: the building transforms in relation to distance. At a great distance, the facade looks totally solid, so much so that it might be assumed that it is made of stucco or concrete. Within a block, the building slips out of focus, becomes blurry, losing detail as the contrast of light and shadow is lowered and the form's hard edges are softened.

Up close, the roughness can be seen at its most extreme, a complete inversion of the distant impressions. Turning to Kazuyo Sejima and Ryue Nishizawa's description of their endeavors, "We wanted to make interiors that expose the way they work in a 'beautiful rough' way…. [W]e want to show what the building is made of and maximize the feeling of openness, but do it in a beautiful way inside the parameters of the toughness."[2] The toughness can be seen in the lobby's structural grid, with exposed beams, aluminum deck, fluorescent bulbs under metal-mesh, and polished concrete floors. The contradictions of its "beautiful rough" quality are unlocked over time and space.

The New Museum evolves over shifting distance. It oscillates between delicate fuzziness and industrial roughness. Its supernatural frame simultaneously projects an enigmatic glow and dissolves shadows. It is fully material and fully an image, the two lock in a perpetual shift in prominence.

1 Clifford A. Pearson, "At New York's Smart New Museum of Contemporary Art, Tokyo-based SANAA Creates an Unambiguous Icon for an Area in Transition," *Architectural Record*, Vol. 196, No. 3 (March 2008), 132–139.

2 "New Museum: Building," *New Museum*, newmuseum.org/building (accessed June 9, 2018).

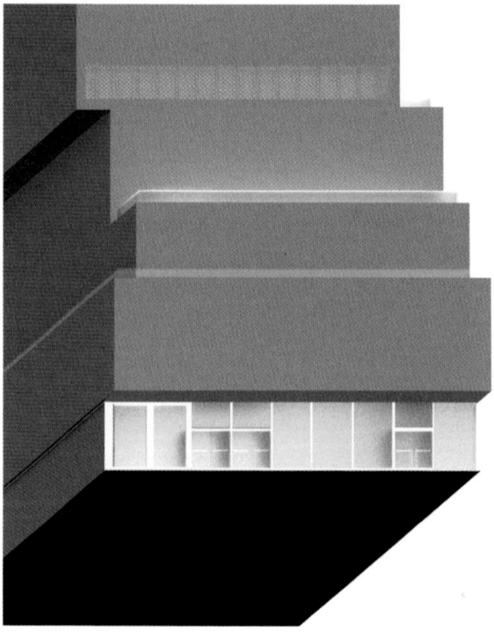

ABOVE: Worm's-eye isometric close-up

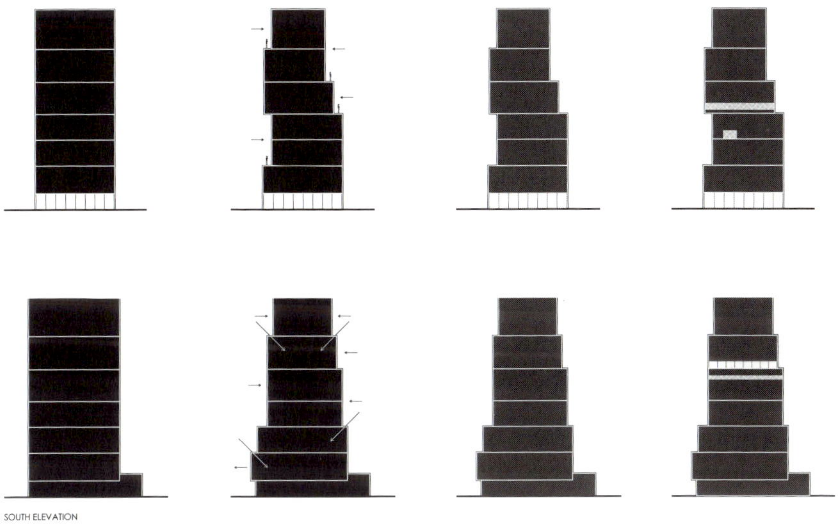

TOP: Diagrams, **BOTTOM:** Oblique elevation with context, close-up

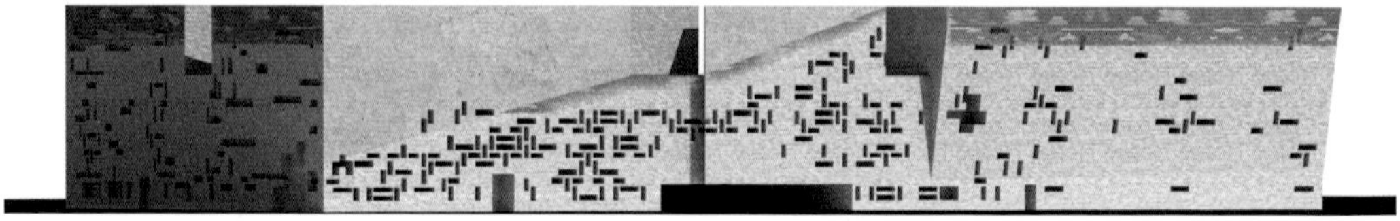

TOP: Isometric, **BOTTOM:** Oblique elevation

2.25 Ningbo Historic Museum, 2008

Architect: Amateur Architecture Studio, Wang Shu and Lu Wenyu **Location:** Ningbo, China
Project Type: Museum
Material: Brick, Concrete and Recycled Tiles

Ningbo Historic Museum is a radical departure from the global idea of the icon, challenging the idea that icons are universal and can be easily exported. The museum collapses history through the superposition and adaptation of formal and material strategies from traditional Chinese and contemporary architecture. Given this focus, the iconicity of this project is found neither in its overall massing nor its silhouette. It is the surface materials that make this project absolutely distinct. The rubble walls — piled together like a giant ant farm or a geologic cut revealing a sedimentary formation — are composed of recognizable individual elements but also have a new accumulative aesthetic.

Sited on a former rice field in an expansive landscape typical of contemporary China, the museum is located a dozen kilometers from Ningbo's historic center; the museum is at a remove from the surrounding new residential, retail, and government buildings. An isolated object, the museum is bordered only by a park and empty fields that await future development. It appears as a collection of multiple buildings or city fragments, a 12-meter tall miniature skyline or large model of a town sitting atop a 12-meter plinth. The gashes in the upper form create an accessible roofscape, and in so doing, recreate the proportions of a traditional Chinese village.[1] Surrounded by mountains to the south and west, the building's toothed upper half could also be said to resemble its craggy backdrop — in Wang's own words, it is an "artificial mountain."[2] The building fuses constructed and geographic context while it recalls past and present, occupying monumental and residential scales.

With the muteness of its Platonic geometry, the form appears to be derived from an ideal rectangular volume. Angular cuts in its massing cause the facade to tilt outward at the top, reeling unsteadily forward. The rectangular prism is carved away by a low gateway at the first floor and is further depleted at its upper half by three carved valleys in the roof, one of which is filled with a giant staircase. Two sunken courtyards pierce through the center of the building and two more exist on its periphery. The character of the building is fortresslike, given its rough material, massive scale, and formal attributes. The roofline could be reframed in another scale to resemble the crenelations of a castle. To the north, the project is surrounded by a man-made pond, separating it from the ground and producing a moat to secure its independence as an object in the landscape.

The Ningbo Historic Museum is a strange presence in the landscape and a literal exhibition of a lost technique of building. The Jury Citation for the 2012 Pritzker Architecture Prize described the museum as "an urban icon, a well-tuned repository for history" and Wang's work as having "the unique ability to evoke the past, without making direct references to history."[3] The museum — dedicated to the history of humanities and the arts on the east coast of China — contains history not only in its collection but in its very facade. The rubble wall borrows from Wapan construction, a regional construction technique deployed after typhoons.[4] In Ningbo, old villages were razed to clear the surrounding land for the two new government administration buildings, an extensive plaza, and a cultural center to the east of the museum. Wang repurposed the broken bricks and tiles from demolished villages, "collect[ing] traces of time"[5] by composing the facade out of the shards of its site.

The complex, layered facade deploys one system of bamboo-formed structural concrete and another composed of stacked rubble — the salvaged remains of the farmers' razed homes —

including 20 different types of grey, red, and black brick and tile. Both systems are striated, echoing horizontal lines up the facade, a cross between geological sedimentation and archeological ruins mixed with the fossilized remains of bamboo groves. Additionally, both are scattered with small horizontally- and vertically-oriented rectilinear openings that resemble the piling of irregular units in the rubble wall.

The project is determined in part by the architect and in part through the ad hoc invention of the construction process, free from the strictures of precisely patterned elevations. The rubble wall was only loosely controlled by Wang, who would guide the builders but did not determine the entire process.[6] Wherever the facade of the museum tilts out at an angle, the wall shifts to bamboo-formed concrete, while the bricks and tiles cover the straight, vertical facades. A concentration of recycled tiles can be found at the top half, the dark layers of which give a heaviness to even the vertical wall. All that said, the distribution of material units and their relationship to labor falls between rigor and inexactitude. Certain qualitative combinations are achieved, but it is hard to say what, if any, controls are placed on the deviations within the rubble walls. The constructive fact of the facades' imprecision and unique relationship to craft makes this project far more elusive and singular than it first appears.

The brick and tile surfaces meet the bamboo-cast concrete surfaces, creating a paradoxical hybrid of a monolithic and an aggregate building. The disparity between the two construction systems is so strong that the continuity of the folded surfaces is challenged. Moving around the elevations, there is a unifying discontinuity, associating and distancing one face from the other. The surface treatment and articulation constitute a different kind of brutalism, one that can't be reduced to béton brut or surface rustication.

The uncanny combination of these textured surfaces and their monumental scale make the building an iconic ruin. The Ningbo Historic Museum is a contemporary historic project that is indicative of China's complicated history and relationship to modernization. It elucidates the possibilities and limits of assembly and craftsmanship at a large scale.

1 Evan Chakroff, "Recasting History: The Ningbo Historic Museum," *Log*, No. 24: *Architecture Criticism*, (Winter/ Spring 2012), 59.
2 Wang Shu and Hsieh Ying-Chun, *Illegal Architecture: Wang Shu and Hsieh Ying-Chun* (Taipei, Taiwan: Garden City Publishers, 2012), 17.
3 "Wang Shu Jury Citation," The Pritzker Architecture Prize, pritzkerprize.com/ laureates/2012 (accessed May 28, 2015).
4 Chakroff, 58.
5 Wang Shu and Hsieh Ying-Chun,17.
6 Chakroff, 58.

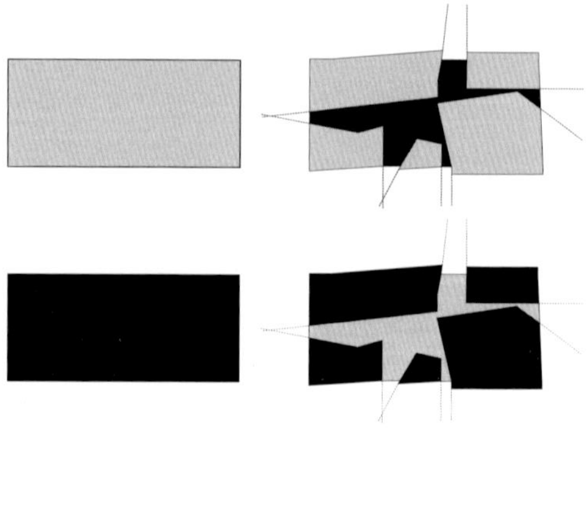

ABOVE: Diagrams

TOP: Isometric close-up, **BOTTOM:** Plan oblique

TOP: Plan oblique with context, BOTTOM: Oblique elevation with context

2.26 Caixa Forum, 2008

Architect: Herzog & De Meuron
Location: Madrid, Spain Project Type: Museum
Material: Perforated Corten Steel

Herzog & De Meuron's Caixa Forum is a difficult whole, a singular image of multiple figures balanced between multiple possible histories. The existing brick building is sandwiched between the two halves of the addition; atop the roof of the existing building a monolithic protrusion has been added, and at the base, a cavernous plaza has replaced the removed lower portion of the existing building in a subtractive operation. This building hides behind its context and through cursory formal references to that context; but, its form is also in clear opposition to its surroundings as are its tectonic, material, and chromatic qualities.

Located in Madrid's Golden Mile high-end fashion district and Paseo del Arte museum quarter, the Caixa Forum takes up nearly the entire block. The dense urban fabric is open around the museum due to the demolishing of an old gas station at the southeast corner of the block and an empty lot to the northwest where a building burned down. As a result of this relief at its edges, the Caixa Forum is a discrete object and exists as an iconic presence, partially detached and isolated in an area that is otherwise defined by narrow streets and buildings tightly packed to the sidewalk's edge. But for all its iconic qualities, its form is withdrawn. The building is set back from the Paseo del Prado to the east, tucked behind a row of existing buildings that line the boulevard. Its east facade is exposed only in part by the southeast entrance plaza. It is further isolated from the context by the freestanding green wall that lines the plaza. This green wall forms a graphic barrier and masks the adjacent hotel's heavily ornamented facade.

Appearing to levitate, the Caixa Forum is theatrically unmoored from the ground and defies gravity. The pink masonry walls of the former power station are imbued with a surreal weightlessness. This is amplified by the proximity of the wall to the ground — as low as two or three feet above the rising street level at the rear of the site — such that the walls remain in tension with the earth's crust. Even the entrance staircase is suspended just inches above the ground. Barely perceptible, dark, reflective glass conceals the three points where the building ties into the ground, dissolving these structural and circulation elements in the shadowy underbelly of the building.

The obsolete power station with twinned roof pitches is an industrial brick relic. Found in a state of ruin, it is clearly from another time, strangely preserved with parts of its walls having been patched with two slightly different colors of brick. The original brick remains but is filled in by the second color of brick following the stepped profiles of once-collapsed portions of the walls. That second brick is repeated in all of the original windows, which have been bricked over and made coplanar with the facade during the course of the building's life. A third brick color is introduced at the edges of the windows' bricked surrounds, amplifying their ghostly presence. Like a restored object in a museum, traces of its deterioration and reconstruction remain visible.

Despite its appearance as an honest historical reconstruction, the building depicts false narratives. The sills and architraves on its facade always told and continue to tell a lie about the interior of the building. Even at the time of its conception and construction, these elements "suggested floors and rooms that were never there."[1] In its original state, it was merely a hollow shell containing massive iron wheels.[2] Even now, the galleries within are indifferent to the sealed windows' placement. The Caixa Forum is "a decorated shed,"[3] an image of a building. The closure of these windows flattens the facade, abstracting the envelope and turning the project into a pseudo-monolithic form. It is an unarticulated solid that withdraws from any expression of its superficial depth or interior organization.

For all its reconstruction, the existing building is moreover mutilated, amputated, and defaced. The granite block base on which its weight was formerly borne is removed. It has been excised, following a stepped edge that does not mark a singular datum on the elevations. A few idiosyncratic cuts are taken out of the facade, creating windows that are independent of any existing order of the brick facade. The brick shell is not an object of reverence, but a weightless clay mass on which the indifferent systems of the new project come to bear.

In direct opposition to the existing building's antigravity, the material and massing look heavy and heavier still at the top. It is as if a rock made of roughly-textured, oxidized iron were bearing down on the existing building, This rock is a darker, ruddy color, a distortion of the light pink brick of the existing building. But for all its apparent density and opacity, this top-heavy attachment shifts to a delicate lattice-work toward its top. At its pinnacle, the mass on the roof becomes a porous screen that contradicts its own massiveness, with small glimpses of the blue of the sky able to be seen from the interior through its perforated surfaces. Its thinness is concealed at the corners, and its pattern doesn't reveal the structure behind, leaving it to appear like a solid mass in spite of its delicacy.

The project's iconic identity as an object comes not only in its detachment from the ground and surrounding context but in the way that it is amplified in the identifiable profile of its roof. While it conforms as an extrusion of the existing building's footprint, the uppermost extent is an irregular, jagged outline that resembles oversized castle battlements. The facade looks absolutely foreign to its surroundings, and yet its form is oddly familiar. The roof reflects a strange affinity with its context; its inlets are analogous to nearby pocket courtyards in the dense urban block, and its stepping silhouette mirrors the low, staccato skyline of the surrounding buildings. But these affinities are not overt — they are subtle, contradictory links to the context that are overruled by the building's abrupt and alien character.

Even with the bold identity of its roofline, the Caixa Forum cannot be reduced to a simple silhouette. Instead, the building projects a composite of its many conflicting profiles. There is the irregular line that defines the plaza's ceiling, the pitched roof of the brick building, the pixelated edge between solid and perforated panels, and the roofline of the crystalline top. And even the new roofline is a multiplicity unto itself. The profile of the facade shifts as it moves across from one side to the next, as the chunks of mass are carved away from the solid prism on the oblique. The experience is of a shifting roof profile as visitors move around the building.

The covered plaza is as alien as the roof. Enveloped in a cloud of triangulated facets of welded aluminum panels, the plaza is the chiaroscuro realm of an otherworldly cave. Reaching down to pull visitors up the stairs and into the museum, the folded and inverted landscape that creates the ceiling of the plaza is flexibly untethered from the mass above. Water percolates in small fountains, emphasizing its grotto-like attributes. Light reflects near the perimeter on the silvery surfaces, but these faces appear black as they fold away from the street and are deeply inset under the building's shadow. The plaza's gray-scale coloration and faceted geometry contrast with the reddish brick yet relate to it in their mirrored locations and radical difference.

Following a long architectural tradition nowadays referred to as "adaptive reuse," this project neither harmonizes the addition with the existing nor stands in complete opposition to it. Rather, it creates a new complicated whole, one that is both iconic and mute. It is iconic in the immediacy of its profile and the relentless and vicious interventions exacted on the old. Its muteness emerges in its ability, against all odds, to equalize its image, appearing almost natural. Formal violence towards the existing building is disguised, a crippling restoration is normalized, while the actual addition is neither celebrated nor foregrounded. Instead, everything is compacted together. Resulting material contrasts and differences are all resolved on a single plane, accentuating the dichotomy of being both dissimilar and unified at the same time.

1 Justin Mcguirk, "Caixa Forum," *Icon Magazine*, July 8, 2008, iconeye.com/404/item/3368-caixa-forum (accessed October 27, 2017).

2 Ibid.

3 Ibid.

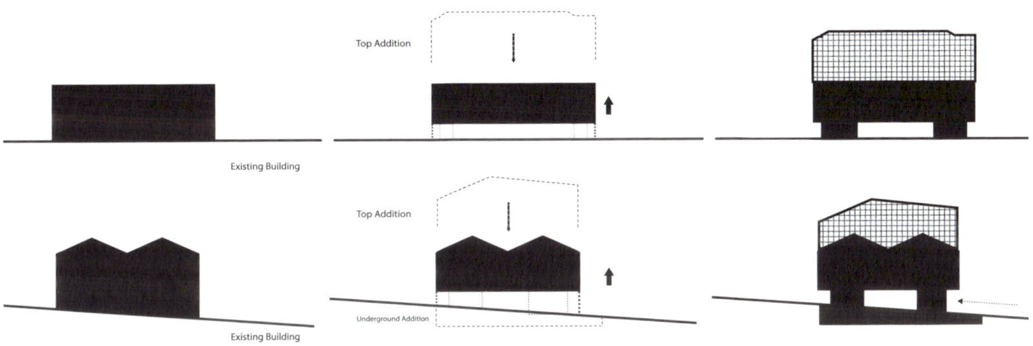

TOP: Diagrams, **BOTTOM:** Worm's-eye isometric

2.26. Caixa Forum

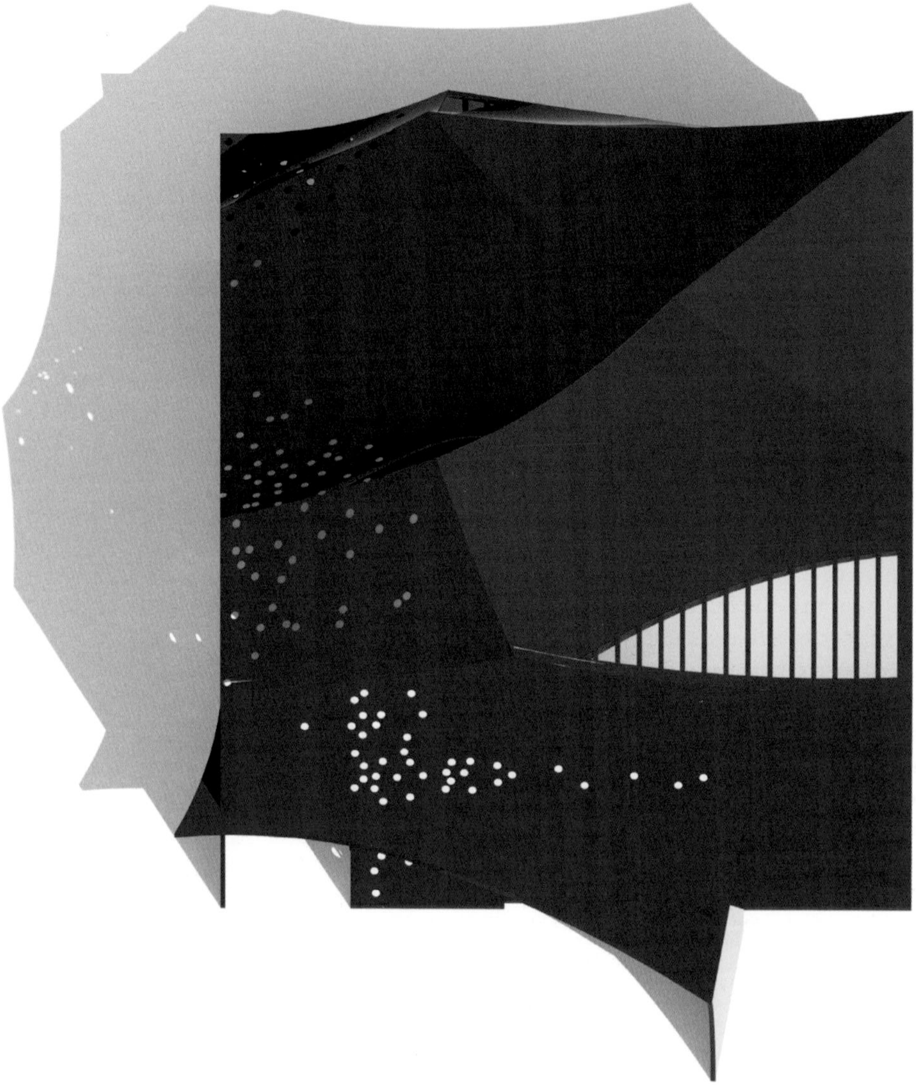

TOP: Plan oblique

2.27 Za-Koenji Public Theater, 2009

Architect: Toyo Ito **Location:** Tokyo, Japan
Project Type: Performance Space
Material: Black Corten Steel

The shadowy figure of Za-Koenji Public Theater exists as a contradiction. A top-heavy black iceberg, the building has three levels above and three levels below grade. It responds to its site while also rejecting it: it is immaterial and massive; it operates as a form on one hand and a shape on the other. These oppositions create a building with multiple characters, one that is both inviting and withdrawn.

The mass is bound by the same height-restrictions as the surrounding urban fabric, but, in every other way, Za-Koenji is the black sheep of the low-rise skyline. At a distance, it appears strangely cropped, filling up the constraints of its tight square plot and leaving only a sliver of space untouched on its site. In plan it is clear that the building is offset from most of the surrounding buildings, withdrawing from the street front by rotating off-axis and aligning to nothing. Its Platonic shape is pushed into the corner located at the intersection of the back and side alley. This misfitting of its square perimeter with the densely packed context produces wedge-shaped gaps between the two. The gaps are stitched with ground treatment, overhangs, and outbuildings that negotiate the irregular offset. The theater's relationship to context is in tension, balanced between rejecting and responding to its surroundings.

The Theater is further alienated from its predominantly light, neutral-colored neighbors in its obscuring darkness. Cloaked entirely in black steel, blackness shrouds the building causing it to appear as an ominous shadow that has fallen over its site. Only the faintest sheen of the satin fluororesin coating reveals the curvature of its form through subtle highlights. Where the walls meet each other and the roof, there is no chamfering, no blended cuts, clearly privileging mass over surface. Even though it is composed of parts, Za-Koenji's uniform darkness and seamless corner connections imbue it with a powerful monolithicity. The project hovers between being an immaterial shadow and massive monolith.

The facades appear to be undifferentiated at a glance, but there is a shift in the character across the project. Its height increases from northeast to southwest; it is at its lowest point when seen from the back of the site and reaches its highest point on the facade that faces the main street. Pointed summits punctuate the roof and consequently shape the elevation and interior public spaces. The only thin surface that projects out from the cube creates an entrance canopy at the south, primary facade, overhanging the entrance and the rotated subterranean theater that remains unseen below. At the ground plane, the subtle projection and rotation of one of the Theater's three performance spaces is revealed in the groundscaping and the projection of the canopy that slips just past the corner from the south onto the west facade.

As a result, the entire roof of the Za-Koenji Public Theater is visible from the back, producing a deep, mountainous backdrop. By contrast, its primary facade is flat, a cartoonish silhouette that looks like an oversized, uncanny house with a sagging pitched roof. Its character fluctuates between the severity of formal complexity at the rear and a playfully simple profile at the front. Za-Koenji is a contradiction within itself, one that is introverted in its seriousness and inviting in its ludic quality.

Aperture is made to play into the building's divergent characters. The austere black figure is punctuated by small portholes that contradict its severe nature and give it a graphic quality. The only significant opening that is not a portal is a curtain wall that fronts the offices, but it is hidden behind the context at the building's southeast corner. The punctures in the facade slip onto adjacent surfaces, emphasizing the continuity of the corners and monolithic quality. The facade remains conceptually opaque, concealing its interior organization via the indiscriminate location of portals relative to its floors and decisively hidden windows, tucked behind a high parapet at the offices.

While the square plan remains relatively static and mute, the complex roof geometry breaks from this regularity to create a spiky meringue silhouette. Five cones and two cylinders articulate scooped removals in the roofs terrain. Ito described his intention for these operations saying, "On one hand I want to regulate it, not with pure geometry but with a kind of geometry generated by algorithms, yet I also want to keep it free. The two feelings are continuously entangled."[1] Using an algorithm allows the geometry to convey a minimum degree of intention.

This geometry resembles a frozen tent, the fabric shell of which is turned into rigid steel with a false material behavior. In fact, Ito likens the building to "a tent cabin"[2] with large steel templates cut to form the profile of built surfaces, like fabric panels cut from a tailor's pattern. Ito deployed a steel plate with reinforced concrete construction technique, wherein concrete is cast on the steel plates and remains in place as permanent reinforcement for the incredibly thin wall construction. Ito's fascination with the form and thinness of tent structures is realized, but with their temporality, tensility, material fluidity, and optical and auditory transparency turned upside down to behave in precisely the opposite way.

This tent enwraps the interior's floating structural system, with every floor slab, wall, and ceiling being insulated from its main structural frame. Each theater is offset on nearly every side from the perimeter, acting as nested objects that are doubly enveloped by their autonomous shell. Accommodated within are the three black-box theater halls: the main auditorium, a subterranean civic hall directly below that, and the subterranean Koenji Awa-Odori festival hall that is rotated by five degrees from the rest of the plan. The last of these is echoed in the awning that protrudes from the front of the building, introducing its strange eccentricity above ground and alluding to the building's iceberg-like quality in the fact of its doubled mass below.

A material and formal enigma, the Za-Koenji Public Theater resists any singular interpretation. It stands out against its context and defies it, but is generic and responds to its surroundings. Even the way in which decisions about its design were made levitates between categories, incorporating nonhuman and human actors. Its character shifts and exposes multiple systems that act in unison to create an unknowable whole.

1 Toyo Ito, "Liquid Space and Fractal Boundary," *El Croquis: Toyo Ito 2005–2009*, No. 147 (2009), 19.

2 Toyo Ito, "Za-Koenji Public Theatre," *El Croquis: Toyo Ito 2005–2009*, No. 147 (2009), 128.

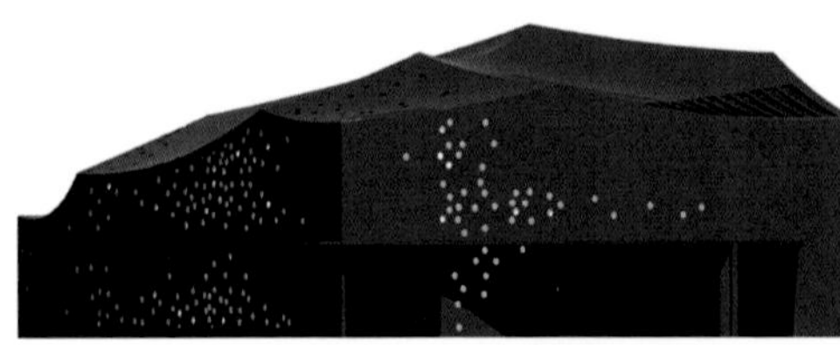

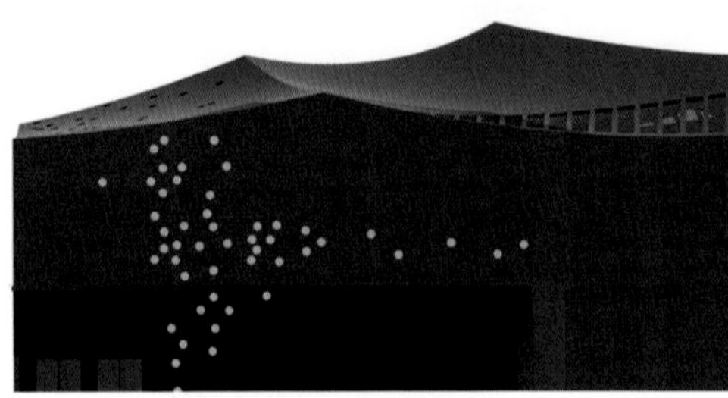

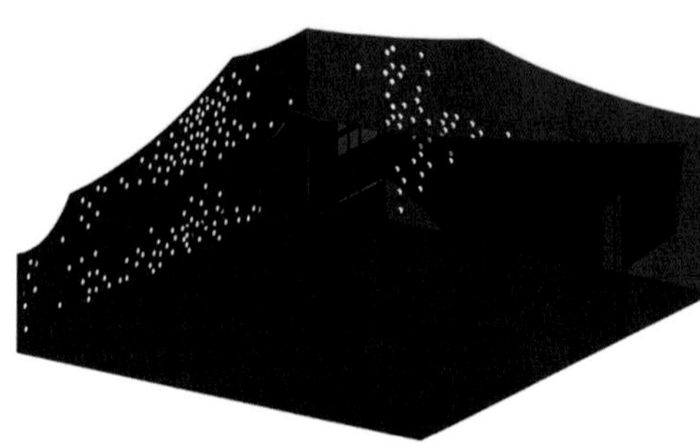

TOP: Elevations, **BOTTOM:** Worm's-eye isometric

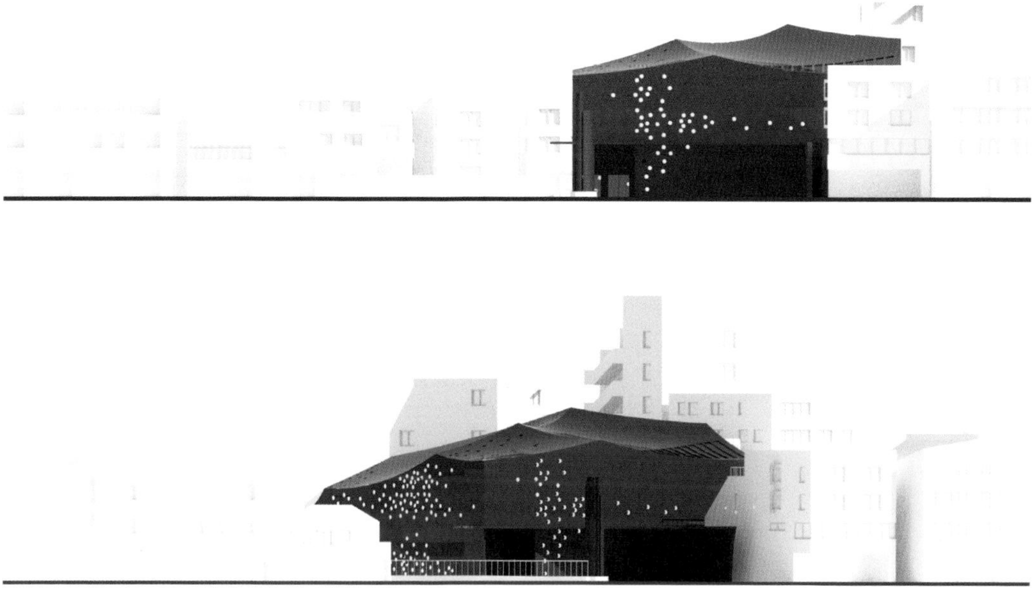

TOP: Elevations with context, BOTTOM: Diagrams

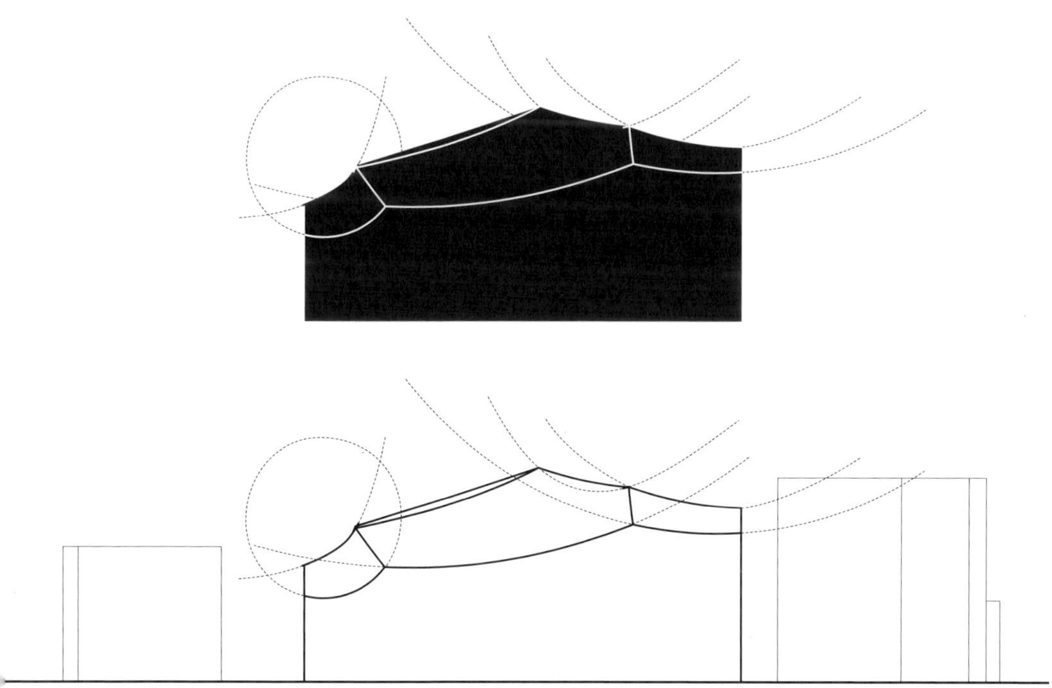

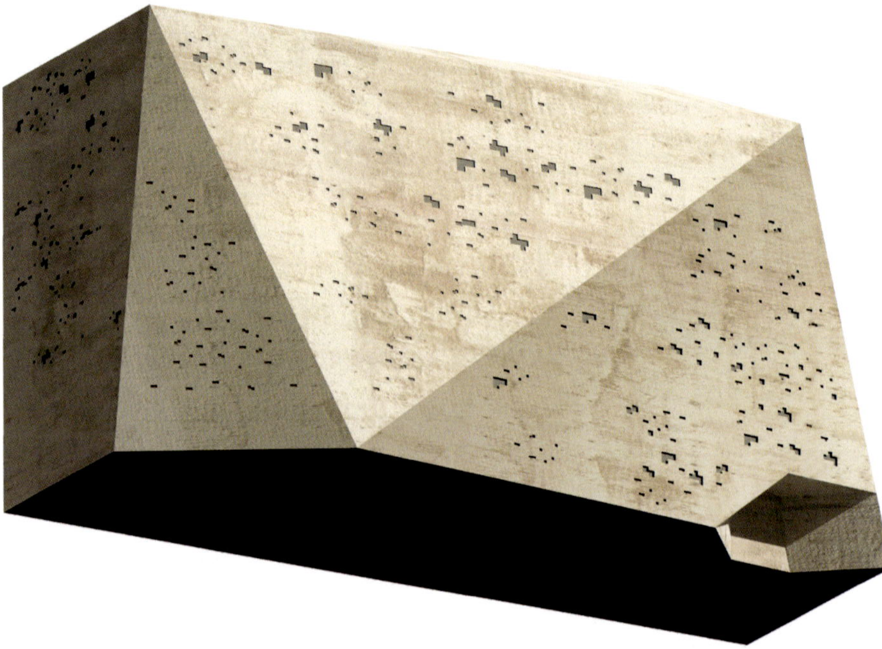

TOP: Worm's-eye isometric, **BOTTOM:** Elevation with context

2.28 Bern Historical Museum, 2009

Architect: :mlzd Architects
Location: Bern, Switzerland
Project Type: Museum
Material: Cast-in-Place Concrete

History is at stake in the aesthetics of the Bern Historical Museum. The extension by :mlzd — located at the head of the Kirchenfeld Bridge in Bern's museum quarter, just north of an enclave of additional cultural buildings — is a crystal-faced and partially submerged tower set into a podium that appears to stand in radical opposition to the existing building. Upon closer examination, it is clear that the project acknowledges and responds to the historical structure, while at the same time creating a duplicitous mirror and unlike analog.

Planimetrically, the project stages a dialogue with the existing building of 1894, designed by Swiss architect André Lambert. The extension is located in a formerly vacant plaza left by an absent wing that would be symmetrical with the western one. The new building is proportionally identical to the existing west wing in length, width, and height, and is placed at the same distance from the center. But, rather than resting in the precise location that would complete the symmetry, it sits in front of and frames the absent wing of the castle, producing a loosely bounded void.

This controlled contextualism is paired with a radical stylistic discontinuity between the extension and the existing. Appearing as a ruin or a geologic boulder, the tower, referred to as *Kubus* or cube, seems as if it may predate the castle, a prehistoric remnant of a geologic past that its predecessor's ornate form was built around. Unadorned, simplified, and evoking the image of a rock from three cardinal directions, the polygonal block acts as a visible landmark that reproduces the mountains — Eiger, Mönch, Jungfrau — visible in the background. The geometry of the facade has even another likeness; it is akin to the combination hip roof of the historic building. The extension's visual coincidence links it to these as a form that is a roof, a mountain, and a rock.

As it were, neither building belongs to the time it summons. The Lambert building harkens back to 15th- and 16th-century castle design.[1] Loosening the relationship to a linear history, the building shakes the very center of the program it contains. Thus, Bern presents its own history through collections in an envelope that implies multiple fictive histories. The extension to the Bern Historical Museum is both object and ground, mass and plinth. The monolithic mass looks to be discrete; however, it is internally interconnected with the plinth. The two are both filled with an exhibition and storage program that is connected by a vertical shaft of circulation. Sharing visual and material qualities as well, both are clad in a yellowish, textured concrete implying that they share a bedrock-like solidity. The plinth is fronted by a monumental staircase that is intersected with a set of switchbacking diagonal stairs. These zigzag profiles imbue the constructed ground with similar oblique geometry that echoes the concrete mass. Two corners on the western side of the south elevation meet at a landing and at the base of stairs in precise alignment, alluding to their possible continuity and solidity.

The facade of the extension is an interplay of textured concrete littered with small openings that are disguised amidst a pattern of similar deeply imprinted or subtly embossed pixels. The openings reveal the depth of the 14-inch-thick concrete shell, as they are deep set in the facade and create dark shadows. Their scale and scattered arrangement reveal nothing about the interior beyond. The envelope further reveals the faint lines and the texture of the oriented strand board formwork. This, paired with the yellowish tinge of the concrete, imbue the surfaces with the patina of artificial time. Playing into its fictive past, the facade of the extension seems to be eroded and weathered instead of constructed. The textural figuration of the surfaces resembles a medieval wall in a state of advanced ruination, wherein individual or groupings of bricks are arbitrarily missing.

At the same time, the extension of the Bern Historical Museum can be seen as an allusion to the articulation of the older museum's facades. In fact, 14 photographs of the partially-carved stone block quoining found in the old building were repeatedly enlarged until only pixels could be seen, and then these were used in the production of the pixelated windows.[2] Normally a source of scale and proportion in a building, aperture here reinforces the scalar indeterminacy of the mass. The small size of these openings relative to the monolithic whole augments the building's perceived monumentality.

The front, south facade is nearly impenetrable, with the exception of a chunk of the mass carefully excised to form the unassuming entrance to the archives at the boulder's southeast corner. Two concealed additional panel doors indelicately attempt to hide their presence, albeit with less success. This facade juts out, creating room behind the angles of the concrete for a continuous stair that connects to the irregularly shaped apertures. None of the surfaces have a 90-degree relationship to one another or to the ground; all of the building's faces are subtly rotated from normal. The mass returns to a regular prismatic form along its side elevations, capped by a pure rectangle at the north.

Radically different from the others, the north elevation is a fully glazed facade. The apparent solidity of the concrete is undermined on this face; however, its massive appearance is still maintained by the smoothness of the glass. The continuity of the glossy panes is achieved by mounting each pane without a clamp profile to create a nearly imperceptible grid. Like a geode cut open and polished on one face, the rock is cut away to reveal this highly reflective surface. Viewing the north elevation head-on, the rock optically dematerializes, the glazing now mirroring its context across the public plaza and creating an unsettling new symmetry of the castle surrounding its absent wing.

TOP: Plan oblique with context, **BOTTOM:** Plan oblique

The mass is masked by its context, clad in a mirrored realism and an abstract photographic enlargement of the historical building's stone blocks.

This shift in character allows the extension to be mute in deference to the castle, a disappearing geologic background that completes its symmetrical composition. At the same time, the museum can be seen as an autonomous object set off the original plan and made to overhang the plinth. Devoid of any element that may reveal its internal function and program, with no visible fenestration beyond the textured and ruinous punctuation of its geologic concrete walls, the architecture of the museum rebelliously asserts itself while withdrawing from any explicit form of social interaction.

1 Rahel Hartmann Schweizer, "Historisches Museum Bern, Bern, Switzerland," *Architectural Record*, Vol. 198, No. 12 (December 2010), 85.

2 Ibid., 87.

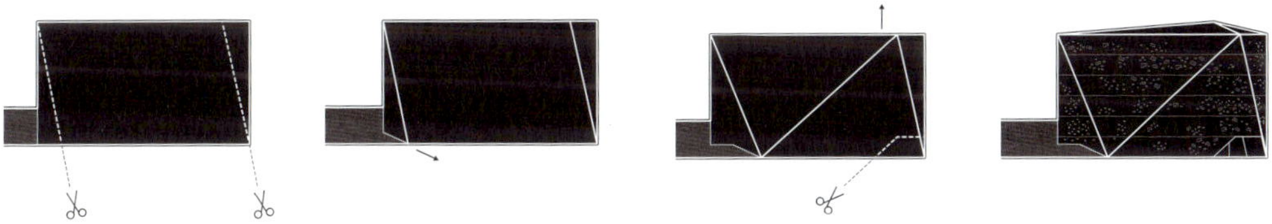

TOP: Diagrams, BOTTOM: Elevation

The Discipline Section acts as a conceptual bridge in the book. It classifies and enumerates notes and concepts which move above and beyond history, projecting possibilities for contemporary architecture to take seriously, reflect upon, and consider enacting. Incomplete by definition, these notes are meant to be both specific and direct rather than exhaustive or dogmatic. Literally exploiting the visual dialectics of diptychs, they aim to suggest and construct relations and exchanges. Opposing historical precedents and recent projects by our office PATTERNS, this section aims to generate "impossible conversations" in its visuals while also amplifying and augmenting established genres within our field.

ABOVE: Olympia, Worm's-eye isometric close-up

3 DISCIPLINE: Current Dichotomies and Their Disciplinary Implications

> Do not believe in the false dichotomies of language versus drama, realism versus fiction, novelty versus tradition. You will experiment with these oppositions in your work until you overcome them.
> —Guillermo Martinez (paraphrasing Paul Bénichou), "Decálogo," *El Malpensante*

Ever since Robert Venturi's influential book *Complexity and Contradiction in Architecture*, the word "complexity" has been on the horizon of architecture as a form of imaginative progress and cultural relevance. In the mid-1980s, architects influenced by the post-structuralist work of Jacques Derrida and affiliated with Deconstruction aimed to create visual complexity through the collision, fragmentation, and dislocation of form and existing canons. Parts were either autonomous or extracted from the whole so as to dissociate them from their origin. The whole's reading was called into question and shattered, with parts reigning as the only legible entities. During the 1990s, theorists such as Sanford Kwinter and Greg Lynn, influenced by the philosophical writings of Gilles Deleuze and Felix Guattari, tried to align architectural complexity with the sciences, especially biology, physics, and thermodynamics. Form followed variegated and intricate fields, along with complex processes of deformation and transformation. Patrick Schumacher's more recent parametric version of complexity, while related to Kwinter's and Lynn's, was more extreme in its intricacy and, polemically and problematically, equated his project to an architectural style.[1] Schumacher positioned parametricism as a vehicle for social communication, accounting for various political, cultural, and economic relationships.

This evolution of the term led to an architecture culture obsessed with control and technological perfection, one that has become so deterministic that refinement and sophistication are now familiar and commonplace. As a result of this shift, we have come to realize that the reliance on only one system, prevailing rhythm, or underlying aesthetic

1. Patrick Schumacher, "Parametricism as Style — Parametricist Manifesto," patrikschumacher.com/texts (accessed August 2, 2019).

principle governing form is a cultural tyranny and aesthetic reductionism that diffuses tension by suppressing dissent.

Learning from Las Vegas by Robert Venturi and Denise Scott Brown

One problematic contemporary response to the technological-driven excesses of the digital is the resurgence of postmodernism. In this cyclical return to Venturi, we see that figure, character, fragment, collage, and an appetite for narrative excess have taken hold as the new status quo in academia. The work associated with this reactionary tendency is neither a pure repetition nor a development of Venturi's project; it lacks complexity altogether and favors only composition and formal conditions against architectural holism. Too bound to history, this branch of discourse tends to rely heavily on the quotation of precedents rather than on speculation about them, focusing on the project of representation rather than on the representation of new projects and resulting in a regressive and nostalgic attitude. Instead, we argue for a dichotomic project that confronts complexity through the tensions of competing mute and iconic qualities.

A Dichotomic Project: A Fuzzier State of Holism

Architecture's disciplinary history has developed in concert with the social and political tensions of its time. More than ever before, we inhabit a field prone to dualisms, oppositions, and strange symmetries. A dichotomic approach in architecture involves engaging dualisms, accepting inconsistencies, and working through constructive incongruities to attempt to overcome them. This approach ought not be confused with the Deconstructivist idea of collage or with a renewed version of Venturi's "difficult whole" which "composes a multitude of diverse parts."[2] Neither is it the intensively cohesive, tectonically intricate, or digitally parametric whole, nor the pure will to figures and character that drives so much of today's neo-postmodernism. The dichotomic project unequivocally favors unified parts and fuzzy wholes.

New speculative realities can emerge from this dichotomic approach, suggesting alternative forms, images, and aesthetics. These novel possibilities may also encourage audiences to question the role and present status of the icon in today's culture and within the discipline of architecture. A significant precedent for such an approach can be found in the literature of the Argentinean author and Jorge Luis Borges scholar, Guillermo Martinez. Using dialectics in a distinct way, Martinez's

2. Robert Venturi, *Complexity and Contradiction in Architecture* (New York: Department of Publications, Museum of Modern Art, 2002, [o.p. 1966]), 92.

literature combines and moves subtly between opposites, not in order to dissolve their contrasting antagonism, but to blur their oppositions. Martinez describes this process, saying, "dichotomies do not dissolve or merge, but instead, they increase to more complex degrees of dualism."[3] As a consequence of privileging dichotomies, the narrative in (his) literature, just as we are proposing for the object in architecture, enters into a more complex state of dualism or a fuzzier state of holism. Making oppositions blurry or making fuzzy wholes is not just a formal and compositional game but also one of reading and legibility. Paraphrasing Martinez, this process implies a kind of concentration, an intensification of attention on things, objects, and even buildings, to create a degree of instability in them; an instability that makes them permeable to other, maybe even contradictory readings and as a result, to different experiences.[4] That is, the parts can have degrees of dissonance within each other.

Implying both maintenance and subversion of existing conventions or genres,[5] as well as a careful infraction of their laws,[6] our present interest in constructive dichotomies stems from the possibility of speculating on a priori antagonist positions, challenging fixed formal and aesthetic notions of both parts and wholes, to arrive at original architectural ideas that have a point of contact with a new sensibility.

This dialectical thinking can also be found in Gilles Deleuze and Felix Guattari's description of "fuzzy aggregates" in *A Thousand Plateaus*, which directly implicates the process by which disparate elements or parts can be combined together. Making an aggregate fuzzy is "not without ambiguity," they insist, since it implies a "synthesis of disparate elements" that share a degree of consistency when combined, but a consistency that still allows for these interleaved elements to be distinguished among themselves. Here, consistency is key, as it is in all design matters, since it assumes that not all parts can be made into a fuzzy aggregate, or unintelligibility results, like "a resonance chamber well on the way to forming a black hole. A material that is too rich to remain too 'territorialized': on noise sources, on the nature of objects."[7]

They caution that aggregation can go too far, as in "the modern valorization of children's drawings, texts by the mad, and concerts of noise, [...] sometimes one overdoes it, puts too much in, works

3. Guillermo Martinez, interview with Marcelo Spina, Buenos Aires, August 16, 2017.
4. Ibid.
5. In literature, Martinez combines the fictional novel with the critical essay format.
6. Martinez, interview with Spina.
7. Gilles Deleuze and Félix Guattari, *A Thousand Plateaus* (Minneapolis, MN: University of Minnesota Press, 1994), 379.

with a jumble of lines and sounds; then instead of producing a cosmic machine capable of 'rendering sonorous,' one lapses back to a machine of reproduction that ends up reproducing nothing but a scribble effacing all lines, a scramble effacing all sounds."[8]

In our view, a resulting aggregate can still be a whole, albeit a fuzzy one, keeping in mind a goal of discernibility. Deleuze and Guattari: "A fuzzy aggregate, a synthesis of disparate elements, is defined only by a degree of consistency that makes it possible to distinguish the disparate elements constituting that aggregate," rather than in the "operations" that have lead to the aggregation.[9]

True Detective opening title sequence.

In the dialectic context of exploring disparity in parts, advancing design by contradiction, and even combining opposites, the mute icon is a fuzzy whole, and maybe the ultimate dichotomy. The following notes, organized according to categories, lay out a series of architectural ideas, qualities, features, and attributes present in both contemporary projects and historical precedents. For the most part, each of these notes implies an opposition or a dichotomy. Altogether, these notes aim to formulate an architectural sensibility for the mute icon, elucidating their strange disciplinary lineage both projectively and retroactively.

8. Ibid.
9. Ibid.

3.01 Indeterminacy & Vagueness

Precedent: Za-Koenji Public Theater **Project:** House of Hungarian Music

Indeterminacy, vagueness, and instability are mobilizing mechanisms that subvert typological and aesthetic fixity, thereby requiring close scrutiny. Indeterminacy prolongs the legibility of buildings and objects, both within their own context and in relation to other objects. This can include the disguise of size and scale and the suppression or subversion of conventional architectural elements or part-to-whole relationships.

While the tendency in contemporary practice is to privilege strong form, and hence limited interpretation, the weak form[10] of indeterminacy avoids the dissolution of difference. Indeterminacy allows multiple formal, typological, and aesthetic categories to complicate and challenge a whole. Wherein form may be static or tensioned, rigid or inflected, it is the precision of uncertainty that makes its indeterminacy productive.

10 Peter Eisenman, "Strong Form, Weak Form," in *Re:Working Eisenman* (London: Academy Editions, 1993), 51–53.

3.02 Incongruity

Precedent: Karola Bunker **Project:** Warner Grand Theater

After more than two decades of interest in formal continuity and incremental variation, current architectural practice favors discontinuities, ruptures, breakages, fuzzy parts, and deep changes in kind as relevant characteristics to be pursued. These discontinuities create a radical incongruity that can be seen in the combination of multiple genres as well as in a renewed interest in collage. Incongruity suggests the possibility that incompatibility, dissimilarity, and contrast can exist within a fuzzy whole that doesn't need to fully cohere. Incongruity also has the power of reestablishing true differences within an unstable, unified whole.

In the last few years, we have been drawn to organizational regimes operating at the border of cohesion and order. For instance, the destabilizing randomness of a "pile" within a monolithic composition suggests a new kind of whole, unified in its violent heterogeneity and cohesive in its ambivalence and multiplicity. This is not a return to collage, which is "an extensive practice wholly dependent on affecting incoherent contradictions within and against a dominant frame."[11] While collage is based on the pure recombination of the known, we understand dichotomies as still fostering the occurrence of the new. In comparison with the postmodern notion of collage, Jeffrey Kipnis

has argued for cases of "coherence forged out of incongruity."[12] In our recent projects, incongruity suggests that the properties of monolithic or megalithic arrangements will enable the resulting architecture to enter into multiple and even contradictory relationships.

11 Jeffrey Kipnis, "Towards a New Architecture," *Architectural Design 102: Folding in Architecture* (1993), 42.

12 Kipnis, Ibid.

3.03 Adjacency & Disparity

Precedent: The Met Breuer **Project:** A4H

Incongruity can be formed through the autonomous combination of disparate forms. While initially in opposition, various formal primitives can be unified within a single object. This object can maintain irreconcilable differences within interdependent regions. Only sharp ruptures, robust adjacencies, and abrupt edge conditions can support these formal relationships. In these situations, the edge is fundamental, affording formal and figural qualities that are revealed in the process of its making. Changes in scale, organization, size, shape, and material are possible consequences of this disruptive procedure. In these cases, scalar shifts no longer reflect incremental variation across a variegated field or growth within a complex system, but instead, divergent effects and dissimilar relationships across contiguous and often disparate regions.

Architects should no longer seek comprehensive fusions or extensive transformations, which so long overpowered essential features and even elements of architectural form. The uneasy unification of aggregates (primitives or otherwise) into monolithic mass is just one of the possible outcomes. Breakages and edges are even more important when it comes to material changes and details. Robert Venturi's MacDonald Research Laboratories and Gonda (Goldschmeid) Neuroscience and Genetics Research Center at UCLA demonstrates this problem. The building as a whole has classical undertones and other historical references. Its treatment of the corner defines it as a difficult whole. Classical — red brick facade with repetitive punched openings — meets the new: a dark, reflectivity of a folded curtain wall — at an impossible paper-thin edge. From each

elevation, its adjacent one is impossible to detect due the hidden depth of both materials and assembly. It is the contrast between the two uncanny compositions and the sudden change that makes this architectural episode all the more powerful and strange. Many Herzog and De Meuron buildings have taken this mantra to a whole other level. Combining increasingly distinct construction systems and material finishes, with or without abstract or figurative patterns, and free from direct historical references, their work produces uncanny (surface) contrasts that both physically emphasize and conceptually disintegrate volume, but are still unified as part of a holistic building.

3.04 Monolithicity

Precedent: Cénotaphe à Newton, Casa da Musica
Project: Peace Corps Memorial, Prishtina Central Mosque

> With the exception of monuments, architecture requires space for inhabitation. If the term monolith is taken literally to suggest material solidity, monolithic architecture would be impossible by definition. However, we understand monolithic to signify monolith-like, and hence to confer a sense of solidity and homogeneity on objects that are not and could not be integrally solid and homogeneous.
> —Rodolfo Machado and Rudolphe el-Khoury, *Monolithic Architecture*

Form cannot be dismissed as insignificant; it is the controlling force of architecture's image in the world and defines the field of activities, cultural habits, and social behaviors that happen around architecture. However, these forces should no longer be taken literally by architects who assume that the field — epitomized by pliant surfaces — should become physical and continuous with the object.[13] During the last six to seven years, we have witnessed a renewed interest in solidity, resulting from an exhaustion with indexicality, the perceived inefficacy of "fields" as buildings, and the failure of the single-surface to produce substantive volume or architectural mass.

The present interest in solidly or "monolithicity"[14] is a viable alternative mode of cultural production, one that offers a means of suppressing formal legibility and of undertaking an introverted approach to building in the city. In a monolithic approach, mass becomes critical once again. In its representational and iconographic nature, latent muteness, scalar ambiguity, and indifference to both program and context, the contemporary monolithic project deploys its "engaged autonomy"[15] as well as its capacity for both resistance and resilience.

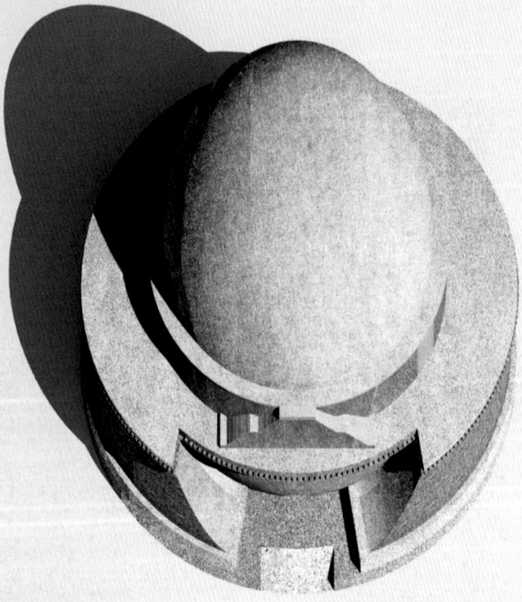

Monolithic architecture, according to Rodolfo Machado and Rodolphe el-Khoury, “exists in its most radical aspect as paradoxical representations: radical in the sense that it self-consciously elaborates its monolithic character into an aesthetic strategy and carries it out to its extreme realization; paradoxical, in the sense that it undermines its own fixity and solidity when its lapidary countenance stands as something totally other with respect to internal and external realities, program, and context.”[16]

Our own generation’s interest[17] in Materialism was never able to account for the finitude and arbitrariness of built objects, just like material or geometry alone could never account for the physical volume of building. This is the inherent paradox of the architectural object: that it can’t simply be reduced to its material constituency, nor it can be completely detached from it. Monolithic forms exhibit and preserve the qualities of mass and those that are derived from it, including weight, instability, discreteness, objecthood, and autonomy. Monolithic architecture embraces a rawness and discomfort in its posture towards both context and ground, stimulating degrees of indifference and independence from these.

Mute icons promote an undeniable degree of formal autonomy while stimulating social and cultural engagement. In fact, they participate fully in the sociocultural and economic context where they are implanted, while simultaneously

claiming autonomy as objects. The autonomy of the mute icon is directly related to Sarah Whiting's concept of "engaged autonomy," which she speaks about in a provocative and elusive manner within her text that bears the same title. In the text, based on an interview by Peter Eisenman, she suggests that projects can be formally autonomous and still engage social conditions around them.

Paul Virilio approached the problem of autonomy in a different, albeit visceral way in his writing about bunkers along the Atlantic Coast of France. In what is among the most provocative chapters of his book *Bunker Archeology*, "The Monolith," Virilio notes that these fortifications confound their own volume and mass by having no foundations.[18] Suggesting solidity, impenetrability, and independence from ground and context, the monolith constitutes an important irritant that allows architecture to continuously reassert its iconographic power and opportunistically negotiate its autonomy.

13 Recent trajectories in Speculative Realism and Graham Harman's theorizing of Object-Oriented Ontology have led to architecture's move away from parametricism's or late postmodernism's preference for objects creating context or context informing objects. Harman argues that objects themselves have real qualities in isolation, regardless of human physical interaction or cultural interpretation. See Graham Harman, *The Quadruple Object* (Winchester, U.K.: Zero Books, 2011).

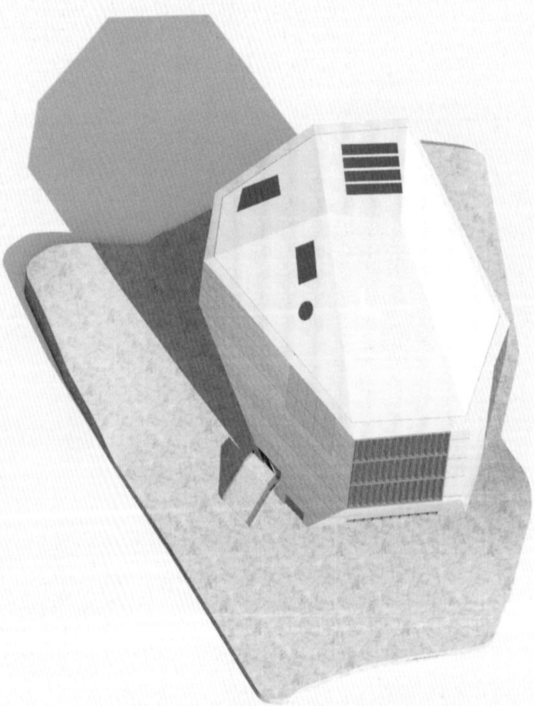

14 One source that does address this important topic is Rodolfo Machado and Rodolphe el-Khoury, *Monolithic Architecture* (Munich: Prestel, 1995). Following the important contributions of *Monolithic Architecture*, we felt there needed to be a single term which could be used to define those properties consistent with a monolithic project. Hence, we introduced the term "monolithicity" that aims to define such conditions as a noun and, therefore, as both a problem and a project. Various studios at SCI-Arc, a studio at Yale, and one at Syracuse were instrumental in developing the agenda associated with monolithicity.

15 Sarah Whiting and Peter Eisenman, "I Am Interested in a Project of Engaged Autonomy" *Log*, No.28 (2013): 109–118.

16 Machado and El-Khoury, *Monolithic Architecture* (Munich: Prestel, 1995), 13.

17 Here we are referring to a group of people educated mostly during the '90s and 2000s under the advent and establishment of the digital in architecture at universities and schools such as Columbia, UCLA, and The Architectural Association.

18 Paul Virilio, *Bunker Archeology* (New York: Princeton Architectural Press, 2009), 37.

3.04. Monolithicity

3.05 Cuts & Outward Voids

Precedent: SESC Pompéia Sports Complex
Project: CEFE Chapinero

If, at least at the most visceral level, we understand architecture as primarily a matter of volume and mass, then articulation or the lack thereof becomes essential. Voids and other interruptions to mass are fundamental. Cuts are sources for shaping volumes, adding crystalline features at times or simple holes at others. Voids are a different matter altogether; they are dimensional subtractions destined to negatively emphasize that which is not there, or sometimes, that which came before or will come after. In these instances, voids are connective separators. They reveal depth and create opportunities for other articulations, either at the scale of volume, system, or material. Individual or collective, centralized or linear, static or dynamic, voids are the invisible spatial and volumetric substance that interacts with building mass internally or externally.

Cuts and voids are fundamental assets in the articulation of architectural volume and mass. In the tradition of solidity, constructing a gap can also create new features within a mass. While a building can demonstrate coherence in its silhouette, its internal cuts, with depth and shadow as resulting characteristics, can imply either fragmentation of mass or volumetric assembly.

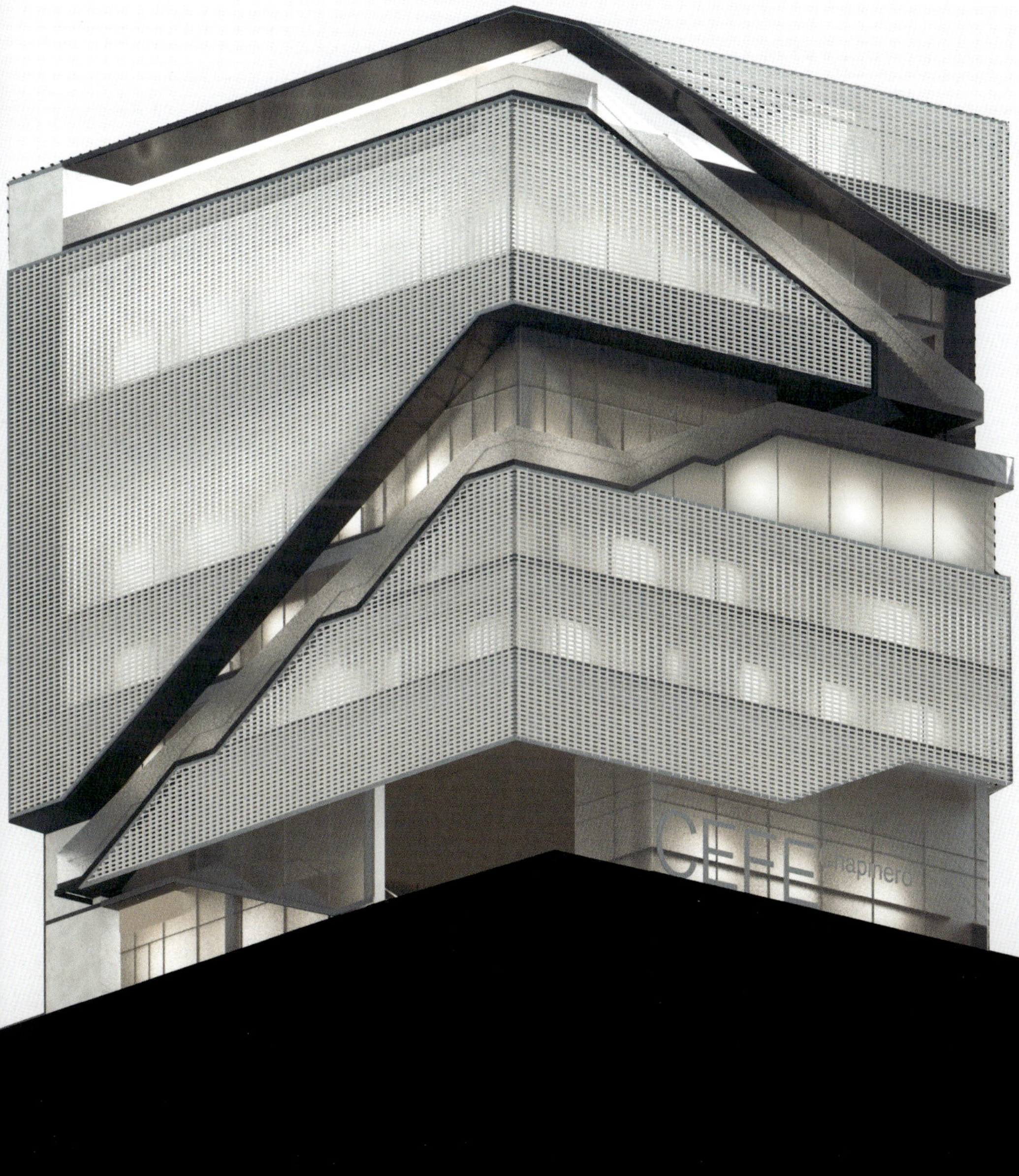

3.05. Cuts & Outward Voids

3.06 Obscure Character

Precedent: Pilgrimage Church of Mary, Queen of Peace **Project:** Museum of Ethnography

> These buildings are no longer just receptacles but binnacles, which is what distinguishes them from ordinary architecture and what gives them this anthropomorphic character. There is here a close relationship between the function of the arm and that of the eye.
>
> —Paul Virilio, *Bunker Archaeology*

An anthropomorphic characterization of architecture provides a coherent representation of something other — perhaps larger — than what a physical building actually denotes.[19] [20] Many representations are applicable to this: outline, contour, shape, figure, and silhouette. The silhouette is perhaps the lowest resolution acceptable for satisfactory representation. While still adequately signifying, the reduction of building to silhouette elicits the most direct communication. Its compressed character offers a common language, free from the complexities of architecture and relatable to wide audiences for mass consumption. The communicative quality of the silhouette-as-symbol solidifies the possibility of an icon. That is, the icon is ultimately not constructed by architects but recognized by the public and sustained by culture.

Given the ever-higher stakes of our present "Instagram" culture, there is an even greater power in silhouettes that are animate and yet ambiguous. This type of silhouette stands for something, but something that is ever reconstituting itself. The "calculated vagueness"[21] of a mute icon's silhouette requires precise indeterminacy. Architecture of this kind is an obscured character. Evacuated of detail and even unpleasant to the public, it becomes increasingly stimulating to gaze upon as time passes.

19 Character here is not meant to imply the abuse of low-resolution cartoon, as seen in the 1980s at the height of the postmodernist movement. Cartoons come and go quickly, commenting on, or perhaps joking about, a subject for an immediate reaction. Architectural character, which is not completely outside the world of typology, is fruitful and has a longer duration.

20 Joseph Altshuler's "Animate Architecture: 12 Reasons to Get in Character" — an expansion and amplification of R.E. Somol's "12 Reasons to Get Back into Shape" — defines character as an anthropomorphic architectural communicator that stimulates our measurable intellect and irrational indulgences. See Joseph Altshuler, "Animate Architecture: 12 Reasons to Get in Character" *Log*, No.33, (2013): 127–135. See also R.E. Somol, "12 Reasons to Get Back into Shape," in *Content*, eds. Rem Koolhaas and OMA (Cologne: Taschen, 2004), 86–87.

21 Ibid. Altshuler revives R.E. Somol's term "calculated vagueness," which Somol uses in his description of the complexities of architectural shape.

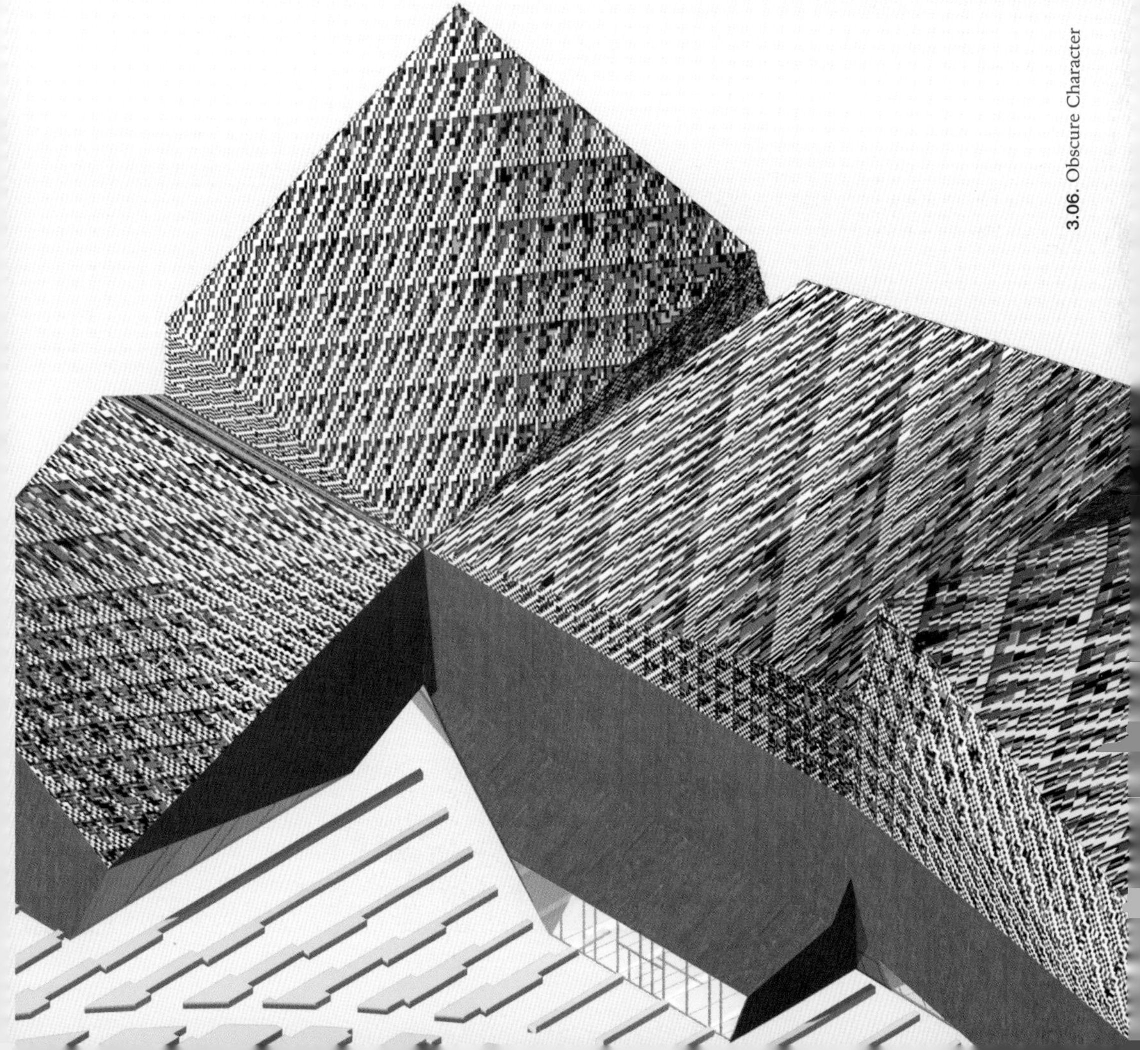

3.07 Physical Abstraction

Precedent: Bruges Concert Hall **Project:** League of Shadows

Digital media and technology continue to affect material and spatial problems in architecture. With the controlled refinement of advanced manufacturing processes, form has become dominant over assemblage. The materialization of form is no longer bound to connections between parts, but rather by the physical abstraction of composites that conceal traditional building processes. The immaterial qualities of output objects suggest that technology is altering aspects of visualization in combination with materialization. Two-dimensional drawings are layered onto form as representational information with material consequence. This overlap of material and representational systems has the potential to create new forms of coherence.

Some of these advances push towards a technological "superflat" — a physical conflation of information, material, and object into a single composite surface. Rather than celebrate representation's role as distinct from building, contemporary media can integrate with physical form and advanced materials, creating synthetic vitality in their ambiguity.

3.07. Physical Abstraction

3.08 Shade & Shadow

Precedent: The Metropolis of Tomorrow **Project:** Olympia

> Architecture is the masterly, correct and magnificent play of masses brought together in light. Our eyes are made to see forms in light; light and shade reveal these forms; cubes, cones, spheres, cylinders, or pyramids are the great primary forms which light reveals to advantage; the image of these is distinct and tangible within us without ambiguity. It is for this reason that these are beautiful forms, the most beautiful forms. Everybody is agreed as to that, the child, the savage, and the metaphysician.
>
> —Le Corbusier, *Towards a New Architecture*, 1923, translated by Frederick Etchells

Since antiquity, architecture has consistently celebrated analytical and quantitative drawings of pure form.[22] The celebration of form is amplified and complicated by physical phenomena of shadow.[23] Now, in the post-fact era, tangible form is not as desirable as it was when it was argued for by Le Corbusier. The formal ambiguity of the mute icon is a productive target for our time. The implied depths or flattening effects of shadow offer a rich multiplicity for formal ambiguity and delayed legibility. A single shadow line can disguise a tectonic seam or a geometric edge, as it can a surface of a dark shade. This erasure reduces the immediate registration and perception of objects, momentarily neutralizing features and turning things into silhouettes.

Things become even murkier when shadow is cast on a dark mass and shade is lost in black. In color theory, shade is a move towards black. When an object in and of itself looks like a shadow, or when the shadow that it is projecting starts to not only to look like an extension of it but becomes a part of it, an unexpected doubling occurs. An *anexact* or partially obscured form or a form that continually reconfigures itself under shadow offers a slowed apprehension of its architecture and maybe, an increased awareness of the world around us.[24]

22 See drawings from Leon Battista Alberti, *De Re Aedificatoria* (Munich: Prestel, 1975, [o.p. 1452]).
23 For examples, see Claude Perrault's French Renaissance drawings that explored classical architectural elements rendered with shadow in his *Ordonnance for the Five Kinds of Columns after the Method of the Ancients* (Los Angeles: The Getty Center, 1993).
24 Jason Payne, "Variations on the Disco Ball, or, The Ambivalent Object," *Project: A Journal for Architecture*, Issue 2 (Spring 2013): 21–22; see also Greg Lynn, "Architectural Curvilinearity: The Folded, the Pliant, and the Supple," *Architectural Design* 102: *Folding In Architecture* (1993): "Anexact geometries, as described by Edmund Husserl, are those geometries which are irreducible yet rigorous. These geometries can be determined with precision yet cannot be reduced to average points on dimensions. Anexact geometries often appear to be merely figural in this regard. Unlike exact geometries, it is meaningless to repeat identically an anexact geometric figure outside of the specific context in which it is situated. In this regard, anexact figures cannot be easily translated."

3.08 Shade & Shadow

3.09 Texture & Fuzziness

Precedent: First House of the Lumbermen
Project: National Gallery and Ludwig Museum of Contemporary Art

Surface articulation and indiscriminate ornamentation have long been formulaic and cliché, a sign of formal and aesthetic weakness. In order to preserve and further emphasize architectural mass, contemporary projects must stop right before the level of ornamental articulation. This results in texture, coarseness, grain, and a toned-down approach to enunciation that could almost be confused with noise. Drawings, with their two-dimensional information and infinite capacity for projection, are central to this since they afford volume with features that are both elusive and penetrating. Noise can irritate the surfaces of a mass, disguising known and expected architectural features — such as windows or fenestration — while maintaining a form of vagueness and constructive indeterminacy.

Considering the case of *béton brut* [25] — a manufacturing material anomaly that became a doctrine and later a style in the emergence of Brutalism in Europe — contemporary architecture has begun to embed the qualities of drawings as a form of glitch. Rather than untainted articulation, glitches are utilized as means of decreasing the resolution of surfaces while increasing an overall capacity for rawness. The glitch is not best deployed wholesale, but rather as a new way of understanding transitions, edges, and articulation.

25 Béton brut refers to the reinforced concrete style pioneered by Auguste Perret and Le Corbusier.

3.10 Ruination

Precedent: Bern Historical Museum **Project:** Fuzzy Monolith

Historically, architectural ruins have been considered in terms of restoration. John Ruskin was against restoration, defending the aesthetic value of buildings as ruins.[26] On the contrary, Eugène Emmanuel Viollet-le-Duc was pro-restoration and devoted a career to imagining the restoration of French monuments, including castles and fortifications. In his drawings, he put forth a speculative approach to completion, in which nothing was ever seen as finished. He added to the original a variety of features and elements that complicated its character.[27] In yet another example, Bernard Tschumi noted the physical dilapidation of Le Corbusier's Villa Savoy, with its chipped corners and peeling white paint. In bringing attention to its ruined state, Tschumi projects new intrigue onto an otherwise quintessential modern masterpiece.[28]

In the mute icon, ruination is a process that relies on the controlled and partial erosion of an object to produce specific aesthetic effects. Instead of waiting in anticipation for a building to produce ruined features, we are intrigued with a possible alternative mode that presents architecture in reverse — celebrating its incompleteness and wear as features rather than consequences of its robust permanence. Partial rustication and fragmentation are preferred over an idealized pure form. These techniques of articulation extract qualities from architecture, revealing an image of decay in an otherwise contemporary work. This creates an indeterminate relationship to time, causing architectural objects to flicker between an image of solidity and one of local instability.

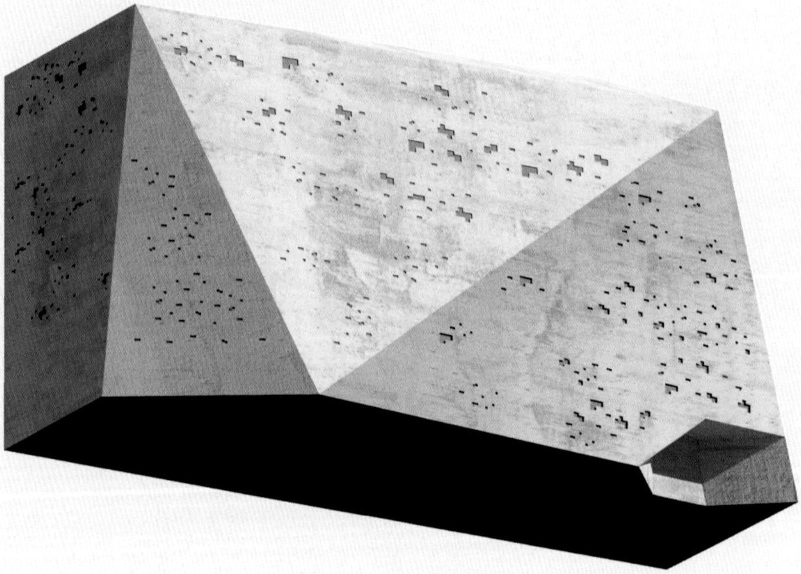

26 David Spurr, "Figures of Ruin and Restoration: Ruskin and Viollet-le-Duc," in *Architecture and Modern Literature* (Ann Arbor: University of Michigan Press, 2012). John Ruskin's theories on architectural preservation remain essential texts on the continued debate between restoration and conservation.

27 Ibid. John Soane's Bank of England drawing also speaks to this interest. Soane's drawing of the bank in a state of ruin was produced long before the building was constructed, giving a sense of nostalgic anticipation of a dire future that never was. While this is a technique of representation, it raises interesting architectural provocations concerning incompleteness and impermanence.

28 On Le Corbusier's Villa Savoy depicted in a state of ruin, "...the most architectural thing about this building is the state of decay in which it is." Bernard Tschumi, *Advertisements for Architecture*, 1976–1977.

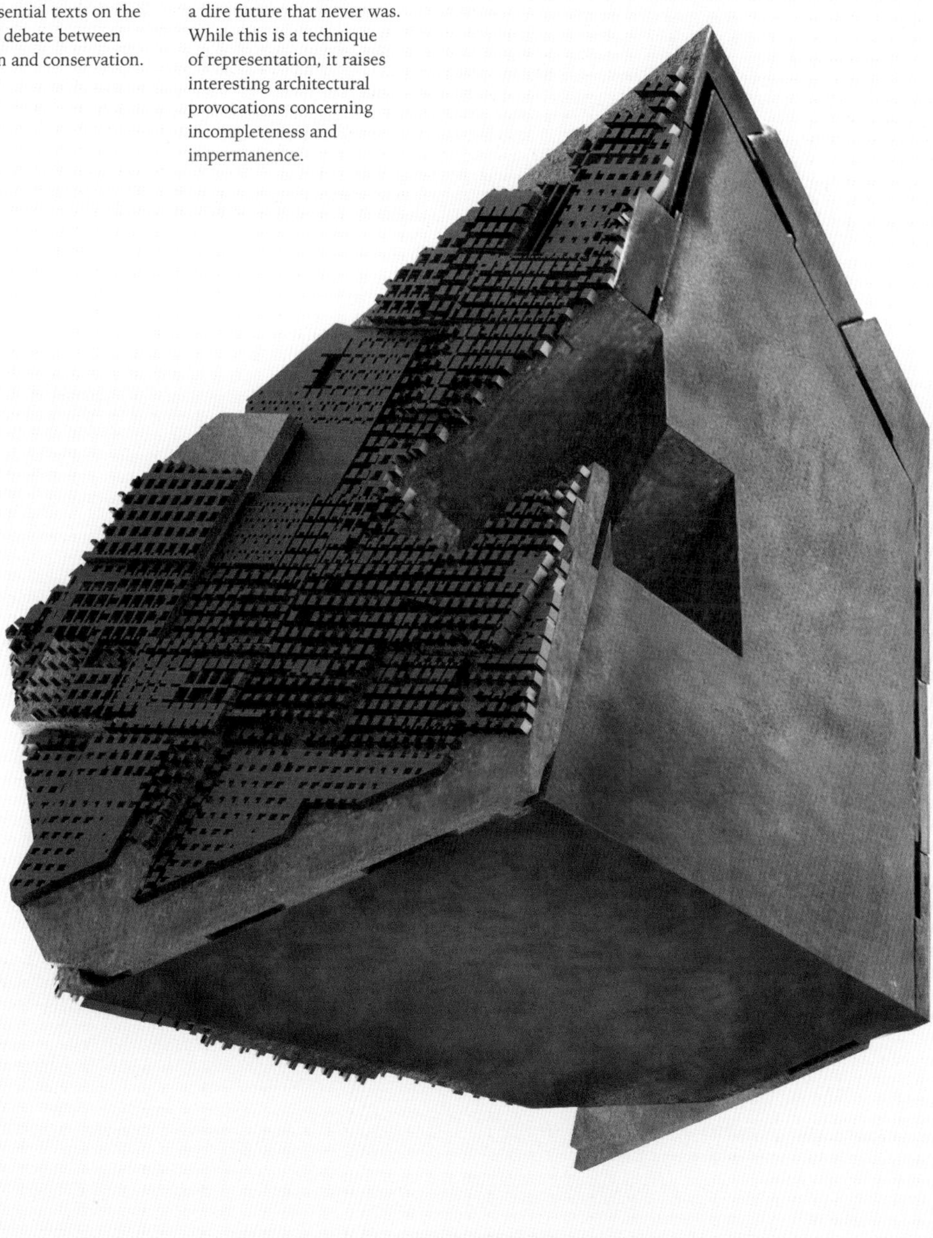

3.11 Groundless Objects

Precedent: Qasr al-Farid Tomb **Project:** Keelung Crystal

Linked to the ground, the surrounding earth, the bunker, for camouflage, tends to coalesce with the geological forms whose geometry results from the forces and exterior conditions that for centuries have modeled them. The bunker's form anticipates this erosion by suppressing all superfluous forms; the bunker is prematurely worn and smoothed to avoid all impact. It nestles in the uninterrupted expanse of the landscape and disappears from our perception, used as we are to bearings and markers.

—Paul Virilio, *Bunker Archaeology*

During modernism, the idea of plinth or podium was a compositional notion establishing a clear difference between a horizontal and a vertical volume. For formal, programmatic, or even social reasons, detachment from the ground was seen as essential. However, both history and the present reveal different and more ambiguous relationships between plinth and building, wherein the elevated podium still exists, but it is integrated into the body of the building. This melds the distinct elements of ground, plinth, and building into a composite whole. In the best cases, it is difficult to assess if the integrated plinth is an elevated ground,

a rotated lower building, or perhaps both. Akin to a Constantin Brancusi sculpture, the base still elevates the presented object, but it also undermines that same object by competing with its formal intricacy.

The muffled distinction between these two traditionally separate elements engenders the possibility of new more accessible grounds, pulling the external world into the architecture.

The groundless object still defines a formal autonomy as it withdraws from the ground. Nevertheless, that autonomy splinters to create interdependencies between building and plinth, plinth and ground, or ground and building. The flickering hierarchy and newfound composite nature between these elements create a fertile public realm.

3.12 Excavated Objects

Precedent: Church of St. George, Lalibela **Project:** Lima Art Museum

The notion of objecthood[29] or formal autonomy in architecture on one hand and the idea of grounding architecture on the other, are very rarely reconcilable. Autonomy suggests precisely a desire of architecture to exist independently from a ground. However, "grounded" is not deployed here in a traditional sense, wherein buildings are grounded simply because they are implanted on a given context. Grounding entails precisely the opposite: submerging an object so as to position it beneath or within the ground rather than on it. An excavated object (an object with grounded autonomy) suggests a rare paradoxical situation, whereby architecture can assert its autonomy from and partially disappear beneath the ground at the same time. This kind of object can align itself and coexist with the ground and, at the same time, separate itself from it both physically and conceptually. This kind of architecture does not only rely on the massing of an object, but rather on the void produced between that object and the ground that surrounds and contains it. This void is produced as a result of the relationship between container and contained. Furthermore, the total or partial alignment and the congruity or incongruity between object and ground — be it through their relationship, shape, or material — will have enormous consequences on the way an architectural object exists in the world.

29 Michael Fried, "Art and Objecthood," [o.p.1967]; *Art and Objecthood: Essays and Reviews* (Chicago: University of Chicago Press, 1998).

3.12. Excavated Objects

3.13 Displacements & Disarticulations

Precedent: New Museum of Contemporary Art **Project:** Olympia

Displacements, shifting, and other forms of disarticulation are the opposite of volume and mass and, at the same time, a direct reversal of articulation. Removing parts from whole, creating dissonances that are sudden, unexpected, and local, can lead to the production of fuzziness within otherwise legible objects. This is where the "glitch" becomes conceptually interesting in its ability to introduce qualities and features within a given object that were, a priori, completely outside its original genealogy.

A glitch is a momentary deviation from what is considered conclusive; it is information that is *almost* correct but displaced in a critical way. System glitches suggest a specific failure in computation, manufacturing, or any other similar production. It is an undesired outcome in the production of efficiency, often a momentary mistake. There are qualities of the glitch that are aesthetically productive for the mute icon, leading to clumsy forms and pixelated tectonics.

A glitch has limits; there is a tolerance point at which the glitch stops being an anomaly and starts becoming new. The glitch is not an incorrect representation of conclusive form; it still refers to conclusive form, though it flickers somewhere in between completeness and incompleteness. When controlled, these momentary displacements and disarticulations reveal a plausible and productive alternative to strong form and legible aesthetics.

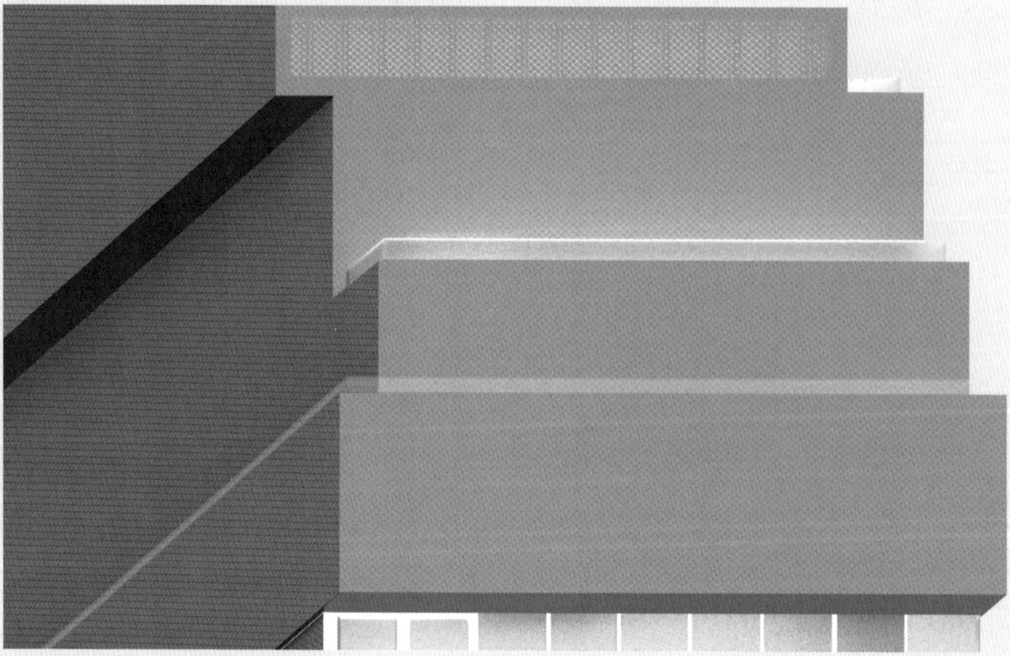

3.14 Context & Conformity

Precedent: Caixa Forum **Project:** Victory Healthcare

Historicist postmodernism, critical regionalism, and various permutations of contextualism have all claimed to address the neglect of local and specific conditions that were so dominant during modernism. Central to these ideas concerning context is the idea of conformity: the act of matching attitudes, beliefs, and behaviors to group norms. In fact, it is this tendency to conform that is both necessary and problematic when it comes to contemporary attitudes towards context.

Of particular interest to the mute icon is a contextualism invested in the possibility of the new as an uncanny combination between future and past. The fusion of the known or familiar surroundings with the foreign object creates a subversive conformity. Additionally, there is a pressing need to adapt to the current state of culture as political leaders intervene in the architect's sphere of influence.[30] This preempts radical formal expression and suggests architects adopt a more modest formal attitude in response to context. Rather than simply aiming to design instant icons for quick cultural consumption, we advocate addressing and subverting cultural contingencies. This allows for a new focus to be placed on how an architectural object — no matter how locally strange — could be absorbed by culture in the production of an icon.

30 One such case of this is the President of the People's Republic of China, Xi Jinping's declaration that there be "no more weird buildings" built in China. The comment suggests a unified national desire to take the power of image away from the architect and redirect architecture to represent a government-mandated image. What does it mean for architecture to have to face regressive cultural and political criticism? Rory Stott, "Why China's President Says 'No More Weird Buildings'," *ArchDaily*, October 21, 2014, (accessed March 15, 2019).

3.14. Context & Conformity

3.15 Strange Vernacular

Precedent: Steinberg Hat Factory Dyeing Hall **Project:** Infonavit Rural Prototype

The vernacular in architecture is characteristically concerned with visual performance that is for "real people" and by "real people." More often than not, the vernacular requires no architect as it needs no cultural argument or architectural ingenuity. What the vernacular offers is the easy communication of familiar forms and locally accepted images. Brushing up against the banal, the mundane, and the everyday, the vernacular can be deployed as a productive foil, bastardized, and hybridized to produce strange speculations of political forms, social spaces, and cultural aesthetics.[31]

The vernacular is nevertheless problematic, particularly for its claim to define a universally agreed upon reality. On the contrary, strange vernacular offers much-needed friction to this otherwise static category. The irritating combination of an outside abstract source with a vernacular feature can be used in the production of new kinds of architectural objects that avoid a totalizing singularity. In line with contemporary approaches to iconicity, these productive hybrids acknowledge indeterminate and even contradictory sources. The expectation is not only to produce an architecture that looks strange but, at the same time, an architecture with near familiarity. When dealing with the vernacular, we must remember that a truly uncanny object is the one that we see every day but that is made extra-ordinary in a critical, previously unexperienced way.

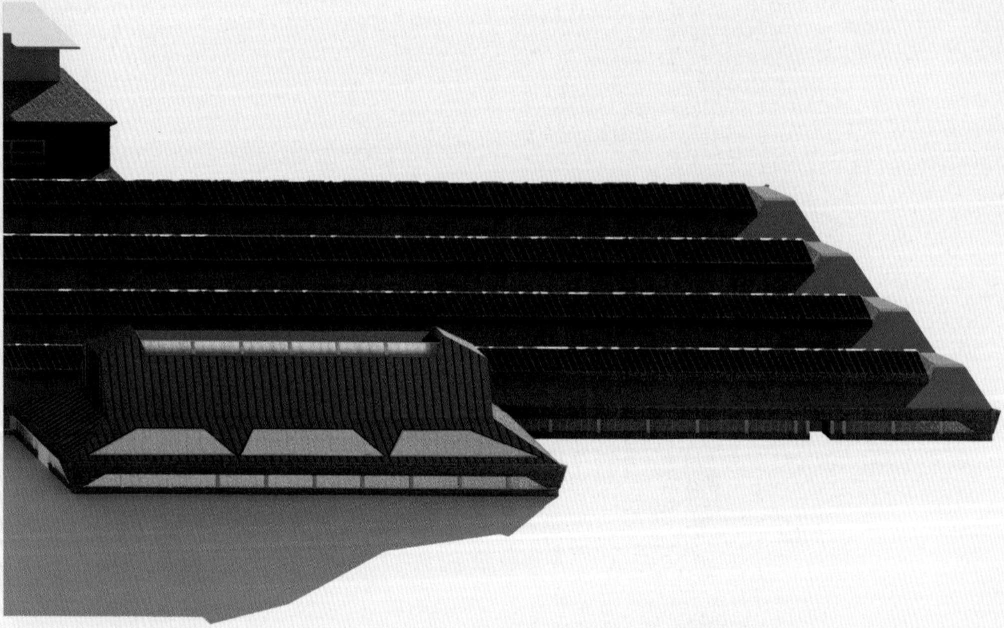

31 Another issue with the vernacular is its potential meaning to local conditions. That is, local vernacular means something different to a particular place. More than often, it functions as a false signifier, a semantic reminder of something we had no memory of in the first place. We see the strange vernacular as a productive alternative to the excess of abstraction, itself an already exhausted form of modern representation.

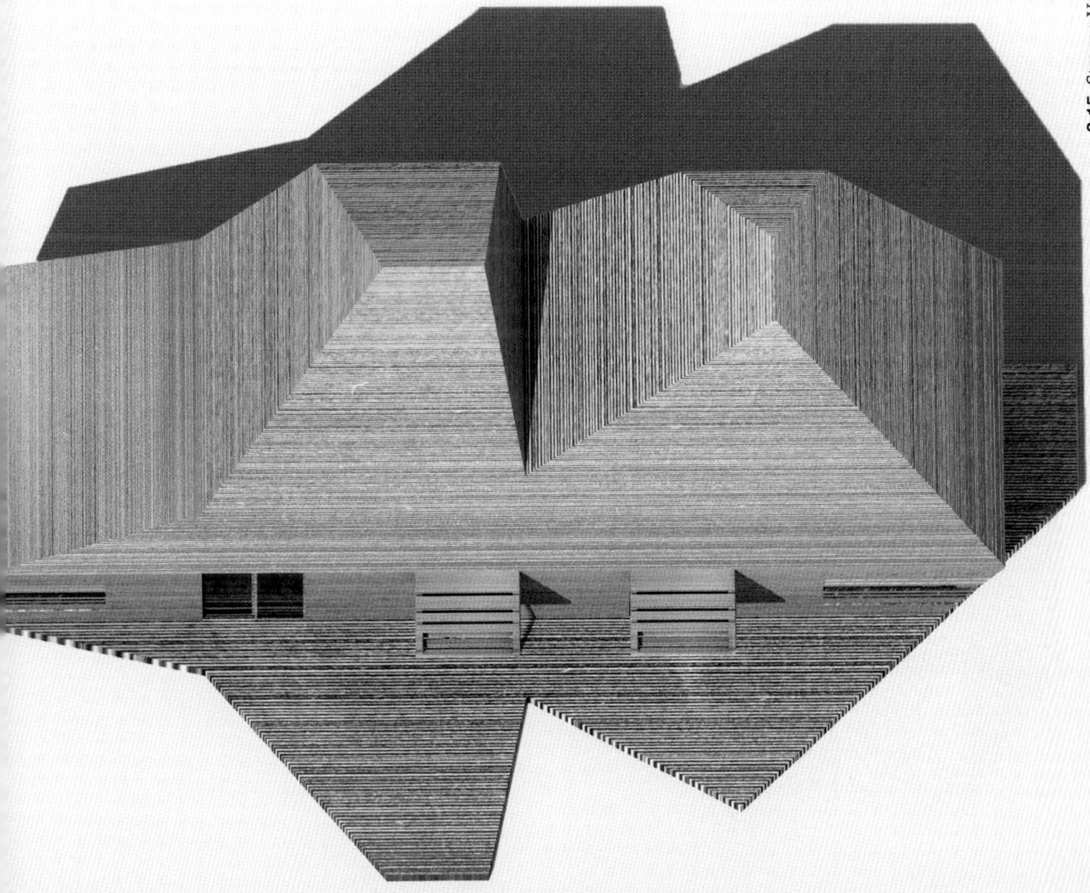

3.15. Strange Vernacular

3.16 Cohering Wholes

Precedent: Ningbo Historic Museum **Project:** Casa del Sol

> It's really about trying to make it feel like you're journeying through a photograph. You don't want it to be as crazy and intense as watching footage, because footage is about a series of events happening, whereas this is just about the compositions themselves.
>
> —Patrick Clair, creative director of Elastic, on the *True Detective* opening credits

Part-to-whole relationships have been central to the discipline of architecture and its discourse since Alberti.[32] However, of interest to the mute icon is a productive tension that promotes difference between discrete and disparate parts in a cohering whole. Frank Stella's early minimalist work *Polygonal Combinations* and a few of his supporting maquettes and studies for paintings suggest another model for coherence. We have come to call these "cohering wholes": formal combinations that are at the edge of coherence. A cohering whole is both a composition problem and an image problem for the mute icon. The flickering tension between layers of information allows discrete parts to be independently legible while they simultaneously cohere into a fuzzy and even stranger whole.

As an archetypal case study of dichotomic images, the opening credits of HBO's series *True Detective* produce an elucidating example of this tension. By placing photos on top of slowed-down footage, the creators aimed to produce "living photographs."[33] This surreal form of motion produces the effect of being in a dream, while the ambiguity of the images — a lifeguard station set against wildly flowing

hair, a freeway running through a silhouette of a face — give a brooding sense of what's to come without revealing too much. This eerie image-based sequence manages to communicate distinguishing features of intervening characters and contexts while conveying with ambiguity the obscure narrative.

32 Leon Battista Alberti, Joseph Rykwert, Neil Leach, and Robert Tavernor, *On the Art of Building in Ten Books*, (Cambridge, MA: MIT Press, 1997).

33 Patrick Clair, the creative director of Elastic, quoted in an interview by Elizabeth Stinson "How They Made *True Detective*'s Opening Credits So Eerie," *Wired*, June 22, 2015, wired.com/2015/06/made-true-detectives-opening-credits-eerie/ (accessed March 15, 2019).

3.16. Cohering Wholes

4 Projects

The Projects Section is an embedded atlas of PATTERNS' recent built and unbuilt work, organized by means of representational categories. Diagrams, axonometrics, plan obliques, physical models, photorealistic perspectives (digital renderings), and photomontages are featured individually, as part of diptychs, or within curated constellations. They aim to depict original architectural ideas and features so as to interrogate the problematic and ever-shifting relation between architectural abstract means of representation and the real.

ABOVE: A4H, Worm's-eye isometric close-up

2012 Keelung Crystal
Keelung, Taiwan
200, 201, 218, 251, 256, 268–271

2013 Prishtina Central Mosque
Prishtina, Kosovo
200, 201, 221, 231, 249, 254, 257, 264, 272–275

2013 League of Shadows
Los Angeles, California, USA
190, 191, 222, 237, 247, 253, 255

2014 National Gallery and Ludwig Museum of Contemporary Art
Budapest, Hungary
190, 191, 207, 236, 256, 276–277

2014 Hungarian Museum of Architecture and Fotomuzeum
Budapest, Hungary
192, 193, 210, 278–279

2014 Museum of Ethnography
Budapest, Hungary
194, 195, 208, 236, 280–281

2014 House of Hungarian Music
Budapest, Hungary
192, 193, 209, 239, 252

2015 Post Castle Kaliningrad
Kaliningrad, Russia
192, 193, 219, 238, 250, 282–283

2015 Karma Bequia
St. Vincent and The Grenadines, Caribe
196, 197, 227, 242, 256, 262

2015–2020 Victory Healthcare
North Hollywood, CA, USA
194, 195, 223, 232, 237, 244, 250, 252, 256, 265

2016 Infonavit Rural Prototype
Morelos, Mexico
196, 197, 215, 238, 239, 257, 265

2016 Lima Art Museum, Contemporary Art Wing
Lima, Peru
202, 203, 217, 245, 247, 253, 254, 255

2016 Fuzzy Monolith
Los Angeles, California, USA
190, 191, 206, 259, 261, 262

2016 The Long Table
Los Angeles, California, USA
202, 203, 216

2017 Warner Grand Theater Expansion
San Pedro, California, USA
200, 201, 205, 213, 228, 246, 248, 250, 252, 254, 284–287

2017 MMBA Museum Expansion
Rosario, Argentina
194, 195, 220, 230, 233, 249, 251, 256, 288–289

2017–2021 A4H
Glendale, California, USA
187, 189, 198, 212, 228, 234, 235, 246, 248, 250, 252, 255, 260, 261, 263, 264, 267, 290–295

2017–2027 Olympia
Los Angeles, California, USA
198, 199, 211, 225, 229, 234, 235, 240, 241, 247, 248, 253, 254, 255, 256, 265

2017–2020 Karma Sanctum
Nusadua, Bali, Indonesia
196, 197, 214, 246, 248, 250, 261, 296–297

2019 CEFE Chapinero
Bogota, Colombia
198, 199, 224, 229, 230, 246, 248, 249, 253, 254

2019 Casa del Sol
Mykonos, Greece
202, 203, 226, 231, 247, 249, 251

ABOVE: A4H, Worm's-eye isometric close-up

FIG 1

Fuzzy Monolith, SCI-Arc Close-up Exhibition

Los Angeles, California, USA, 2016

Fuzzy Monolith was exhibited in the SCI-Arc Gallery in Los Angeles, California, as part of the group show *Close-Up Exhibition*, curated by Hernan Diaz Alonso and David Ruy. Fuzzy Monolith explores complex levels of material and tectonic assembly that are often in contrast with a monolithic form. Given the impossibility of actual monolithic architecture — or as we like to call it, monolithicity — its very attempt suggests an internal disciplinary riddle: a dichotomy that connects issues of abstract representation, visual aesthetics, and those of material and building assembly. The proposed crystalline object combines actual solidity with a panelization system of changing scale, which becomes increasingly fuzzy with a pixelated texture, calling into question the actual make-up of this dark object.

FIG 2

National Gallery and Ludwig Museum of Contemporary Art

Budapest, Hungary, 2014

The New National Gallery and Ludwig Museum stems from a paradox: the problematic need to partially integrate two distinct cultural institutions within a single building so they can coexist independently from and yet be interrelated to each other. Conceptually and physically, the building is a composite monolithic mass of two distinct, discrete, and adjacent volumes, which, leaning against each other, engender a larger, albeit fuzzy whole.

A decidedly idiosyncratic silhouette of tapered hyperbolic shapes and truncated pyramids disrupts the horizontality of the park. Like medieval castles in Budapest City Park, the building is both imposing and sublime, appearing autonomous and yet completely grounded, since unlike its neoclassical counterparts, it is socially engaging by being permeable and accessible to pedestrians at ground level. The surfaces are articulated with an abstract dazzle pattern of stamped metal panels. Projected on the building following the main public promenade across the City Park, the flickering pixelated nature of the texture intensifies towards the entry passage, where the two building volumes connect, enhancing and obfuscating the legibility of the architecture.

FIG 3

League of Shadows, SCI-Arc Graduation Pavilion and Multipurpose Event Space

Los Angeles, California, USA, 2013

League of Shadows is a large, outdoor, semi-permanent event structure located within the SCI-Arc campus, at the core of the Arts District in Downtown Los Angeles. Strategically positioned at the corner of the 4th St. Bridge, the pavilion is both a visual landmark and an institutional beacon, a natural yet strange marquee for SCI-Arc's mission and culture. Shaped vertically by joined fingering volumes, the pavilion addresses sustainability by creating enough shadow so as to allow for comfortable zones away from the sun while disturbing parking at a minimum when not in use. Its band-shell shape acts as a natural backdrop for events, providing students and families controlled views of the ceremony during graduation in what is otherwise a fully open parking lot. Volumetric and graphic, the project offers a dichotomic legibility that alternates between an idiosyncratic silhouette from far away to a radiating texture at close range. Its vaulted interior serves as a natural choreography for ceremonies, while it affords the audience favorable acoustic, visual, and environmental conditions during events.

FIG 1

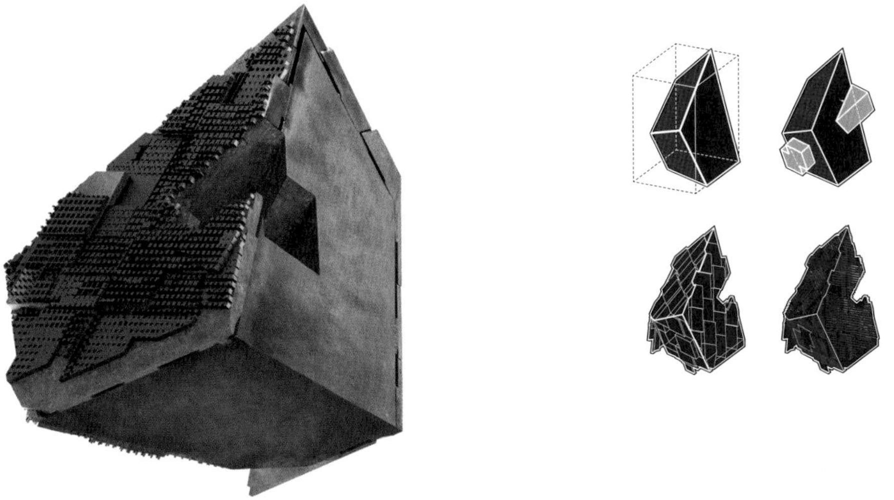

FIG 2

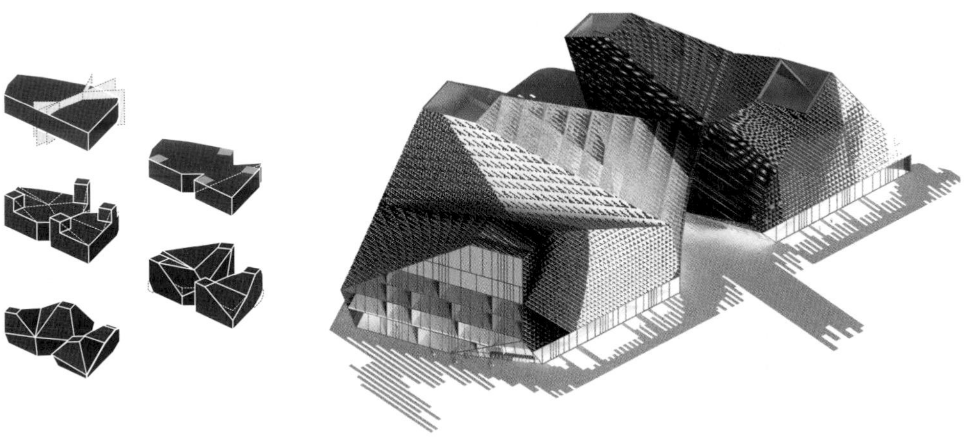

FIG 3

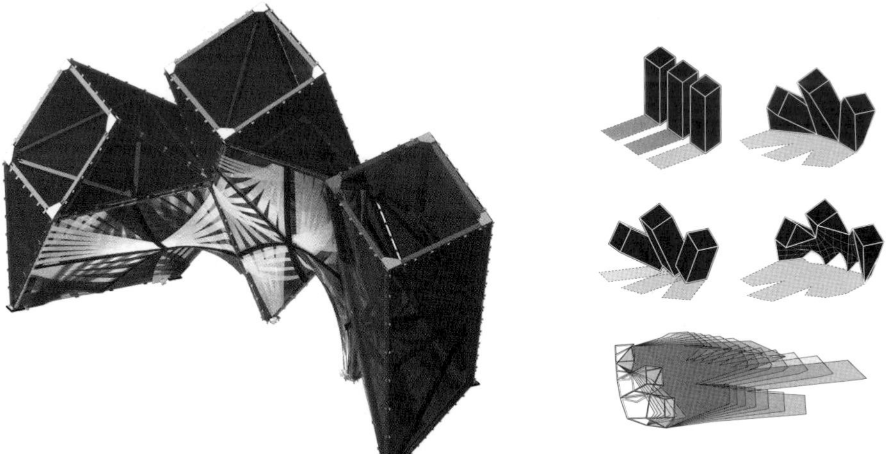

FIG 4

House of Hungarian Music

Budapest, Hungary, 2014

The New House of Hungarian Music is conceived as a cultural fortress, and much like the medieval castles within Budapest City Park, it drastically distinguishes itself from its context. A single monolithic and semi-autonomous object, this dark-shaded crystalline mass is conspicuously grounded within the park. Autonomous and contextual at the same time, the project's outline is seemingly compliant with the neoclassic Varosliget circle, while its posture is relatively indifferent to it. The monolithic nature of the building is severely challenged in its interior. The mass partially cracks into two separate volumes which, leaning against each other, generate an interior multilevel atrium apt for music performances and presenting stunning views of the park. The building surfaces are articulated with an abstract dazzle pattern. The pixelated gradient nature of the building texture makes its presence simultaneously graphically pleasing and tectonically mute. As a result, the building is like a strange rock: a silent idiosyncratic object in stark contrast with the lush and idyllic landscape of Budapest City Park.

FIG 5

Hungarian Museum of Architecture and Fotomuzeum

Budapest, Hungary, 2014

Our proposal for the Hungarian Museum of Architecture and Fotomuzeum departs from the inherent paradox presented by the brief: the need to conceive and integrate two distinct and discrete cultural institutions within a single scheme. The new building is comprised of two discrete, contrasting, and conceptually unified objects. Sliced into two objects, akin to perfectly cut rock, the resulting volumes exhibit polygonal crystalline shapes facing each other. Conceptually, the fracture reasserts the physical significance of two distinct wholes: a black and a white object that cohere into a single split object, presenting a spatial dichotomy with reciprocal equilibrium wherein each object balances and completes the other. As a result of this operation, the open promenade generated in between two institutions induces the public to gravitate towards both culture and history, architecture and photography. The willfully fuzzy texture of both buildings' surfaces visually intensifies and enhances this cultural experience.

FIG 6

Post Castle Kaliningrad, Main Square, Government and Cultural Buildings

Kaliningrad, Russia, 2015

Seeking a strange balance between such distinct historical periods and architectural styles as modern and medieval, exemplified by the Brutalist House of Soviets and the ruins of an old medieval castle, this cohering whole is in fact an urban "ensemble" that aims to reinstate the lost visual consistency, physical harmony, and civic meaning of the public square. The new complex seeks to create an integral fragment, generating a diverse and unified skyline for the new city center. Consciously but without nostalgia, the design draws inspiration from the castle's medieval outline, constituent elements, and eroding materiality to create a contemporary "open" fortress. Arranged around a monumental courtyard, the public square is flanked by "pillars" and "minerals" on each corner — building masses with surfaces cladded in dark brick and grey stone. Conforming and standing out from its context, the new ensemble is brutally articulate, monumentally idiosyncratic, and mysteriously powerful.

FIG 4

FIG 5

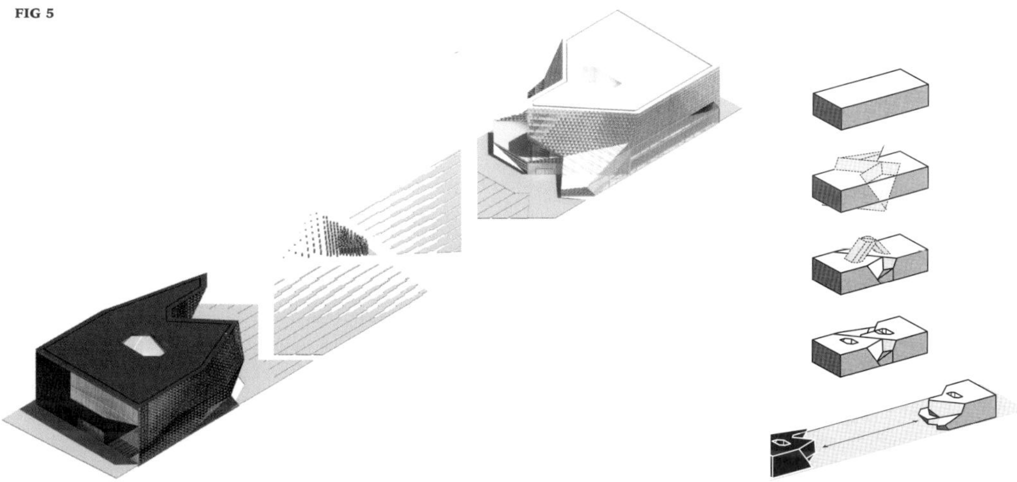

FIG 6

FIG 7

Victory Healthcare, Adaptive Reuse, Medical Offices

North Hollywood, CA, USA, 2015–2020

Entailing the conversion of an existing bowstring truss warehouse into medical offices, this project conserves and subverts a generic object and its suburban environment, bestowing it with an idiosyncratic character and the capacity to transform an otherwise undistinctive context. A careful exercise in surgical subtraction and meaningful addition, the approach assesses, critically and inventively, the notion of 'adaptive reuse', maintaining while amplifying the spatial, formal, and aesthetic possibilities offered by the building's internal structure.

Four carved-out courtyards and a large wedge plaza create a necessary open space connecting all levels of the building. A diagonal promenade connects front and back while a series of crystal-like pod-offices meaningfully conclude and challenge the mono-volume status of the bowstring structure. A reconditioned existing sign provides the project with a commanding vertical element and a newfound iconicity both integrated with and distinctive from its context. The result is a more accessible and nuanced, multidimensional, and engaging project for an area of Los Angeles in much need of urban regeneration.

FIG 8

MMBA Museum Expansion

Rosario, Argentina, 2017

The expansion of MMBA intends to intensify the inherent duality present within the existing museum: a cultural institution that meaningfully participates in its urban context and a quasi-fascist modernist building-object that maintains an unnecessary degree of social autonomy.

The new multifaceted building assimilates with and distorts the formal and social status-quo of the existing museum. Located at the edge of a metropolitan park, the expansion would generate a new urban posture and character for the museum, certainly a more integrated and less heroic one. Continuing and questioning the classical heritage of modernist "white cube" architecture, the project offers a less pure logic, both formally and materially. The 'L'-shaped addition is segmented diagonally to create a more idiosyncratic silhouette and provide natural light inside the galleries. The frail graphic vibration of the white zebra marble-striped surfaces disturbs just enough the otherwise solemnity of rationalist boredom.

FIG 9

Museum of Ethnography

Budapest, Hungary, 2014

The New Museum of Ethnography intends to address the dilemma between local culture and global trends, historic conservation and innovation by proposing a building which is profoundly contextual in its abstraction and mysteriously strange in its urban attitude.
A monumental bar-shaped object, which occupies the southernmost edge of the park, is partially fractured into four adjacent and dissenting volumes that both assert and challenge the typological determinacy of the rectangular block. Radically contextual and partially reminiscent of Art Nouveau buildings around Budapest, the concrete monolithic base is crowned with a tile-cladded mansard roof. As a result, the museum communicates its critical mission by opposition: appearing massive, silent, and restrained in the noisiest and most urban part of the city while expressing its most emblematic features against the skyline, hence asserting its urban visibility and status as a cultural landmark.

FIG 7

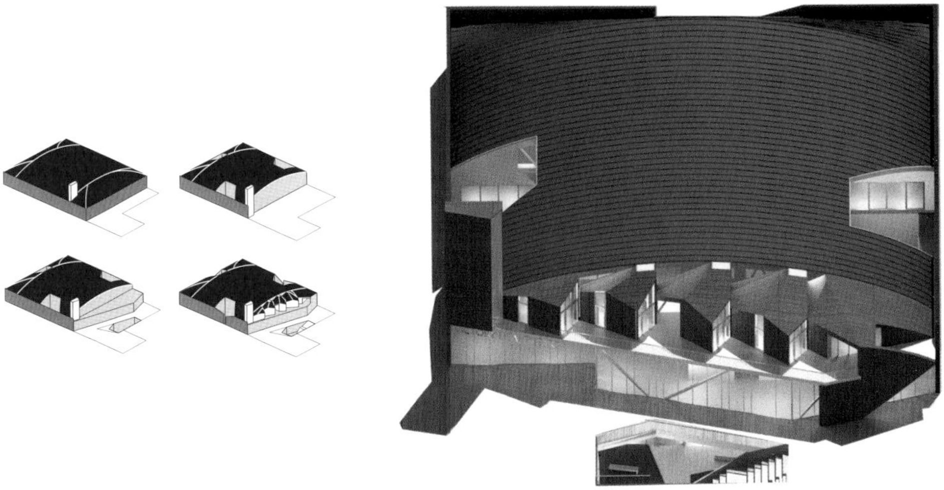

FIG 8

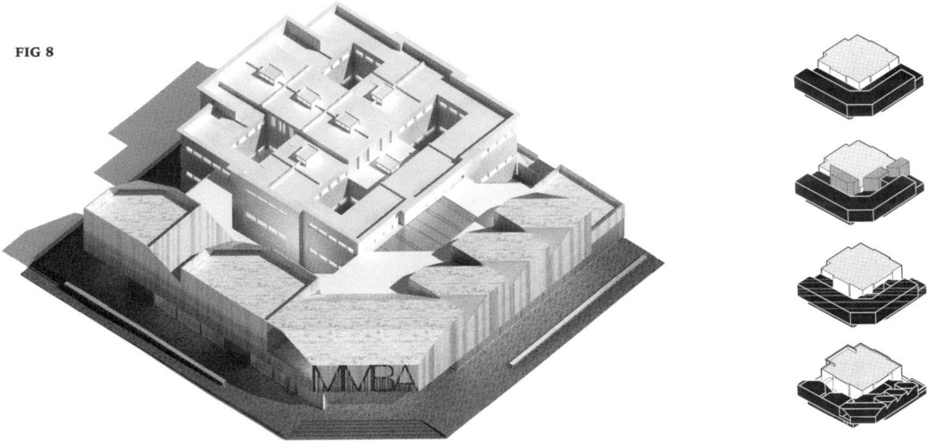

FIG 9

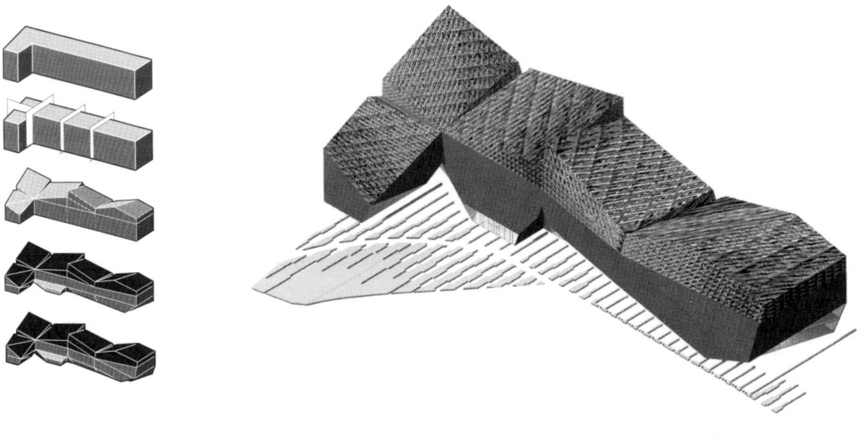

FIG 10

Infonavit, Rural Housing Prototype

Morelos, Mexico, 2016

Rural Housing implies not only building and living in the outskirts, but also a notion wherein architecture and its image exist in close proximity to its surrounding territory and landscape, one that is both agriculturally productive and aesthetically picturesque.

In this context, and conceived to be self-built by owners, our proposal's abstract posture, shape, and silhouette, made real through (strange) vernacular references and locally sourced materials, aims to conceive not just a housing prototype but also a new sense of rural living. As a result, a crystalline barn-shell would be built during the first stage of construction, ensuring a meaningful shelter at the start of the initial effort while providing efficiency, flexibility, growth, and a better quality of life for its inhabitants.

FIG 11

Karma Bequia, Boutique Hotel and Villas

St. Vincent and The Grenadines, Caribe, 2015

Consisting of 16 villas of various sizes and shapes plus other amenities, our proposal for a luxury resort in Bequia, the second largest island of the Grenadines, explores the paradox of thinking and conceiving architecture in such remote and exotic milieus.

The project takes advantage of the site's dramatic slope directly off the shoreline to create a cascading cluster of informally arrayed masses along a stepped terrace that spills naturally towards the ocean, creating a sense of community among guests and visitors alike.

Lush and yet subtle, the architecture incorporates and subverts tropical lifestyle by including ideas of exterior living and elements such as open verandas and shutter systems, enhancing the pristine natural environment and creating an eccentric sense of place. Strange and vernacular at the same time, the austere pitched-roof masses, textured with a dark wooden cladding, appear in stark contrast and yet weirdly familiar in this distant context. Allowing the adjacent ecosystem to seam naturally, the architecture absorbs and intensifies a dramatic and picturesque site.

FIG 12

Karma Sanctum, Boutique Hotel and Spa

Nusadua, Bali, Indonesia, 2017–2020

Standing out from the lush scenery of Bali and the noisy streets of Uluwatu, our proposal for this boutique hotel aims to create an iconic sanctuary: a strangely-black, rocky object that provides a welcoming and relaxing escape to a memorable sensory, spatial, and aesthetic experience.

Shaped as an open prism to maximize ocean views and preserve a small Buddhist temple located onsite, the concave angular mass opens dramatically towards the street. Clad in black volcanic stone in its solid exterior walls and with gold ceramic tile accents on its interior, the project insinuates Balinese motifs from local temples while being distinctly contemporary in its aesthetics. In contrast with the strong crystalline outline of its mass, the building surfaces are irregularly textured, creating a textile feel to the exterior. A frayed-edge treatment on the rooftop allows the interior to blur naturally between shaded and open areas, creating an impressionistic experience that blends architecture with the surrounding picturesque scenery of this exotic island.

FIG 10

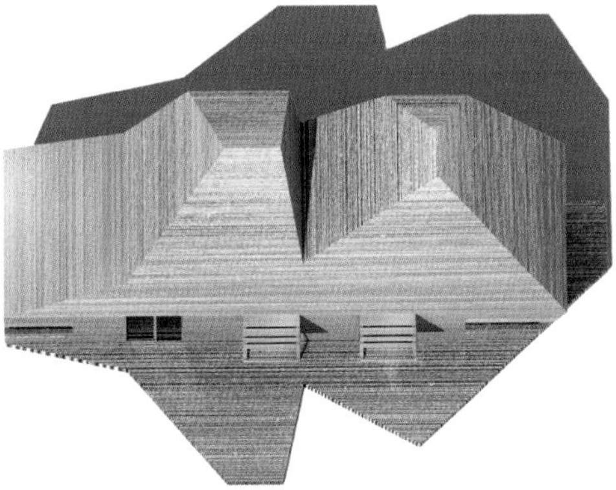
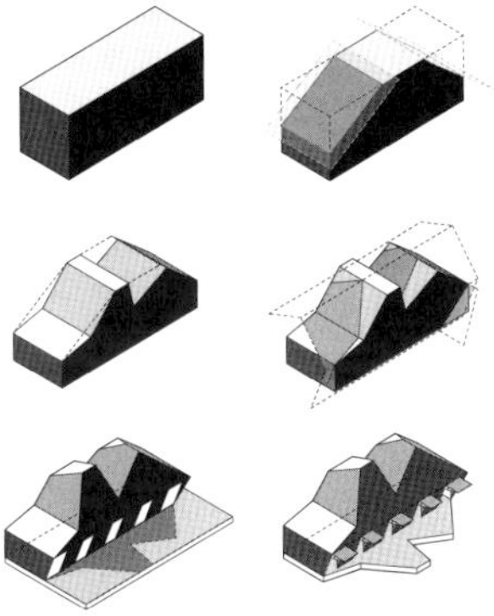

FIG 11

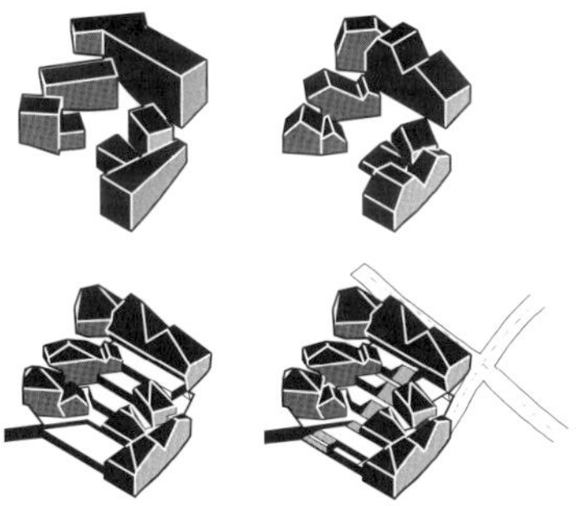

FIG 12

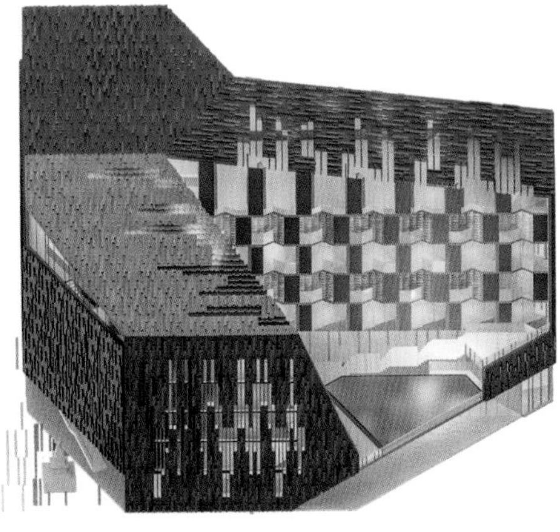
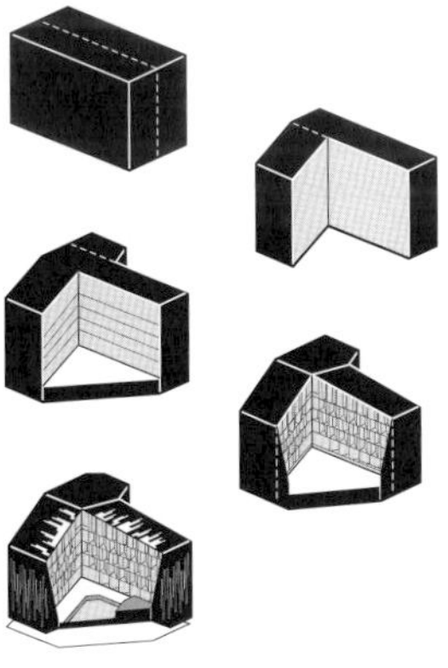

FIG 13

A4H, Commercial and Medical Office

Glendale, California, USA, 2017–2021

Responding to the need for imagining a commercial office building within a civic context, this project aims to construct an authentic dichotomic image: one that can be confused for a strange civic building, too mute to be publicly engaged, but yet too eccentrically unusual to be privately used. A primitive mass is sliced, subtracted from, and split into three separate and yet unified volumes: a large, tilting, dislodged "head," a doubly stepping volume, and a small corner bar. A continuous balcony and a peripheral void that connect all three parts reveal depth through material contrast. Despite its significant corner presence, the project's materiality is decidedly one-sided. While the Broadway facade is cladded in a dark, fritted glass curtain wall, the one that faces the civic center ports a recursively fuzzy brise-soleil made of deep metal fins. An embossed, mirrored, stainless steel soffit completes the incongruity of an obscure character-driven corner composition, adding a level of aesthetic indeterminacy to the entire building. Set back from the street by a small public park, the building affords visitors the necessary distance to engage and experience the top-heavy composition.

FIG 14

Olympia, Mix-Use High-rise Towers

Los Angeles, California, USA, 2017–2027

Poised to become one of the largest and tallest developments in Downtown Los Angeles, Olympia aims to reconsider the visual familiarity and scalar uniformity of high-rise typologies. Through local displacements and disarticulations as well as strong material contrasts, our proposal for three mixed-use towers of 65, 53, and 43 stories each, aims to generate a concentrated iconicity by means of intensity and thresholds of social activity. Collectively, the proposal traces a distinctly new silhouette on the Los Angeles skyline, defined by vertical masses, horizontally displaced volumes, and stacked terraces that create visually interconnected places for leisure, entertainment, and urban life. The facade articulation with shifting intercalated bands of vision and fritted glass affords residents with framed horizontal vistas of Los Angeles as well as the indoor/outdoor lifestyle of Southern California climate. Conceived as a "vertical neighborhood," the project articulates communal space across three discrete towers, creating a diagonally implied sequence of horizontal voids that visually unify the composition while creating a radically distinct scale of legibility and experience for high-rise typology.

FIG 15

CEFE Chapinero, Social, Cultural and Sport Center

Bogota, Colombia, 2019

In a city of extreme social divisions, some of the most fundamental elements to integrate society are culture, leisure, and sports. Our proposal for CEFE Chapinero connects, unifies, and synthesizes these three components into a pure and yet enigmatic whole. The project is conceived as a large vertically stacked volume cladded with a dense concrete mesh and diagonally traversed by an embedded ascending stairwell. The insistent and repetitive fabric of a reinforced concrete mesh works as an environmental veil, revealing and concealing the activities within the building. The frontal character of the project, added to the contrast between translucent volume and the diagonally figural void of the circulation, combines the stability of modernism with the transient obliqueness of human movement and life itself. As a result, the project aims to become an "iconographic" and "utilitarian" reference for its immediate context and for the entire city of Bogotá.

FIG 13

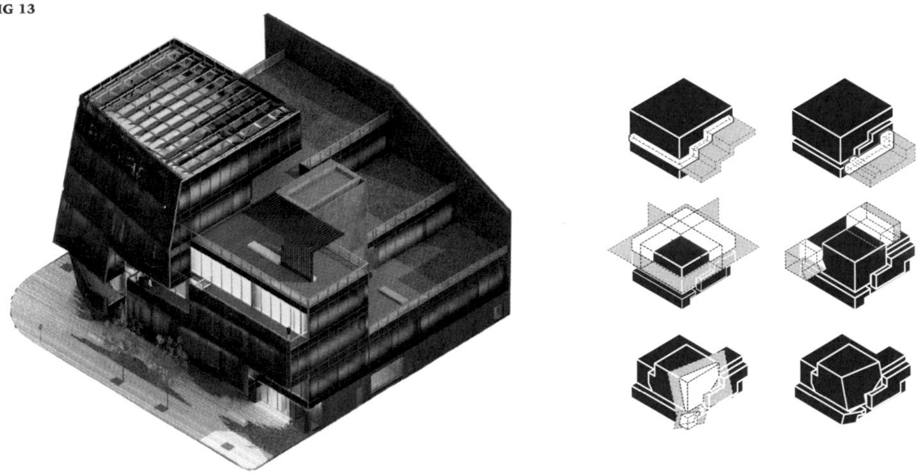

FIG 14

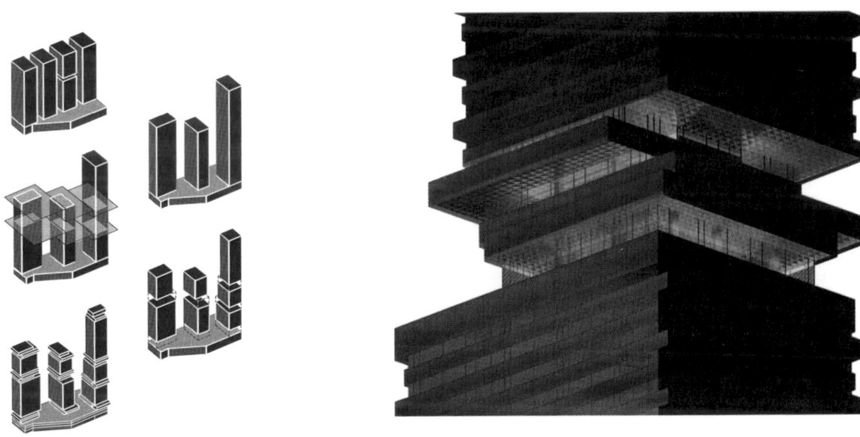

FIG 15

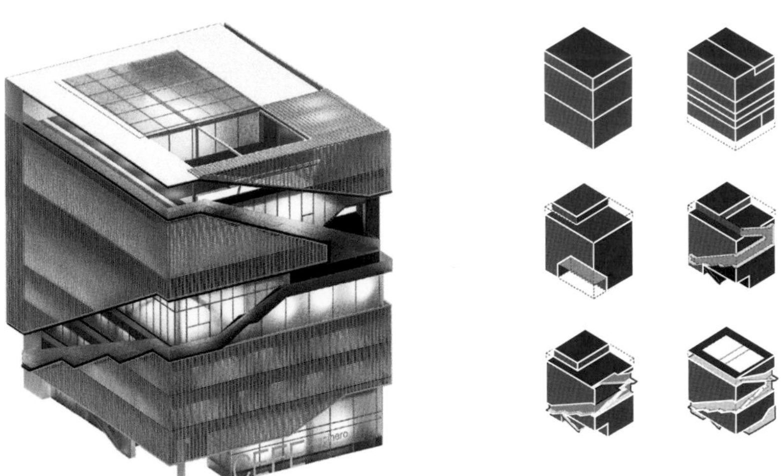

FIG 16

Prishtina Central Mosque

Prishtina, Kosovo, 2013

Seated atop a hollow plinth, and surrounded by a withdrawn courtyard for outdoor prayer, the new Central Mosque prayer hall is a mute, imposing object that hovers uneasily and indifferently over the ground and towards the street, its gigantic mass dominating the overall composition with its brutalist monolithic appearance. Monumental in size, the solid appearing, texture-filled volume of the prayer hall emerges from the ground below, levitating just above the boulevard. Sitting awkwardly above an excavated plinth, the autonomous mass is formally distinct: its mute iconic posture seemingly indifferent to both its ground beneath and the adjacent context. Further in the back, a twisting minaret anchors the horizontality of the elevated ground and is a natural public node for civic identity with its daily calls that create public orientation.

Located in the Dardania neighborhood on the south side of Prishtina, the project is a new kind of urban landmark, wherein the private, spiritual experience of religion is intensified by its public, corporeal manifestation. As a result, the vast and heavenly nature of spaces for mass congregation meet the visual and physical accessibility of their implied public nature.

FIG 17

Warner Grand Theater Expansion

San Pedro, California, USA, 2017

This expansion proposal for the iconic Warner Grand Theater in the port area of San Pedro pragmatically and imaginatively speculates on the future of this Art Deco structure, providing much needed physical accessibility to the 800-seat facility and adding a variety of ancillary functions and cultural amenities in an adjacent, vacant corner lot.

The new cultural tower, a dominating vertical mass cladded in perforated aluminum mesh, glass curtain wall, and mirrored metal panels in the projected soffits of its overhangs, bears an unstable silhouette and therefore a distinctively civic character. In consequence, the new intervention emphatically anchors the theater to its urban context, creating a beacon for the performing arts in an area of Los Angeles in much need of revitalization.

FIG 18

Keelung Crystal, Harbor Service Building and Passenger Terminal

Keelung, Taiwan, 2012

The project's contorted shape generates an ambiguously iconic presence on the harbor: at times solid, smooth, and monolithic; at others, porous, textured, and multifaceted. Atop an urban podium with a public park sits a contorted crystalline shape cracked open by a massive open atrium. The coiling mass shifts direction as it loops and folds onto itself, facing with hovering projections the most important vistas within the site. Consequently, the project soars above its site, a geological form forged in the density of commerce and formed by the crosswinds of urban modernization.

The atrium is articulated with a rusticated facade treatment producing a distinct sense of cavernous interiority. Like a large, amethyst geode, the monolithic nature of the exterior mass contrasts with the extremely ornate environment of the open-air plaza. With the overt intention to create a new identity for Keelung, the project is both a global gateway and a local destination, a metropolitan space for public use and access to the waterfront that visually and conceptually connects the city and its hills with the harbor and the Chinese ocean.

FIG 16

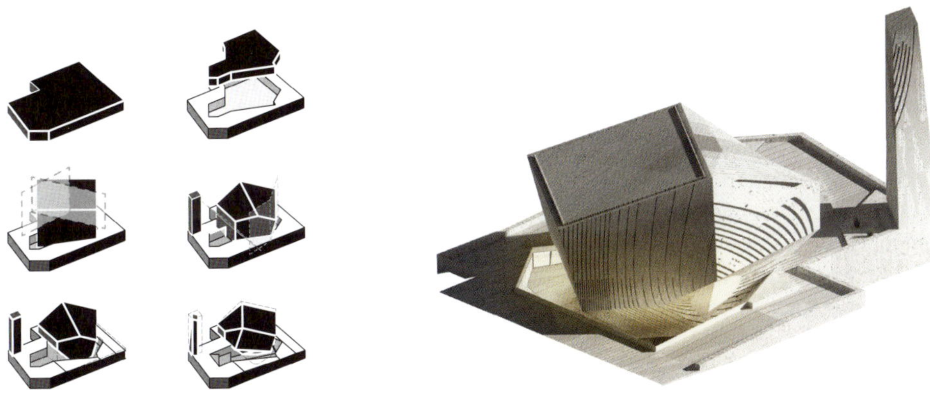

FIG 17

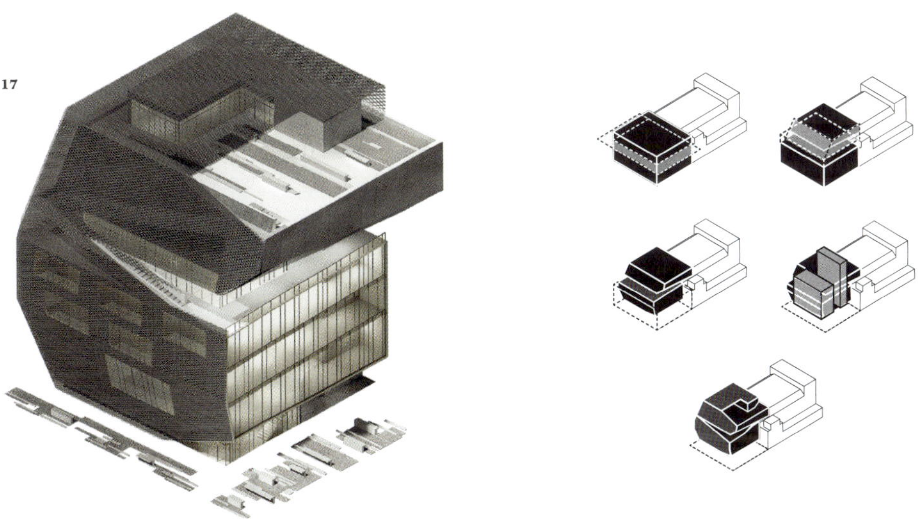

FIG 18

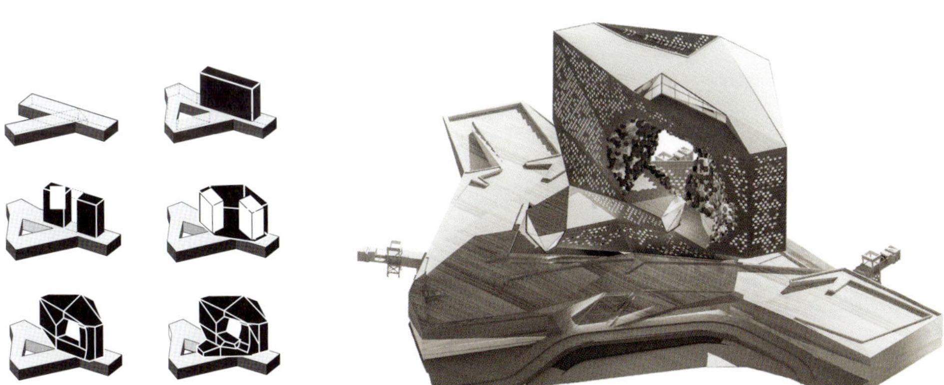

FIG 19

Lima Art Museum, Contemporary Art Wing

Lima, Peru, 2016

Our proposal for the New MALI Contemporary Art Wing is a direct response to the insurmountable conundrum of the brief: the need to position a new building contiguous to the existing one, which would have almost zero presence above ground. Our response was an 'excavated object', a building with agency and autonomy as mass, but entirety submerged within the ground.

Serving as a kind of negative plinth, the project is predicated on resolving an urban condition and organizing the heavy pedestrian traffic of its busy intersection, rather than simply creating an object. The project combines the pragmatic efficiency of the linear bar shape with the crystalline character of its more idiosyncratic protrusions. In the balance between solid and void, object and field, building and excavation, it asserts itself as a "mute icon": an engaged and mysterious grounded object; decidedly introspect and withdrawn while conspicuously iconic and texturally emblematic.

FIG 21

The Long Table, Special Events Table for CAP UCLA

Los Angeles, California, USA, 2016

This proposal for a sculptural-modular table aims to facilitate the hosting of special events at the Center for The Art of Performance at UCLA. The table incorporates various types and sizes of reclaimed blackened wood and, through a process of interlocking assembly, can be divided into three independent parts for multiple uses and easy storage. At a micro level, the table is perpetually under construction. Given the creative and artistic mission of CAP, the table is meant to engage visiting artists, donors, as well as board members in a tactile and playful experience where the very material makeup of its assembly is up for rearrangement, discussion, and speculation.

FIG 22

Casa del Sol, Summer Residence

Mykonos, Greece, 2019

Located right at the edge of a rocky outcrop and steps from the blue Aegean Sea, Casa del Sol entails a large and extensive renovation of an existing pseudo-Italian villa and other ancillary spaces into a contemporary summer residence.

Organizationally and experientially, the project aims to make the large residence feel like a Greek village: a collection of odd parts, small buildings, and pavilions, which never quite cohere into a single whole. The meandering organization provides a choreographed sequence of spaces and interstices, a constant promenade where architecture frames itself as much as object as it does landscape and nature.

In this unique context, material decisions are restricted to variations of white color. As such, texture and stone composition, form, shape, outline, and silhouette are paramount. Consequently, the new residence is an organically loose ensemble of limpid white volumes, broken crystalline masses, and divagating terraces — a 'fuzzy aggregate', a series of autonomous parts not quite cohering into a whole but not entirely fragmentary either.

FIG 19

FIG 21

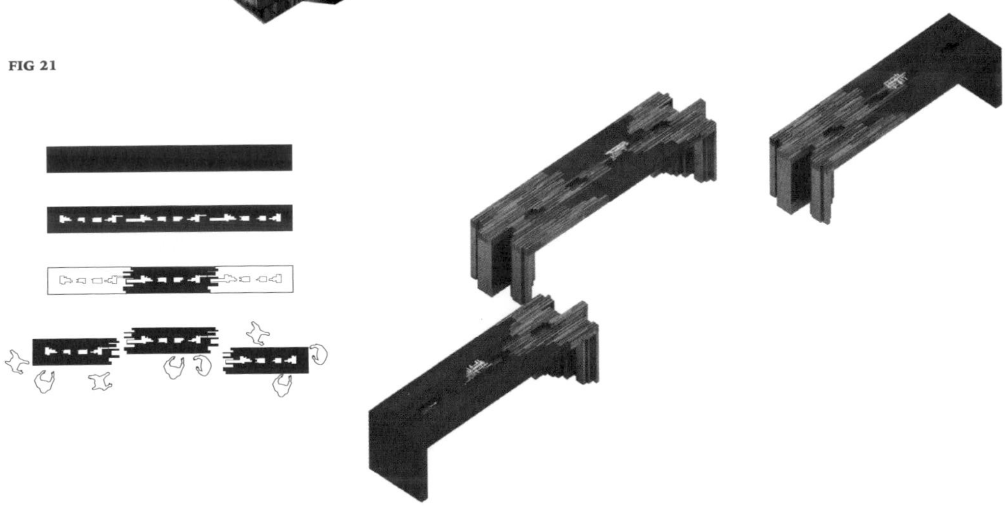

FIG 22

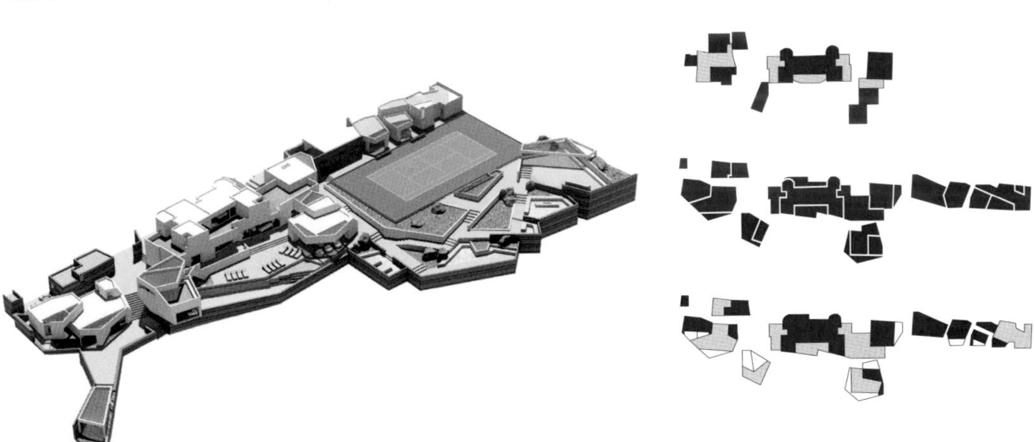

Appendix A — Hyper Obliques: Abstract Distortions of the Real

Orthographic projection is one of the most significant attributes of architecture as a discipline. Portraying architecture as both distorted abstraction and material reality, 'Hyper Obliques' intensify this historical medium and are the ultimate paradoxical means of architectural representation. The images that follow engage in dissimilar levels of abstraction and realism; free from the subjective limitations of perspective, they incorporate the material precision and aesthetic sensibility of the real.

ABOVE: Warner Grand Theater, Worm's-eye isometric

ABOVE: National Gallery and Ludwig Museum of Contemporary Art, Plan oblique,
OPPOSITE: Fuzzy Monolith, Oblique elevation

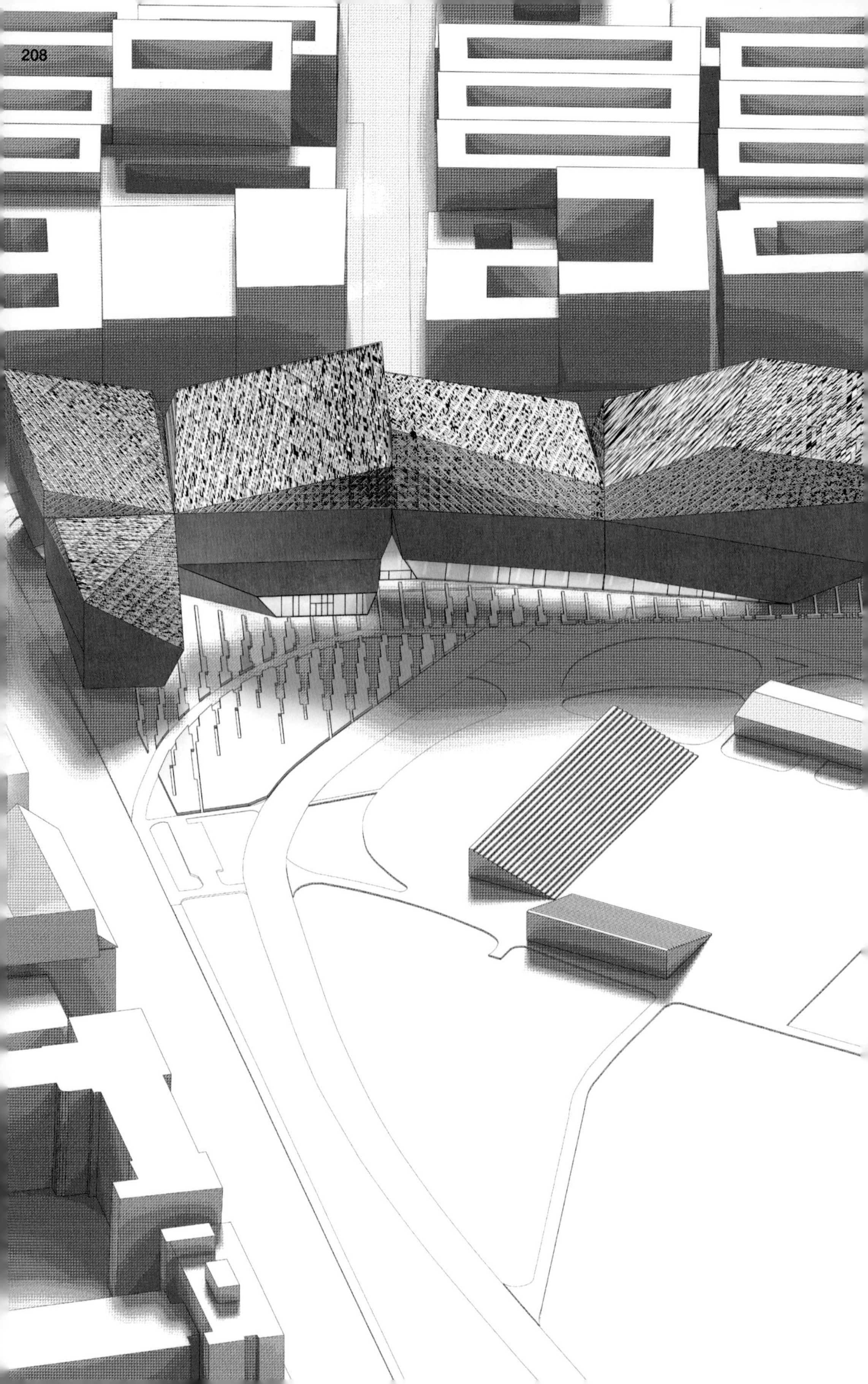

ABOVE: House of Hungarian Music, Isometric
OPPOSITE: Museum of Ethnography, Plan oblique

ABOVE: Olympia, Isometric
OPPOSITE: Hungarian Museum of Architecture and Fotomuzeum, Isometric

Jandiah

ABOVE: Warner Grand Theater, Isometric
OPPOSITE: A4H, Isometric

ABOVE: Infonavit, Plan oblique
OPPOSITE: Karma Sanctum, Plan oblique

ABOVE: Lima Art Museum Contemporary Art Wing, Isometric
OPPOSITE: The Long Table, Top view

ABOVE: Post Castle Kaliningrad, Isometric
OPPOSITE: Keelung Crystal, Isometric

ABOVE: Prishtina Central Mosque, Isometric close-up
OPPOSITE: MMBA Expansion, Plan oblique

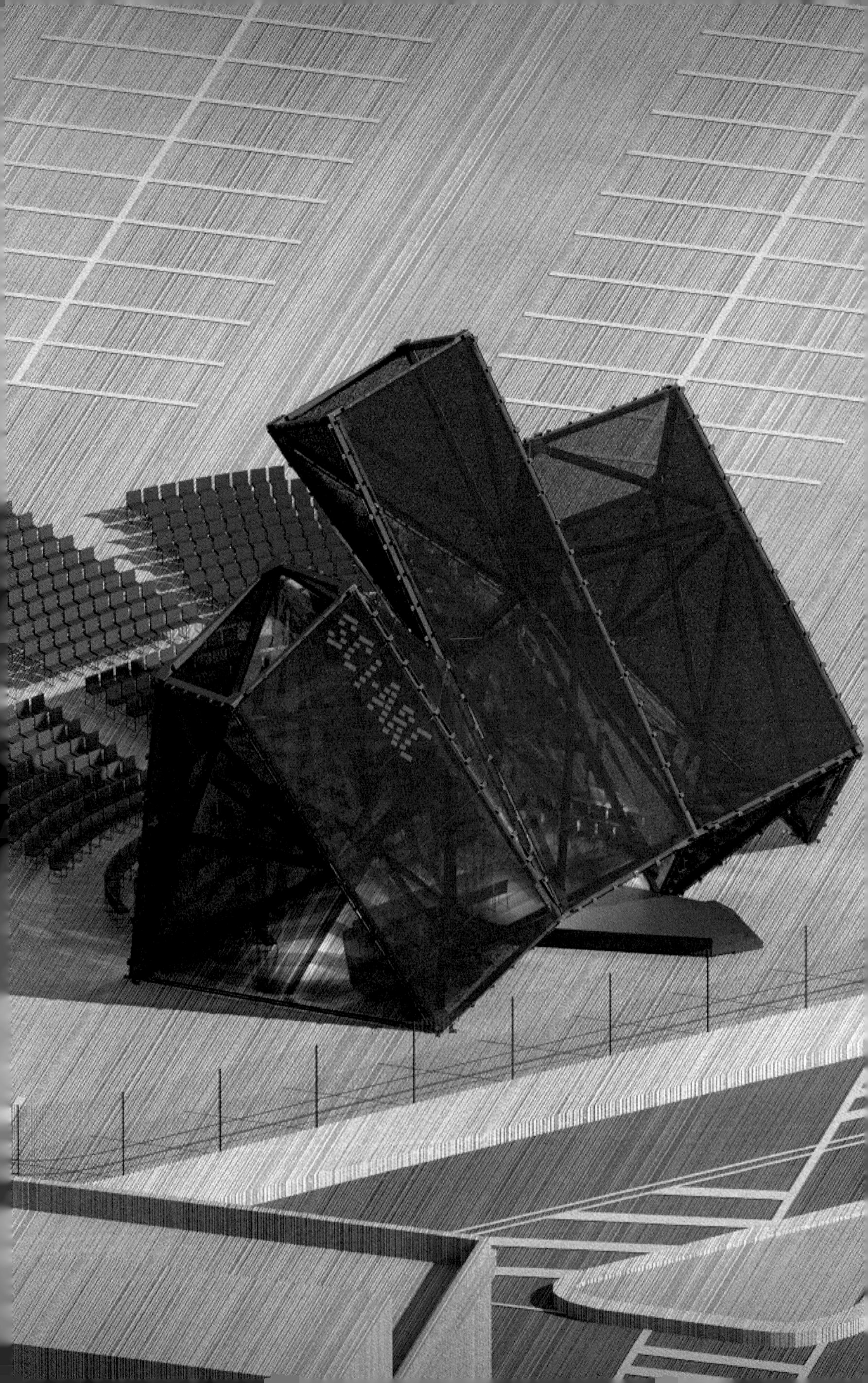

ABOVE: Victory Healthcare, Isometric
OPPOSITE: League of Shadows, Isometric

ABOVE: Olympia, Worm's-eye isometric close-up
OPPOSITE: CEFE Chapinero, Isometric close-up

ABOVE: Karma Bequia, Oblique elevation
OPPOSITE: Casa del Sol, Isometric close-up

ABOVE: A4H, Worm's-eye isometric
BELOW: Warner Grand Theater, Worm's-eye isometric

ABOVE: Olympia, Worm's-eye isometric
BELOW: CEFE Chapinero, Worm's-eye isometric

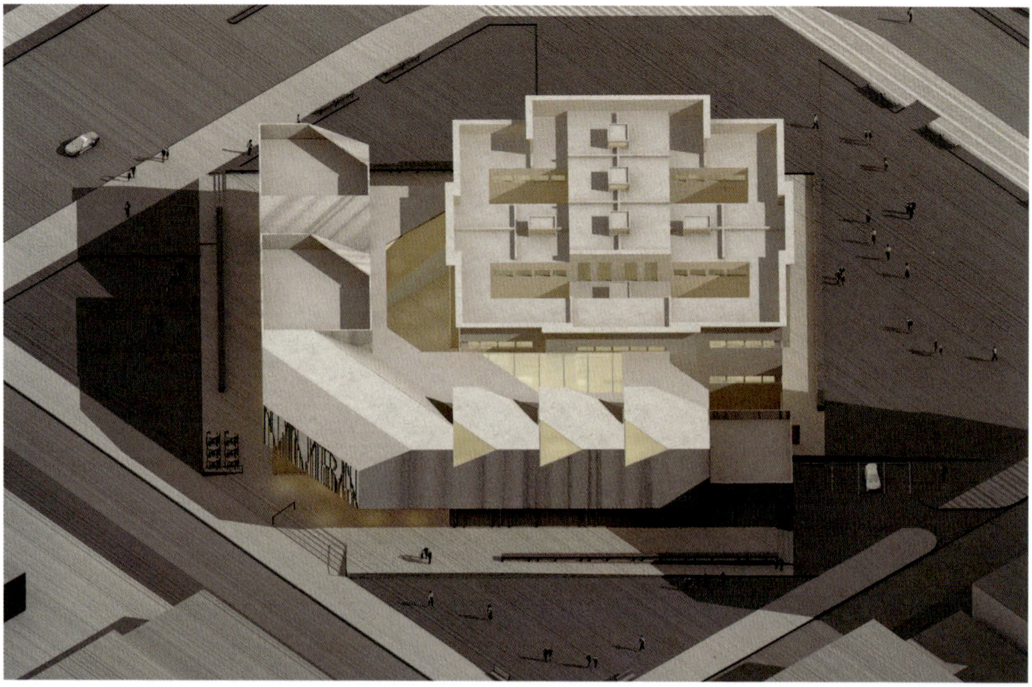

ABOVE: MMBA Expansion, Plan oblique
BELOW: CEFE Chapinero, Worm's-eye Isometric

ABOVE: Prishtina Central Mosque, Plan oblique,
BELOW: Casa del Sol, Worm's-eye Isometric

ABOVE & BELOW: Victory Healthcare, Plan oblique, parallel and perpendicular to street

ABOVE AND BELOW: MMBA Expansion, Plan oblique parallel to existing building and to new addition

ABOVE: Olympia, Isometric, **BELOW:** A4H, Worm's-eye Isometric

ABOVE: Olympia, Isometric, **BELOW:** A4H, Worm's-eye Isometric

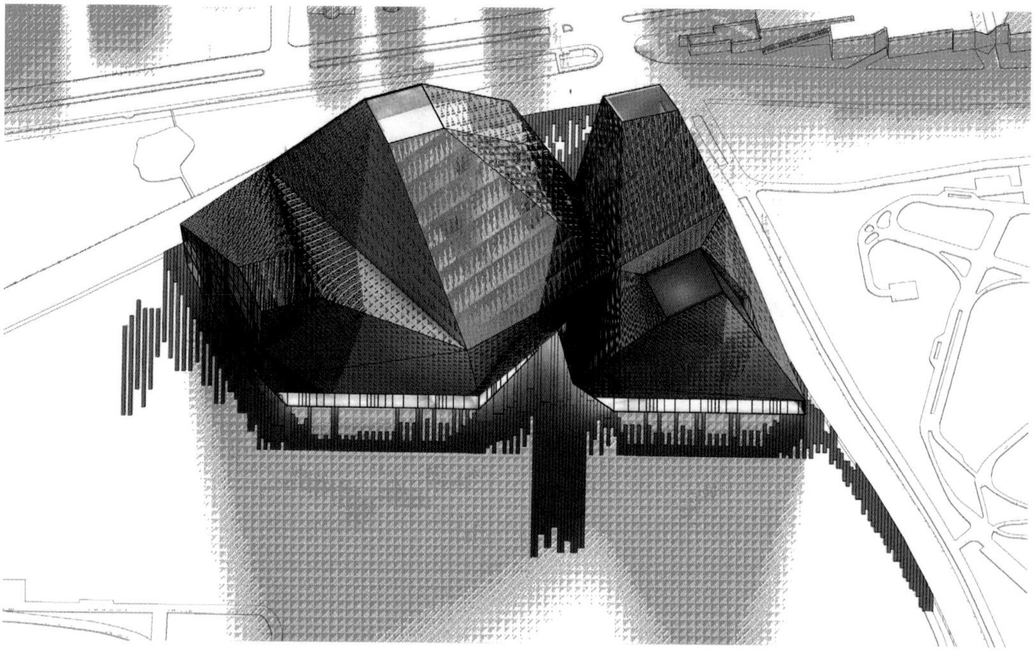

ABOVE: National Gallery and Ludwig Museum of Contemporary Art, Plan oblique
BELOW: Museum of Ethnography, Plan oblique

ABOVE: League of Shadows, Isometric
BELOW: Victory Healthcare, Plan oblique

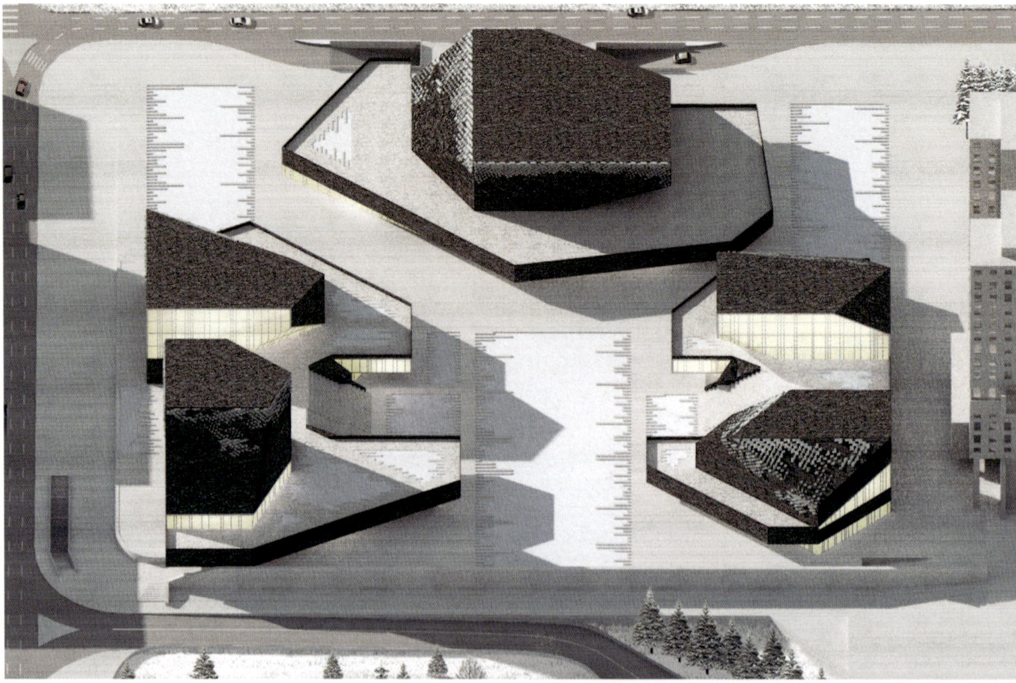

ABOVE: Post Castle Kaliningrad, Plan oblique
BELOW: Infonavit in desert environment, Plan oblique

ABOVE: House of Hungarian Music, Isometric
BELOW: Infonavit in winter environment, Plan oblique

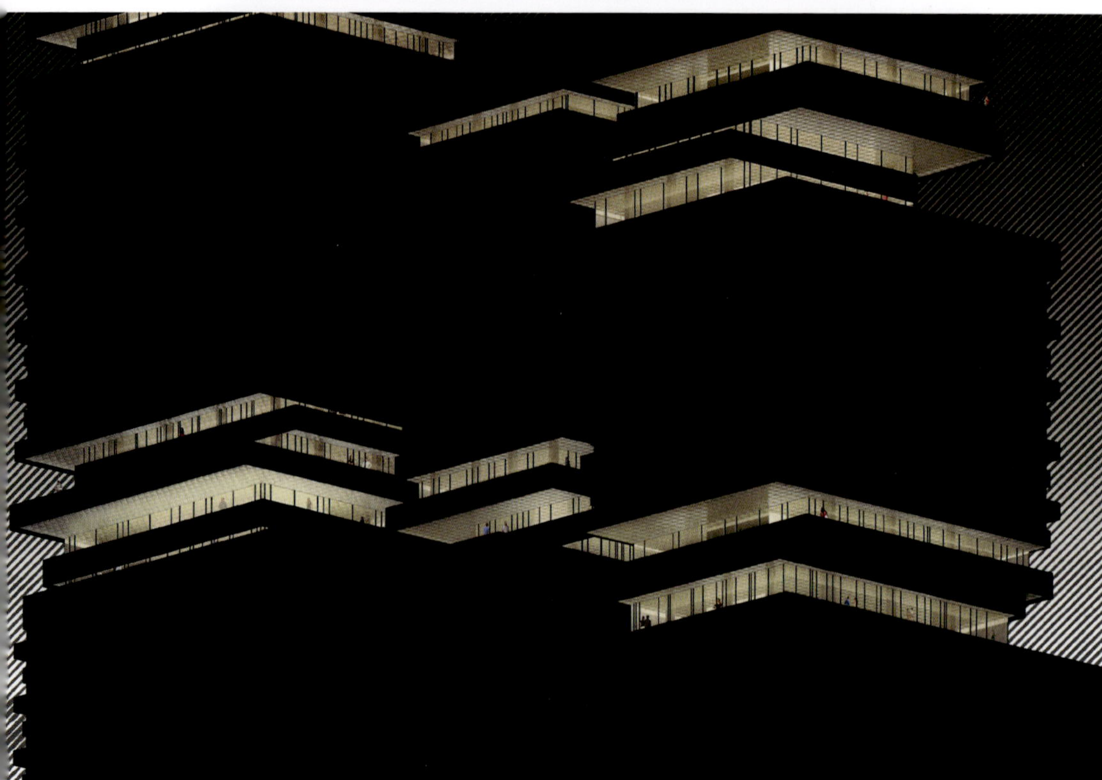

ABOVE AND BELOW: Olympia - single tower and three towers, Worm's-eye isometric

ABOVE AND BELOW: Olympia - single tower and three towers, Worm's-eye isometric

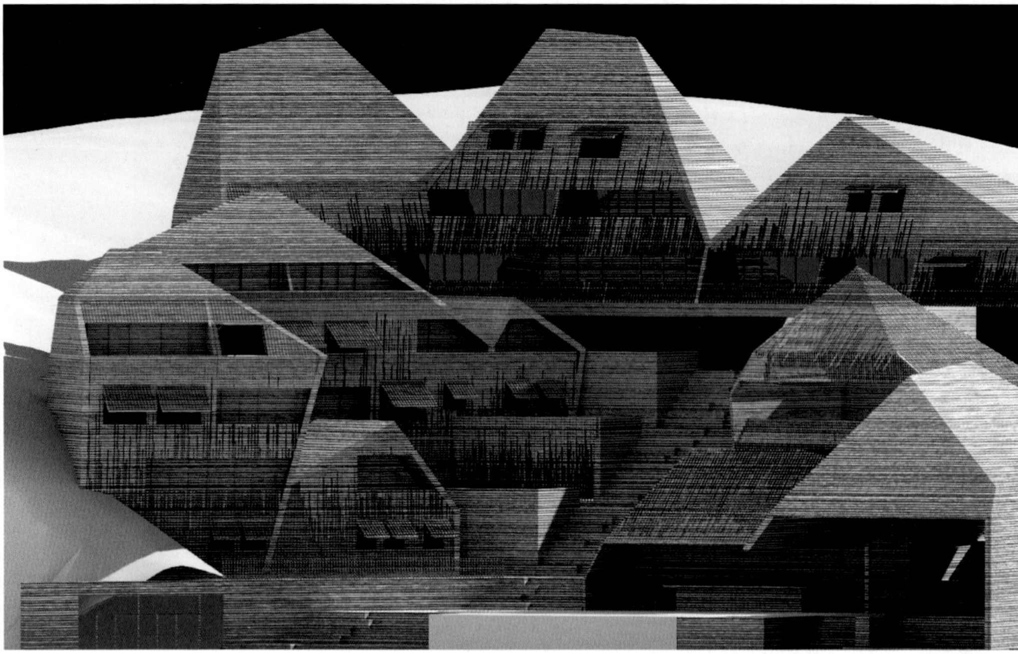

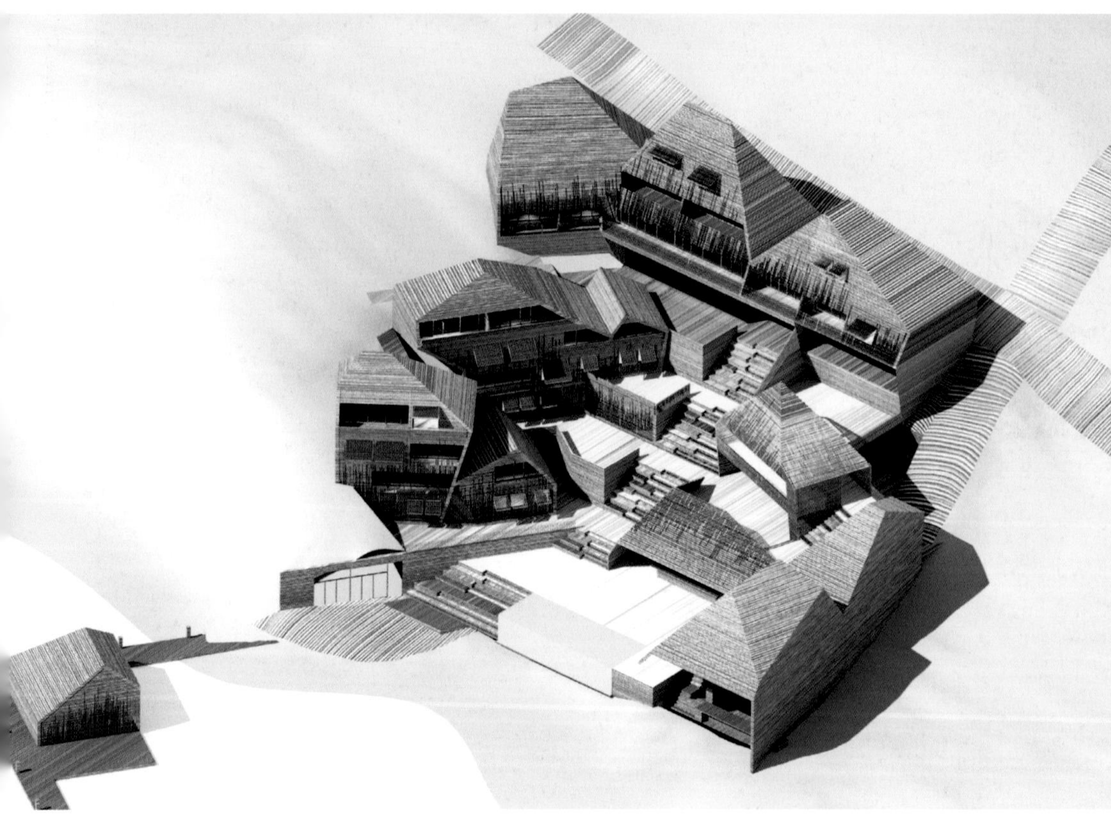

ABOVE AND BELOW: Karma Bequia, Elevation and isometric

ABOVE AND BELOW: Karma Kandara Phase VI, Elevation and isometric

ABOVE AND BELOW: Victory Healthcare, Plan oblique and oblique section

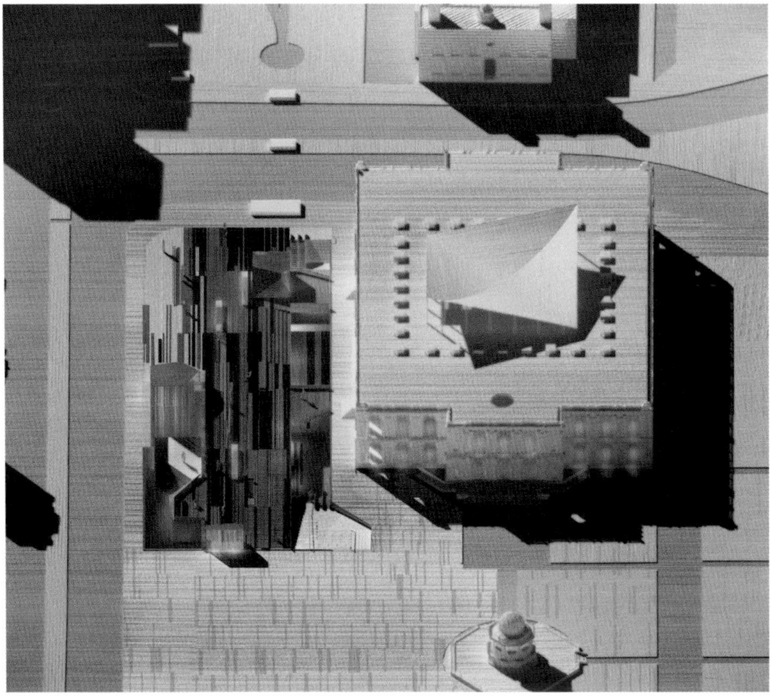

ABOVE AND BELOW: Lima Art Museum Contemporary Art Wing, Plan oblique and oblique section

ABOVE CLOCKWISE: A4H View 1, CEFE Chapinero, A4H View 2, 1099 Mixed-Use, Karma Sanctum, Expansion of Warner Grand Theater

ABOVE CLOCKWISE: Lima Art Museum, Casa del Sol, Olympia, League of Shadows

ABOVE CLOCKWISE: Olympia single tower, Warner Grand Theater, Karma Sanctum, CEFE Chapinero, Olympia, A4H

ABOVE CLOCKWISE: Casa del Sol, CEFE Chapinero, Prishtina Central Mosque, MMBA Expansion

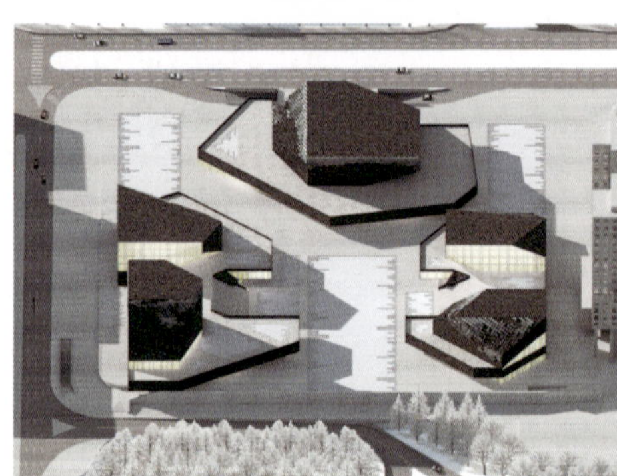

ABOVE CLOCKWISE: Karma Kandara Phase VI, Victory Healthcare, A4H, Post Castle Kaliningrad, Warner Grand Theater, Karma Sanctum

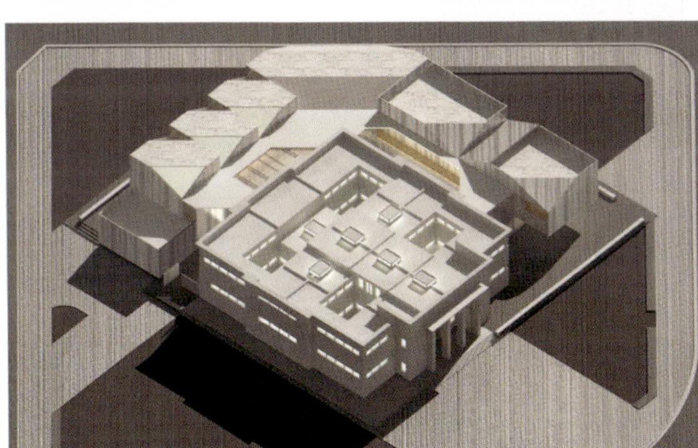

ABOVE: Peace Corps Memorial, Keelung Crystal, Casa del Sol, MMBA Expansion

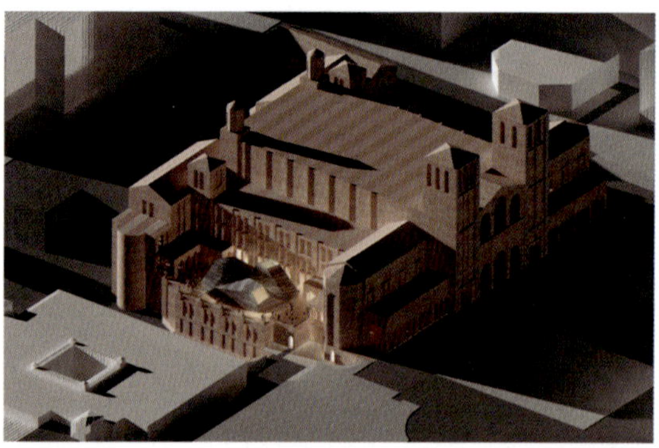

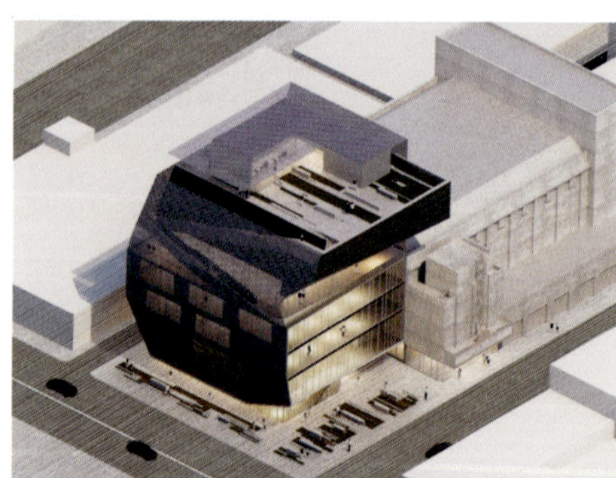

ABOVE CLOCKWISE: A4H, Victory Healthcare, House of Hungarian Music, Expansion of Warner Grand Theater, 1099 Mixed-Use, UCLA Ahmanson Terrace Pavilion

ABOVE CLOCKWISE: Lima Art Museum Contemporary Art Wing, League of Shadows, Olympia, CEFE Chapinero

ABOVE CLOCKWISE: Lima Art Museum Contemporary Art Wing, Expansion of Warner Grand Theater, Prishtina Central Mosque, UCLA Ahmanson Terrace Pavilion, CEFE Chapinero, Olympia

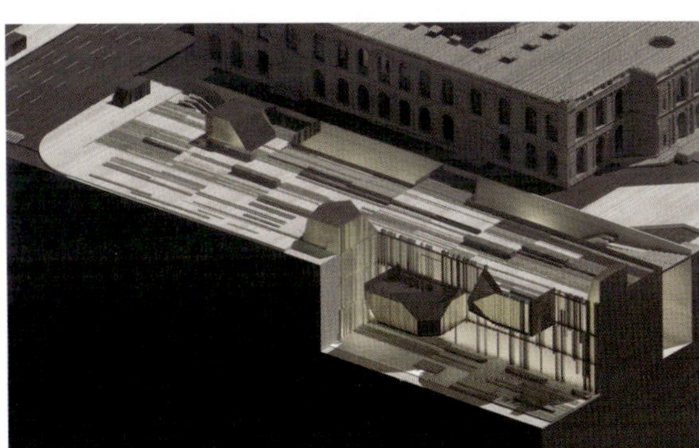

ABOVE CLOCKWISE: A4H, League of Shadows, Olympia, Lima Art Museum Contemporary Art Wing

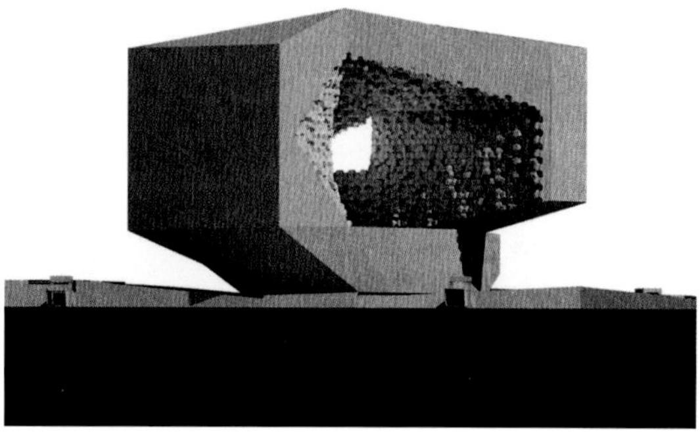

ABOVE CLOCKWISE: Keelung Crystal, Olympia, Victory Healthcare, Karma Bequia, MMBA Expansion, National Gallery and Ludwig Museum of Contemporary Art

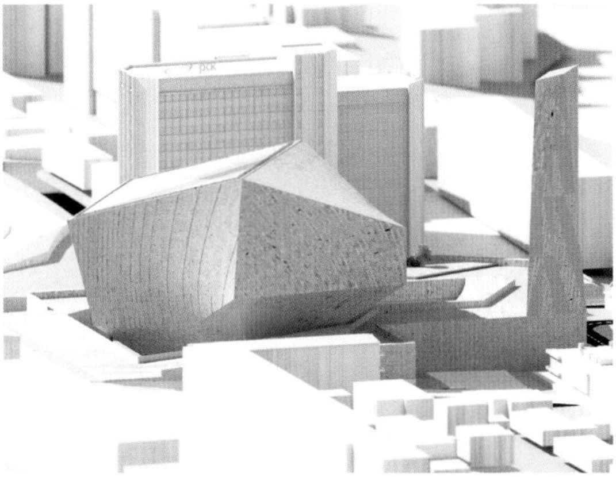

ABOVE CLOCKWISE: Prishtina Central Mosque View 1, View 2, View 3, Infonavit

Appendix B— Physical Models: Material Reductions of the Real

Models are about mass, void, articulation, and texture. As objects, they are unambiguously factual, since they convey the tactile immediacy of physical reality. The material abstraction of models is both liberating and powerful. Their delayed materiality allows us to isolate variables. No one will confuse the materiality of a model with that of the proposed building. Influential mediums, they are real insofar as they exist in their own condensed version of material resolution and physical reality.

ABOVE: Fuzzy Monolith elevation

ABOVE CLOCKWISE: MOCA Textile Room, View 2, A4H, Arts Hotel View 1, View 2, A4H View 2

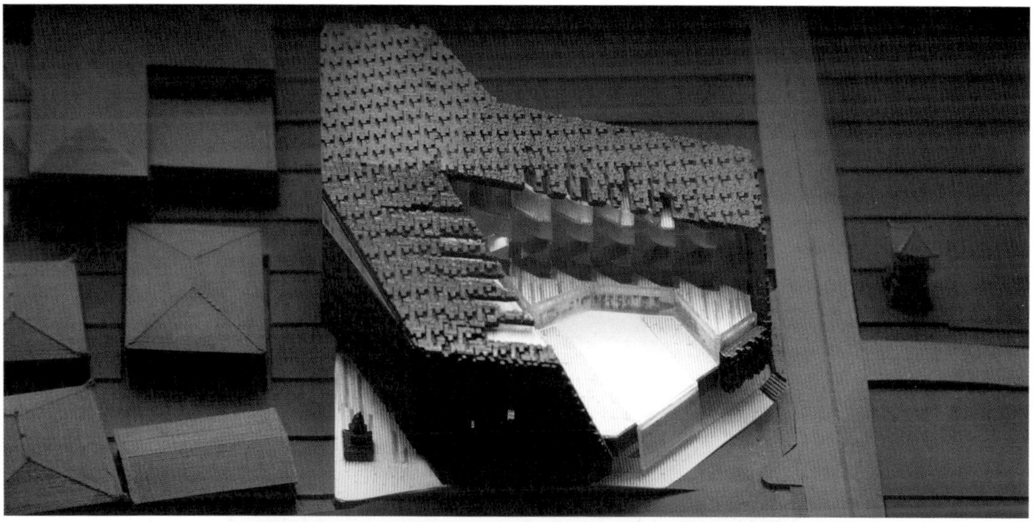

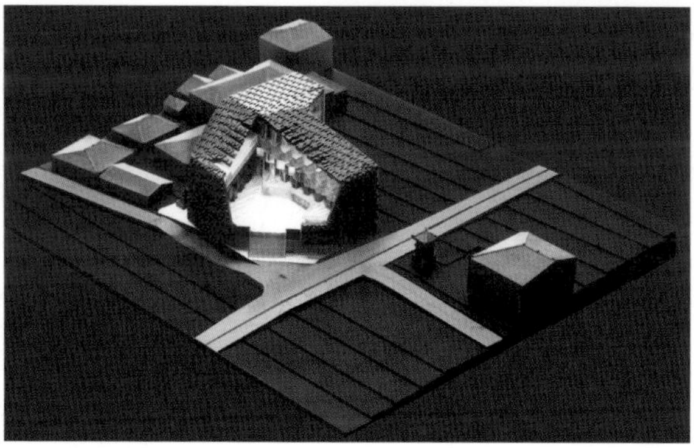

ABOVE CLOCKWISE: Fuzzy Monolith View 1, View 2, Karma Sanctum View 1, View 2

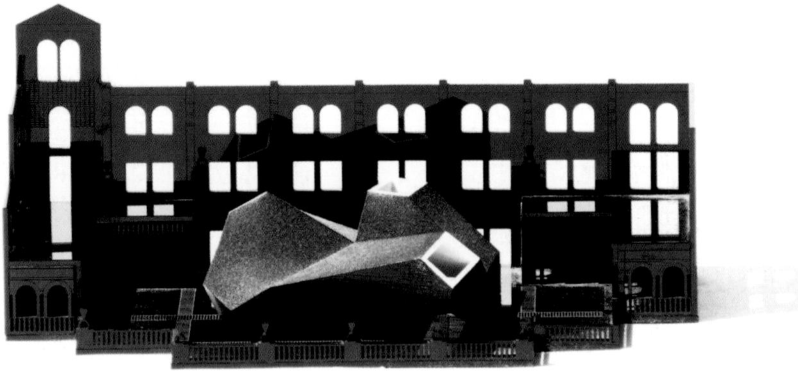

ABOVE CLOCKWISE: UCLA Ahmanson Terrace Pavilion, Study 1, 2 & 3, Karma Bequia, Fuzzy Monolith

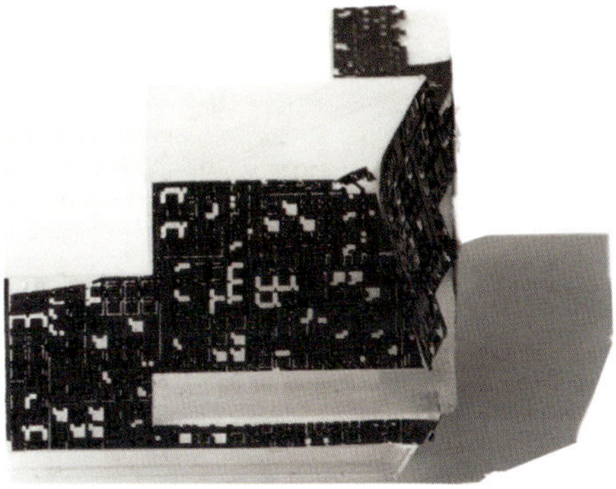

ABOVE CLOCKWISE: A4H Study Model 1, Study Model 2, A4H, Arts Hotel

ABOVE CLOCKWISE: A4H Iteration 1, Iteration 2, Prishtina Central Mosque, Prishtina Central Mosque with context

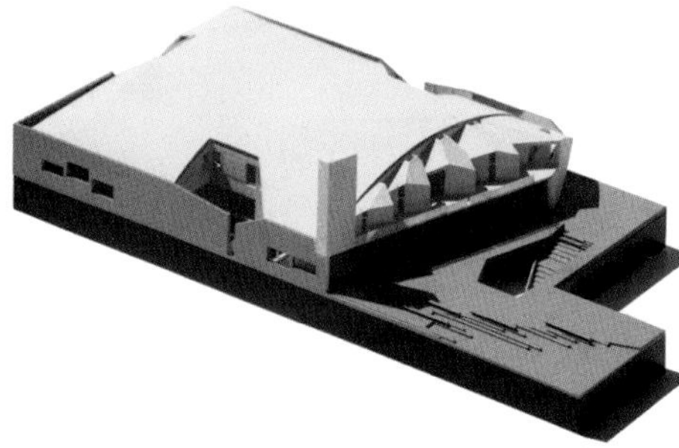

ABOVE CLOCKWISE: Infonavit, Victory Healthcare, 1099 Mixed-Use Iteration 1, Iteration 2, Iteration 3, Olympia

Appendix C— Photorealistic Perspectives: Narratives and Concentrations of the Real

Photography is probably the most real of all art forms, since it deals directly with visual reality as a source. Drawing from artists such as Gregory Crewdson, Todd Hido, and Thomas Ruff among others, the following images situate and describe projects in slightly unfamiliar and perhaps even strange ways. Rather than anesthetize the world from architecture, these (one-point perspective!) images concentrate on unforeseen aspects of architecture's uncanny beauty, constructing fictional yet probable narratives concerning both content and context.

SHIMAHARA ILLUSTRATION

ABOVE: A4H Aerial view

JAMES VINCENT

4.3. Photorealistic Perspectives

FIG 1

Keelung Crystal

Keelung, Taiwan, 2012

Summer Afternoon. The project's contorted shape generates an ambiguously iconic presence on the harbor: at times solid, smooth, and monolithic; at others, porous, textured, and multifaceted. Like a giant, the coiling mass shifts direction as it loops and folds onto itself, facing the most important vistas with hovering projections while creating an unmistakable panoramic porthole towards the China Sea.

JAMES VINCENT

FIG 2 & 3

Keelung Crystal Urban Sight and Interior Atrium

Keelung, Taiwan, 2012

Summer Early Evening and Twilight. A strange mass soars above its site, a geological form forged in the density of commerce and formed by the crosswinds of urban modernization. Articulated with a rusticated and recursive facade, a rising atrium produces a distinct sense of cavernous interiority. Like a large, amethyst geode, the monolithic nature of the exterior mass contrasts with the extremely ornate atmosphere of the gigantic open-air plaza.

FIG 4
Prishtina Central Mosque
Prishtina, Kosovo, 2013

Spring Sunrise. Monumental in size, what seems to be the solid, texture-filled volume of the prayer hall emerges from the ground below, levitating just above it and the boulevard beyond. Appearing awkwardly from beneath an excavated plinth, the autonomous mass is formally distinct: its mute iconic posture seemingly indifferent to both its ground and context.

4.3. Photorealistic Perspectives

JAMES VINCENT

JAMES VINCENT

FIG 5

Prishtina Central Mosque

Prishtina, Kosovo, 2013

Spring Sunrise, Friday Prayer. The new prayer hall flickers with a glitch-like graphic array of parallel lines, asserting the authority of its mass with varying densities and visual intensities. Further in the back, a partially torqued minaret anchors the horizontality of the elevated ground and is a natural public node for communal orientation in the daily ritual prayer.

JAMES VINCENT

FIG 6

National Gallery and Ludwig Museum of Contemporary Art

Budapest, Hungary, 2014

Summer Evening, Opening Night. A decidedly idiosyncratic silhouette of tapered shapes and truncated pyramids disrupts the horizontality of the park. Imposing and sublime, the museum appears as an alluring and newly arrived foreign object, persistently suspended above a light-filled, transparent vestibule glowing in a dense and shadowy Budapest city park.

JAMES VINCENT

FIG 7

Hungarian Museum of Architecture and Fotomuzeum

Budapest, Hungary, 2014

Morning, Spring Mist. Situated somewhere between the regimented row of neoclassical facade edifices and that of the equally disciplined fuchsia trees in the nature-mimicking but picturesque Budapest City park, the Museum building looks away, eccentric and impatient. The willfully fuzzy texture of shimmering and rasterized surfaces enhances the fractured nature of its crystalline mass, creating a haunting aesthetic experience of culture and visual history.

FIG 8

Museum of Ethnography
Budapest, Hungary, 2014

Late Winter Night, Blizzard. Museum Closed. Strangely contextual, the museum appears as a dark ghost, its mass hidden in plain sight and its silhouette outlining a decidedly obscure and withdrawn character. It sits before a nearly empty boulevard, confronting a consolidated block of Art Nouveau reminiscent and other neoclassical buildings along Budapest City Park.

4.3. Photorealistic Perspectives

JAMES VINCENT

JAMES VINCENT

FIG 9

Post Castle Kaliningrad

Kaliningrad, Russia, 2015

Late Winter Night. With the brutalist-inspired House of Soviets barely discernible in the hazy background, pro-democracy activists and other peaceful demonstrators by the thousands long dispersed, a mysterious presence disturbs the now empty and suspiciously clean monumental square.

FIG 10
Expansion of Warner Grand Theater
San Pedro, California, USA, 2017

Summer Afternoon. A helicopter photograph of the new Warner Grand Theater with the Port of Long Beach in the background can easily be read as an establishing shot for a Hollywood crime drama: the vast industrial landscape of the Harbor, a sea of containers, heroic structures, and infrastructure contrast with the smaller and humbler edifices of downtown San Pedro. The still vibrant light and looming shadow of the late afternoon positions the discernible silhouette of Warner Grand amidst landscape photography reminiscent of Andreas Gursky.

4.3. Photorealistic Perspectives

NEPHEW

FIG 11

Expansion of Warner Grand Theater

San Pedro, California, USA, 2017

Summer, Early Afternoon. From the street, the slow loneliness of a traffic jam reminds us of *Falling Down* or *La La Land*. Gary Winogrand's work in Los Angeles during the early 1980s comes to mind, the coincidental beauty that's both high contrast and distant, in a Los Angeles kind of way.

4.3. Photorealistic Perspectives

NEPHEW

NEPHEW

FIG 12

MMBA Museum Expansion

Rosario, Argentina, 2017

Fall Twilight, Cloudy Day. Museum Closed. A decapitated tree in the corner, an unknown piece of clothing hangs weirdly from a nearby branch, and the bright and exaggerated emergency and exit lights of the Museum are on, casting strange effects against the white Carrara-zebra-marbled facade of the empty building. Imagining architecture after hours, a lonely context already strange, will alter the strange quietness of this magic moment, forever. A picture of contrasting intimacies, the worn surfaces and remnant objects archive a presence, but too little to tell a complete narrative.

SHIMAHARA ILLUSTRATION

FIG 13

A4H

Glendale, California, USA, 2017–2021

Winter, Evening Thunder Storm. An early winter storm moves into Los Angeles, a preview of a much-awaited rainy season. Lightning heralds the increasingly dramatic effects of climate change in Southern California.

SHIMAHARA ILLUSTRATION

SHIMAHARA ILLUSTRATION

FIG 14 & 15

A4H

Glendale, California, USA, 2017–2021

Winter Night, Downpour. Heavy rain causes street flooding all over Southern California.

VOICE 1: "It's become the rainiest city on the planet…" "Lot of surf on the sidewalks…" "I don't think I remember it raining like this in a long, long time." "We have been in a drought for a while…" VOICE 2: "The rainfall has been tight this year…" VOICE 3: "It rained like, a lot today, no one knew how to drive, when commuting to work…" VOICE 4: "Take umbrellas everywhere in LA!" VOICE 1: "Who has umbrellas in LA? I think I had two when I moved out here, I think I junked them after the first two years of no rain…" VOICE 2: "We needed the rain, so I think everyone is happy for the most part."

NYT podcast, March 2014

FIG 16

A4H

Glendale, California, USA, 2017–2021

Winter Night, Foggy Rain. "Climate change may put California in a destructive cycle of floods and droughts" (Quartz). With low visibility and a torrential rain, Los Angeles looks like a scene from David Fincher's film *Seven*, where the rain never lets up. Here, A4H is seen through a downpour, and like in the film, the foggy rain adds a dark and moody, noir-type element and ups the mystery of the setting.

SHIMAHARA ILLUSTRATION

NEPHEW

FIG 17 & 18

Karma Sanctum

Nusadua, Bali, Indonesia, 2017–2020

Summer Twilight. Giant bats and ascending treetops extend the bounds of Karma Sanctum's inner court, while opposing color keys cleave the layered composite. The proximity of the Hindu temples nearby makes the black volcanic stone of the hotel's rusticated facades seem oddly familiar. Inspired by old Chinese watercolor paintings presenting a layered arrangement of objects and landscapes, these images contemplate ideas of "view" making, emphasizing a tiered vertical picture plane rather than a strict perspective grid.

Appendix D— Aerial Photomontages: Displacements and Glitches of the Real

Aerial photography, such as that used by Google Earth and other global search and navigation engines, have become ubiquitously real in our understanding of the environment around us. What follows is a one-off experiment on the limits and possibilities of these kinds of images, which reveals both hidden inconsistencies as well as newfound potentials within this medium, defining new speculative realities for architecture and its extended milieu.

PATTERNS & CASEY REHM

ABOVE: Oblicuo, Fragment

PATTERNS & CASEY REHM

FIG 1

Oblicuo

Chicago, USA, 2016

Oblicuo challenges fixed aesthetic notions of beauty and legibility in architectural representation and visualization, using abstraction and defamiliarization to speculate on the generation of withdrawn, irritant, and engaging photo realistic images. Focusing on the paradox between abstraction and realism, the project speculates on the currency of the image in architecture, precisely as it relates to the role and present status of the icon.

PATTERNS & CASEY REHM

By revisiting the Budapest City Park project, *Oblicuo* aims to experiment with the limits and possibilities of the image, the way it can be technologically captured via drones and its realism hyper enhanced, to reveal both the hidden inconsistencies as well as newfound potentials of this medium, defining new speculative realities for architecture and its extended milieu.

Technically, *Oblicuo* leverages the underlying biases and discrepancies in contemporary methods of computer visualization and distributed surveying to generate a novel understanding of both context and field in architecture. By purposefully misappropriating and retooling common algorithms utilized to create coherent representations of urban environments from distributed sources, *Oblicuo* exposes the seams, voids, and flaws concealed by the hidden agencies that continuously manipulate our perception of the world.

In its purposeful dichotomy and vague indeterminacy as both an oblique plan ["oblicuo" in Spanish] and a photo realistic montage, *Oblicuo* attempts to contest long-standing antagonisms such as those between abstraction and realism, simulation and representation, perspective and projection, object and field, drawing and image. The speculative nature of its result attempts to expose the disciplinary potential of these machines in their ability to both perceive and transform our world at ever-finer degrees and scales.

4.4. Aerial Photomontages

5 CULTURE: On Dialectics —

A Conversation with Guillermo Martinez

Translation by Marcelo Spina

MS: Let's talk about dialectics.

GM: My first ideological encounter with dialectics was in the context of my family, with Marxism as a guide. My father was an important [Argentine] leader in the communist party who dealt with all manner of theory, and so in my house, there were many philosophy books. There were books about dialectical logic by Eli de Gortari, Henri Lefebvre, and Carlos Astrada, among others. I attempted my first theoretical incursion in my adolescence and even tried to attend a university seminar dealing with Hegel's *Encyclopaedia*. But I had my first awakening to theory around the notion of dialectical logic upon trying to understand, as much as I could, *Anti-Dühring* by Engels, and in particular, the formulation of the laws of dialectics. I recall this time quite well, and I even try to bring it back from the past: every so often a reference to it appears in one of my books.

Later I committed myself to the systematic, formal study of mathematical logic. In that sense, I turned away from all these philosophical ideas because they were very difficult to formalize. In my practice as a logician, I was able to observe some attempts to formalize ideas of dialectical logic; the principle of contradiction, for instance, which in mathematics assumes that there can be no logical contradiction because from any contradiction, a premise can be inferred from it. And this, in some way, trivializes the system of entailments that happens as a result. However, there are logics that are called "para-consistent" that try to limit the number of statements that can be deduced from a contradiction. Defined by a Brazilian theorist, there is a first attempt to formalize some idea of the dialectic, in the sense that it admits contradictions... that is to say... it is supposed to advance by way of contradictions. However, these logics were not fully studied nor did they have a very wide range, so I turned more towards other branches of mathematical logic and began to move away from that line of thinking. However, I was always interested in these issues, and I will elaborate on the ones that are relevant to my current thinking. One is an essay I wrote about Witold Gombrowicz: "Gombrowicz, Writer of Dialectics."

MS: I've read it on your blog. It's a presentation for a conference…

Witold Gombrowicz: Detachment, Intensification of Perception, and the Instability of Being

GM: Gombrowicz was immersed in the ideological discussions of his time, contemporary to the rise of Marxism, of which he was critical. What I find interesting is Gombrowicz's exposition of those ideas, even if he didn't absorb them entirely; and even with the critical reservations he may have had about dialectics, they appear in many of his narrative procedures in a very natural way.

What do I mean by this? First, there is a recurrent issue that appears in his characters — situations in which he begins to look with casual attention at a hand or a face, for instance… If his attention strays and he moves on to something else, nothing happens. But if he takes a moment longer than expected, critical reflection happens about why he was delayed there in the first place. This produces a form of detachment, and from here on, by intensification and concentration, it leads him to see a potentially sinister or even monstrous side of what he was looking at. Thus, this is one of the first laws of dialectics: that which exists, exists in an unstable way, and it is enough for one to pay attention to it, noticing and studying it, so that it also reveals that which it is not. That which it is not, appears from what it is. This is a procedure that Gombrowicz uses a lot and even explains in the introduction to *Cosmos*, which I was recently rereading.

Gombrowicz, who emigrated to Argentina, was originally from Poland, and his novel *Transatlantic* takes place when the Second World War had just been declared in Europe. In it, there is a character who seeks help at the local embassy, and none of the Polish ambassadors dare to say anything about the war. They do not want to be trapped in any statement that could damage their reputation, so everything they affirm, at the same time they also deny, just in case. There's a moment of madness, of schizophrenia, that spreads throughout the work and is incarnated in one of the characters. For instance, they invite him to eat dinner, and the food he eats is at the same time both known and unknown. He thinks he knows what it is, but it is also something else, because he is in another country. So again, there is a type of instability of being that corresponds to that moment of war.

There are also famous passages that I try to salvage throughout that article. One is the notion of quantity and quality, which appears in an emblematic way in some of Gombrowicz's characters: like the Analytic, as he calls him. I see this also as an influence from Sartre, who also had a character who was self-taught, somebody who tried to read the entire library in alphabetical order. These are characters that embody the theoretical idea of how quantity becomes quality. But at the same time, quantity also deteriorates quality. In my opinion, these reflections are all part of a literary incarnation of dialectics.

The other question that interested me came from Todorov's book *Critique of Criticism* [1991], which has resonances with a book that I had read earlier, *Six Memos for the Next Millennium* by Italo Calvino [1998]. In that book, Calvino affirms and puts forward some of the attributes that would be aesthetically pleasing for him to be preserved in literature of the future. Nevertheless, for each attribute he advances, he perceives and incorporates the opposite attribute as well. This is the germ of the idea of dichotomies. For example, he speaks of lightness, but as soon as he begins to argue in favor of lightness, he realizes that there are also excellent novels based on the idea of weight, of that which is heavy. Then, despite stating his preferences, he doesn't stop recognizing the value and place of the opposite preference. He does this to such a point that, in one of the final essays, he begins to contradict his preferences from the beginning. For example, he speaks in defense of multiplicity, and then arrives in an almost unforeseen way at the idea of heaviness, the heaviness of filling everything with meaning. He then sets out some novels that would be severely challenged by the reflections he had made when he started. This is a clear dialectic development, wherein one finds oneself reencountering the opposites that one wanted to put aside. This made me think [about something] I was also able to put down in a chapter of one of my novels entitled *I Also Had a Bisexual Girlfriend*, in which I conceived of a kind of critical theory, also based on the way

[Calvino] discusses Todorov in this book, where one can capture dichotomous pairs in literary criticism. Pairs of opposites that, by the way, can also be seen in architecture; such as weight and lightness.

An Ascetic Exercise: Oppositions, Dichotomies, and the Evolution of Criticism

MS: In your novel *I Also Had a Bisexual Girlfriend*, there is a passage where the main character, the Argentine professor teaching in the United States, very eloquently articulates the problem of dichotomies by stating something along the lines of "dichotomies do not dissolve or merge, but instead, they increase to more complex degrees of dualism." I find this declaration incredibly compelling. Could you elaborate on it?

GM: That was my proposal for how criticism should be. Nowadays, criticism, as it is generally professed in reviews and scholarly works, develops somewhat like this: from the possible set of dichotomous pairs, a predetermined choice or preference is set, let's say randomness over determinism, or the fragmentary over the complex, an ideological preference a priori, from which one plunges into the work to see to what extent it responds to the expectations of the critic. That is how I see criticism now: a critic who approaches the work with his repertoire of elements from the pair already chosen.

What is interesting to me is just to realize that there is no a priori preference that one can establish between those pairs. Each of these elements are equally good or equally bad for elevating a work or throwing it out the window; that is to say that, in and of themselves, these elements do not have an assigned value. Therefore, I think that the critic naturally cannot start from tabula rasa or from scratch. He or she begins with certain preferences, but in my opinion you have to put your pairs to the test, just being careful not to use those elements that you already know don't have a pre-assigned value. A more advanced version of criticism should entail challenging preconceptions so as to try to find particular justifications rather than a priori and general ones.

MS: How do you see this kind of exercise?

GM: I see it as a sort of ascetic exercise, an exercise of the critic with him or herself.

Reading Under Aspects of Suspicion: Crime Novel, Essay, and Crossing Genres

MS: Beyond being a critical exercise, what I find most intriguing in your work is that this idea becomes a creative practice as well, and that it manifests in the capacity of the work to exist across genres, attracting different degrees of close reading. Walter Benjamin wrote in *The Work of Art in the Age of Mechanical Reproduction* that the experience of architecture takes place in a state of distraction. One normally does not stop to "read" a work of architecture with the same degree of attention with which one listens to music or reads a work of literature. Your novels, however, combine a level of distraction associated with entertainment with the notion of attention closely connected to the genre of the essay. At first glance, your work could be confused with an airport novel,[1] but very quickly it becomes clear that there is something much denser and deeper at work. The genre of the novel and that of the essay are carefully intertwined — and I am not sure you would agree with this — but in my opinion, it makes for a much more speculative, subversive, and impactful form of narrative. The enunciation of the genre itself is already constructively vague, "an abstract crime novel," as you called it...

GM: Not only do I agree with what you are saying, but I also find the genre appealing. I like it as a reader, and I have tried to give it new levels of nuance. To the degree that what you are saying seems to me correct, that this type of novel can be confused with an airport novel, the fact is that many actually do read it that way. I have conceptualized a novel that deals with a writer's small drama, wherein this exact thing happens to him: the critics do not take him seriously because they read his books so quickly that they overlook them. I even have an image of it in my head: of skating on ice; they glide so fast over the sheet of ice that they never get to see what's under the ice, the figures below. So, in the crime novels, I work on those two levels, the philosophical level that a crime novel has or could have, and the level of clever entertainment, which also interests me as a writer. There is a feature about the crime novel that is usually overlooked — that it is the only genre that requires a close and sophisticated reading from the beginning. In other words, the reader of a crime novel

1 From Wikipedia: The use of the term "airport novel" is mildly pejorative; it implies that the book has little lasting value, and is useful chiefly as an inexpensive form of entertainment during travel. Airport novels are sometimes contrasted with literary fiction, such that a novel with literary aspirations would be disparaged by the label.

knows from the beginning that he has to read between the lines; he can't abandon himself completely to reading. Put in a better way, it is reading, but with a kind of suspicion. So, I find this essential about this genre, that it challenges the very concordance of reading.

MS: I was thinking about ideas of 'close reading' in architecture... When I first encountered *The Oxford Murders*,[2] and I can't remember what a priori expectation I had about what I was about to read, I became immediately fascinated by the ambiguity of the genre itself. The fact that it was full of ideas, and that the entertainment of the novel was less about what was happening but about what wasn't happening.

GM: I'm writing another novel now, and the same idea comes up...

MS: I was thinking about the difference between dichotomy and ambivalence, which are both, to me, forms of dialectic thinking. But ambivalence suggests the state of having mixed feelings or even contradictory ideas about something or someone. I am not sure if this differentiation makes sense to you...

GM: Absolutely. I would like to touch on two more issues associated with the notion of dialectics that I have been thinking about, and are connected to what you are saying. When I left the university about ten years ago, I began to ask myself a series of questions related to the philosophy of mathematics, Wittgenstein, and other topics. Wittgenstein examines the foundations of mathematics and finds things that seem certain but are then revealed as shaky. It is the same idea. As soon as one goes to interrogate the fundamentals, a number of issues appear not as certain as one would think. In that search I reencountered Hegel's dialectic logic, which led me to think about these issues in a more systematic way. At some point, Hegel deduces a formal logic of the basic principles of dialectics. What begins as a reflection on general concepts of being and nothingness then starts getting into the idea of becoming. He goes further, finding justice, quantity, and quality, and arrives at very different concepts for a basic philosophy — to the point where, by studying "Universals," he deduces (or there's the suggestion one could deduce) the formal logic of dialectic thought. That led me to think about the possibility of trying a procedure of clarification of those steps. For me, Hegel's operations are not convincing enough. There are a number of

2 *Crímenes imperceptibles* is the original Spanish title.

passages that are, in my opinion, arbitrary. However, the question should be: Is it possible to articulate the steps embedded in Hegel's reasoning, so as to derive a formal logic from it? That is a first general question.

The other related question is: If it is not possible, what kind of protocols, what kind of laws should govern this reasoning? That is to say, a reasoning that begins with these principles and advances by way of contradictions to the extent to which Hegel does. How should one try to correct Hegel so as to validate his thinking? That is something that remains an idea. I have seen some attempts to formalize principles of dialectical logic but found nothing of interest. An American mathematician was doing something, but it was far from being in the spirit of what Hegel tried to do. That is the problem with trying to formalize something — the feeling is that one ends up with very little.

And I'll end with this final question, which interests me currently and also relates to the fierce political dichotomies that exist nowadays in Argentina:[3] What is it that makes a difference transform into a dichotomy? And furthermore, why, in discussing this tendency, do human beings tend to polarize their opinions? What makes a difference scale up so that it becomes an absolute and irreconcilable opposition? Finally, how can we describe the passage from an ordinary difference to a dichotomy, or to a mere contradiction? With all of this, I believe I have come up with a mathematical model, a way to theorize how we handle judgments, concepts, etc., which can be formalized mathematically as a reticulate structure, with its conjunction and its logical disjunction. That mathematical structure has a close association with Boolean algebra, where these opposite elements exist. So, I believe one can explain, at least linguistically, how you get from differences to opposites.

Mathematics as a Narrative Intuition: Discipline, Seriality, and the Ambiguity of Randomness

MS: This made me think of one of your articles in *La Nación*[4] about "Death and the Compass" by Jorge Luis Borges. The criticism is incredibly rigorous, and I mean geometrically rigorous. When you describe points in space and time, it was impossible for me not to think of visual examples. In fact, I found it fascinating that you referred to a small sketch that Borges did associated with that story. The criticism is one

3 "La Grieta," or "The Crack," has come to symbolize the larger ideological opposition currently dividing public opinion within Argentinean politics and society at large. To a lesser extent, this is probably true in Latin America generally, but is more pronounced in the context of the United States.
4 *La Nación* is one of the oldest and most important newspapers in Argentina.

of a mathematician, and if one didn't know your work, one could have overlooked this line of inquiry as a purely analytical one. On the contrary, that criticism contains, as you said before, a very complex and creative form of speculation about other modes of evolution of Borges' original idea. In your work, mathematical features as well as riddles appear a lot, but there is something far more tenuous, fragile even…

GM: softer …

MS: Exactly. I was thinking about a specific passage of *The Book of Murder*,[5] where, in order to substantiate what appears to be a disconnected but incredibly suspicious set of natural deaths taking place around the main character of the story, you use the actual example of flipping a coin. Thought of as one of the ultimate acts of randomness, the narrator describes how within an extended series of 'coin flips,' one could often find, and this is mathematically proven, a sequence of up to seven repeats. It is an interesting case of calculated vagueness, wherein you use mathematics as a source of both precision and instability by introducing further psychological ambiguity about the supposedly accidental nature of the events. How do you think of mathematics within literature?

GM: Well, you read that essay, but I have another one called "A Return to Aleph," which is a purely literary essay on the Aleph. By taking on "Death and the Compass," I was interested in considering a very specific element of the story rather than doing a literary analysis of it. What I tried to illustrate is what happens when one brings up the idea of serial crimes. It's commonly understood; which is to say, when establishing a series of crimes associated with a series of symbols, there is a sort of riddle with a unique solution that only a sufficiently intelligent detective will be able to figure out. That's the whole point.

MS: Following your mention of Borges' sketch, I was wondering about the role of mathematics in your writing. As an architect, it's impossible for me not to think visually, in diagrams, drawings… so I'm wondering if you ever have a parallel, abstract formalization of your narrative, one that is closer to mathematics or even to geometry than to literature?

5 *La muerte lenta de Luciana B.* is the original title in Spanish.

GM: No. I deal with mathematics in my work in a very gentle way, more like the intuition that a reader might have about it. I know the reader hardly ever has the tools to understand exactly what I am talking about. I want to convey a sensation that leads the reader on the right path, and which won't be totally confusing. Somehow, a watermark is also established there: readers with a mathematical knowledge can access that meaning more clearly, but those without it can still have a sense of it. When introducing mathematical elements in his fictions, Borges operates that way too. In "The Aleph," when Borges writes [that the application of] "the name [of The Aleph] to the record of my story is not an accident," it has a precise meaning.[6] Aleph is the name with which we define the infinite. He makes the connection because within the infinite, the part can be equivalent to the whole. That has to do with the Aleph, that is to say, the sphere is equivalent to the universe. Therefore, he establishes a plausible analogy.

A Kind of Concentration: Dimensions of the Real and the Strange

MS: Before, when talking about Gombrowicz, you said, "When he stops to look at something or when he concentrates on something," something happens... To me, that something, be it an object or a subject, appears as a latent possibility for instability. I thought about a parallel with Viktor Shklovsky's notion of estrangement — the idea that through the automation of our day-to-day experience, we create such familiarity with the objects that surround us that we stop seeing them for what they are and instead, only begin to recognize them. A certain concentration of perception, as you describe it, creates the possibility of that 'other' to appear, for the strange to appear within the real, or the uncanny from that which is...

GM: That which is expected ...

MS: Exactly. But the results suggest more than they reveal. It is fiction, but it is not science fiction. There is also fantasy...

GM: Yes, fantasy literature is based on that kind of mechanism. I tried that in my last book of short stories, *A Repulsive Happiness*. In one of the stories entitled "A Dead Cat," an old lady stares at another woman

6 "El Aleph" is the title of Borges' story as well as the record of his narrator's encounter with an Aleph in his rival's basement.

through a window. The kind of concentration in the old lady's eyes begins to turn the other woman crazy. She starts to believe that a curse is being transmitted, that her son is going to be born with — and this ends up becoming reality — a kind of self-prophecy.

MS: You touch on reality, which is also different from the notion of the real. To me, reality has an almost oppressive immediacy, but it can also be manipulated; it's possible to subvert its conventions, to construct something different, something strange. What is your take on the real?

GM: Today I wrote a sentence in the novel that I am working on that says: "The real is always a projection, the crushed footprint of something that walked in other dimensions..." One sees the real, but in the background the real has vestiges incorporated within it of its own construction. There's a history that remains imprinted, and not all of it can be read in the mark, though sometimes it can be salvaged in a story; the real is what remains fixed, but in less dimensions. This is the same in physics, where in order to study the electron, you have to observe it in one place. The electron lives in a kind of limbo of possibilities. When you make it real, that is, by studying it, you have to choose one of those possibilities.

MS: Going back to the idea of estrangement, Viktor Shklovsky suggested that the function of art is to defamiliarize us from our immediate surroundings. In discussing this notion, he talks about "de-automating" and goes on to famously say: "To make the stone stony again, man has been given the power of art."

GM: Exactly. Kundera has a very interesting essay that speaks about prophetic novels, arguing that what they do is to take a phenomenon at the moment of its germination and manage to project it into the future. Once the phenomenon is settled and normalized, nobody sees it anymore. He explains this using Kafka's novels. We are now living in a Kafkaesque world; nobody would be surprised to have to waste an entire day on bureaucratic procedures. The role of the novelist is to take the phenomenon when it is beginning to appear, when it is a seed. Once it settles, the phenomenon disappears — it becomes invisible, which is a bit like what you say.

The Delicate Infraction of Laws:
The Weight of Cliché, Novelty, and True Originality

MS: Reading an interview of yours, I was struck by a quote that I believe deals with the idea of novelty and originality in literature but also in the arts in general: "… of course, there are also writers who continue to believe in the imagination, in the possibility of going beyond the 'already said,' and who still propose the challenge of originality and the writing of a literature that can be measured in subtlety, in complexity, in ambition, alongside the great works of any literary tradition." What role does the new or the original play in your work?

GM: Well, I wish one could do something like that. When writing a crime novel, you have the weight of what is considered cliché. Then somehow, you try to shake something out of it. Borges had a very nice idea. He said, "The crime novel lives on the delicate infraction of its laws." That is, you can't blow up all the laws at once because you end up with a kind of joke. But, it seems to me that by way of "the delicate infraction of the laws," as he puts it, the genre actually lives and survives.

MS: In your *Decalogue*, which I always found a very provocative declaration of principles, almost a manifesto, you refer to the "avant-garde tradition" as an idea in and of itself. You write, "Before you proclaim yourself avant-garde, you must remember that the avant-garde is also a tradition, one that just turned one hundred years old."

GM: I criticize the idea of wanting to present as vanguard those ideas which have been not only already theoretically delineated, but have been exhausted as of a hundred years ago. Duchamp's urinal [*Fountain*, 1917] has already been made, what is one to do? A bathroom? A shower? That's it, period. *Black Square* has been done already; you can't just do the *Café-au-lait Square*. [laughs] There is something that is exhausted in those proposals. I always found the idea of the new very appealing, especially the notion of the original, which I distinguish from the new. To me, what's original is almost the demarcation line for my appreciation of literature. But that which is truly original, and doesn't sound like a rehash of things we've all seen before, is only original in the sense that it leaves a mark and has a point of contact with a new sensibility. In that sense, Gombrowicz is an original writer. He positions a distinctive sensibility, paying attention to certain issues, with a kind of humor and a type of criticism which until then I had not found in any other author. Sometimes the original is a voice and not necessarily a form. Sometimes it is a way to illuminate problems or issues in a society. For example, Michel Houellebecq is a writer who does not interest me, but in his work, I recognize a distinctive gaze through the kind of problems he detects. I have the same opinion of Herman Koch's work. In his two novels, *Summer House with a Pool* and *Dinner*, he incorporates contemporary themes in an authentic manner. The original exists in different ways. Sometimes it can be in the form, but everything is not necessarily played out in form, as the vanguard generally believes. I believe the original thrives on a new sensibility, on the kind of human experience it elicits, on a particular point of view, and on new ideas…

The Limits of Abstraction: Art, Science, and the Cunning of the Original

MS: You just mentioned *Black Square* by Kazimir Malevich. Does art interest you? If so, is there any relationship between art and your literary work?

GM: Some things interest me, but I confess that what I am interested in, beyond the medium, are works that have some kind of atmosphere. For example, there is Malevich's *Black Square*. Reading a book called *A Musical Offering* by Luis Agasti, I found out about a precursor to Malevich, the satirical writer Alphonse Allais, who exhibited a [plain white paper] he called *First Communion of Anemic Young Girls in the Snow* [*Première communion de jeunes filles chlorotiques par un temps de neige*, 1881]. The title is everything. In Agasti's book, he talks about the avant-garde, dialectics, John Cage, etc. This is related to what we were just discussing. What is reality? It is what one projects. Notice how the title is the operative, which brings the anemic girls into being.

Kazimir Malevich,
Black Square, 1915

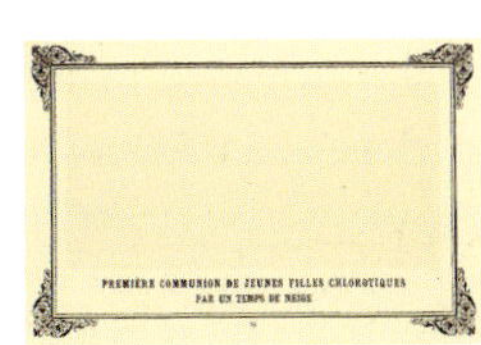

Alphonse Allais,
First Communion of Anemic Young Girls in the Snow [Première communion de jeunes filles chlorotiques par un temps de neige], 1881

MS: What's essential here is the relationship between the extreme visual abstraction of this work and the narrative title. As an avant-garde development in painting, I think today, extreme abstraction represents a form of production that is nearly exhausted, although there are exceptions. But photography is a medium that brings a form of abstraction to the real. Photographers such as Gregory Crewdson, Todd

Hido, or Thomas Ruff interest me greatly in that regard, since they aim to sublimate the real, making photographs both atmospherically beautiful as well as unusually strange. Crewdson, for instance, uses artistic sets more akin to filmmaking productions, including lighting, actors, and carefully choreographed locations. His pictures take the idyllic suburbs of New England and make them first feel familiar and then strange, even sinister. The interesting aspect about these photographs is that they are the opposite of abstraction. Moreover, one could say these are intensifications of a certain real, which make scenes of everyday life both mysterious and weird. What do you think is the role of abstraction in the arts?

GM: On the subject of abstraction, there is an interesting analogy with science. That's what I try to say in my article, "An Exercise in Swordsmanship." Abstraction is an operation widely used in science. When you have a certain problem in mathematics, you also have the tools to solve it within a given context. Suddenly you find another context, which may be completely different, but wherein the same tools not only reappear, but with them, the minimum elements that made you solve the first problem. One tries to "abstract" the procedure used before, to see if the same game can be played, along with any necessary variations, so that what was articulated in a certain way here can also be articulated, generally in a more astute way, over there. One seeks what's essential, what made the game work, and tries to bring it to new terrain. However, the translation of this game in science has a very precise limit, which is that sometimes, when the new situation is too simple, the craftiness of the reasoning does not translate well enough. For me, that is the limit of abstraction. Abstraction is interesting, but only if it manages to keep the sharpness of the original. This is an idea that is very clear in mathematics, and that in my opinion, is not that clear in art. Often times in art, abstraction amounts to nothing. I use the example of a spider whose legs you take off one by one to see when it stops crawling...

MS: Right, or, when it is no longer a spider.

Buenos Aires, August, 2017

POSTSCRIPT: A Few Secrets of the Mute Icon—

Restraint, Doubt, and Darkness in the Architecture of Marcelo Spina & Georgina Huljich

Ciro Najle

00_Genealogy

The Mute Icon opens up a new lineage in the genealogy of iconic architecture, reframing its tradition along a complexity-driven, materialistic ethics reloaded with phenomenological effects, internal friction, and a loose-fit approach. These ethics offer a radical alternative to the effect-driven visual tradition of the iconic, commonly articulated by figurative manifestations.

01_Analogy

The Mute Icon genealogy operates analogously to the materially-rooted notion of architectural style, as opposed to the idea of style that is built upon autonomous formal resources and ready-made cultural figures. This notion does not classify, appropriate, restate, or combine figures but constructs the representational-material continuum for the expression of moods and character.

02_Representation

The Mute Icon is a piece of architecture operating as a materiality-based block of representation rather than as a representational means, a spongy medium of absorption that paradoxically appears as a mass and redefines architectural representation as a virtual material problem, autonomous of a priori contents and free to inspire open-ended appropriations.

03_Concept

The Mute Icon does not illustrate a branding concept operating from above and governing its construct from outside of its material reality, but rather manifests itself as a rarefied material concept: a concept-thing that functions as an enigma. Its tectonics are driven toward the appearance of a slippery effect and therefore rendered inherently inapprehensible.

04_Communication

The Mute Icon is not steered to effectively communicate a single message, but rather to make it abstruse in the very act of facilitating it, eroding content through contradictions of terms. Its iconicity often appears extravagant, remote, and inaccessible, spoiling any didactic form of knowledge transmission and paradoxically claiming communication by being noisy.

05_Expression

The Mute Icon is drawn with apparently primitive digital resources, simulating at once the rough texture of charcoal, the granulated abstraction of pixels, the juxtaposed heterogeneous planes of a bricolage, or the collage of minute fragments, in order to generate a precise formal lack of definition, loaded with rarefied effects, impenetrable properties, misleading contrasts, and blurry figures.

06_Mass

The Mute Icon is made of variably rough surfaces with multiple abstract encounters and instants of friction coalesced without conflict. These are unevenly distributed across a mass that operates as a pluri-dimensional material continuum of formal relationships and produces a general effect of harmless rarefaction and a manifold of devious, slippery concepts.

07_Consistency

The Mute Icon is a consistent, self-standing object that degrades form through the intensification of difference in a consistent field to the point of engendering internal contradictions and uncanny inconsistencies. The poignancy of its evasive and irreducible unity is grounded on the multiplication of these inconsistencies and on the enigma of their presence and origin.

08_Composition

The Mute Icon has relatively differentiated regions, indiscernible as objects, which work rather as peculiar localities, offbeat traits, chance meetings, and weird motifs. It lacks intermediary pieces between them: third parties, articulations, and construction details vanish in the mass, get confused in its coarseness, and are devoured within the continuum of its character.

09_Experience

The Mute Icon erodes the architectural elements and neglects the configuration of stratified relations. It is made of violent clashes within a continuum that fold into one another, preserving the internal heterogeneity of its constituency without discrediting the unity of the whole. Instead of an effective image, this retrained breakdown produces a memorable experience.

10_Mood

The Mute Icon configures an atmosphere closer to a loose way of being, or mood, rather than to an obsessive, performative manifold, articulated through modes. It joins implicit systematicity and explicit intuition in the work of form without relying on figurative signs, which it draws and undraws, or on relational laws between parts, which it emphasizes through their corrosion.

11_Non-straightforwardness

The Mute Icon configures flat and unemotional haptic experiences, both precise and deceitful, whose resources disappear as soon as they become manifest. Its technology of representation operates as a material medium for experience and as a geometric vehicle for formal fuzziness. This involves a radically non-straightforward, anti-literal approach to the thinking of architecture.

12_Continuum

The Mute Icon is apathetically imbued with exterior and absorbs particularities within its difficult formal-material continuum. This apathy supposes the inversion of the relationship between object and context according to an inward, selfish direction, in which context is manifest by omission, or inclusion, through the granular play of the mass, which is both monumental and fragile.

13_Fog

The Mute Icon involves an architecture of the rough surface, the blurry border, the difficult relationship, the complicated dichotomic materiality, and the consciously slippery meaning. Its estrangement works as a crystalized fog, a vaporous environment, concrete and yet elusive, that diffuses form, obscures structure, abstracts matter, and liquefies communicational clarity.

14_Black on Black

The Mute Icon is the architecture of the black on black (on black on black, to the nth power), recursive, intertwined, redundant; architecture that hides itself iteratively, until it hides the very mechanisms themselves. Contrast and nuance merge and get confused in a continuum of internal friction, whose signification, by definition, lacks any logical soundness.

15_Celebrity

The Mute Icon is the ultimate anti-commodity. Its distinguishability lies paradoxically in its lack of definition. It is the architecture of dark light, filtered by sunglasses that, instead of heroically celebrating the healthy, plastic effects of light-over-form, hide any evidence of its presence in favor of the amoral way in which a celebrity relates to the world after a wild celebration.

16_Decadence

The Mute Icon exhibits itself while it veils itself, refusing to be recognized as a discrete identity. It awakens a new form of star architecture, a decadent form with hangover and bags under the eyes, headache and susceptibility, a mellow, pathetic form between paparazziphobia, tourismphobia, and fanphobia. This is not to be confused with austerity, soberness, or prudence.

17_Amorality

The Mute Icon maintains a consistent degree of basic darkness, an opaque shine, a kind of amoral non-religious sanctity, rough, somehow rotten, retreated, primitive, rich and variegated, folded onto itself and turned into itself, just safe enough and therefore somewhat suspicious. Its excessive, yet introverted charisma is sustained by formal fatigue and decline, which are turned into forces.

18_Animism

The Mute Icon embodies an animism of stillborn beings, introducing a new, skeptical form of vitalism in complexity culture in architecture, that is both a ludic form, and yet somber and threatening. Its objects appear as dead stars, arrested dynamics, still life naturalisms, barely activated zombies, fossils of unknown species, and overwhelming harmless monsters.

19_Theory

The Mute Icon can barely be theorized with approximate precision. Its dark form does not admit the illumination of theories that can fully explain its fundamentally devious meaning. In turn, it insinuates wild theories by means of its indistinctness, bounces stable categorizations between its folds indefinitely, absorbs them within its enigma, and holds them in its coarseness.

20_Culture

The Mute Icon breaks down all cultural references across its multi-dimensional materialist plane of consistency into a manifold of rarefied expression and darkened communication. The texture of its deep surface operates as a difficult technology where all external references, operative rigor, and coherent techniques melt down to become a mystery driven to produce perplexity.

21_Poetry

The Mute Icon blurs the mass, folds the envelope, unbalances the object, breaks down any kind of formal detail, and dismantles the figure in an abstract material poetry of vague substance and glassy edges, with no clear meaning, uncertain narratives, and a rich, overburdened expression of indifference to anything that has not been adequately swallowed and formally digested.

22_Scale

The Mute Icon dismantles any reference to recognizable scales by means of non-figurative resources. Commonly huge things are minute, and vice versa. Size is turned into a game that finds perpetual relish in the out-of-scale or non-scalar limbo created, generating abstract tensions between proportions and values, the sheer uncertainty of which becomes disturbing.

23_Monstruosity

The Mute Icon is a hard to define monster due to its formal and scalar undefinition, a minor Godzilla, paradoxically incommensurable because of the ungraspable scalar references of its formal features and traits, because of which it is impossible to say if the whole is far too large or just too small. Its terror, a light form of terror, lies in the haziness of this scalar obscurity.

24_Infrastructure

The Mute Icon appears as a piece of infrastructure or as an element of urban equipment, like a traffic light, a railroad barrier, or a streetlamp, without any hint as to its possible use. Between perverse and childish, both sympathetic and terrifying, and even terrifying as a result of being sympathetic, its abstract bewilderment consists in not knowing what it is really all about.

25_Legibility

The Mute Icon muddies the waters, pollutes the fields, corrupts the grid, and dissolves the object. It does not do so at an organizational level as much as through the darkening of its legibility. The monumentality resultant dissipates as the edges blur. The low-res generates vagueness and projects a temporary dark light over the world, similar to the one cast by a total eclipse.

26_Mundanity

The Mute Icon acquires a quasi-autonomous self-standing status through the apparent ambiguity and ambivalence of its expression. This ambiguity, resulting from the multiplicity of contained internal contradictions, is neither erudite nor ironic, and has no message as such, but is rather unemotional and mundane noise. Its message is its meticulously crafted lack of one.

27_Abstinence

The Mute Icon is simplistic, abstinent, and plain; it limits all expressive stridence, conceptual sharpness, or technical virtuosity in favor of a ruthless, indifferent status loaded with numerous, internal, mutually neutralizing differences. This global indifference operates as a mantle that buffers and veils rapid and direct readings, which remain explicitly ignored or postponed.

28_Endurance

The Mute Icon generates a light, arrested, dazzling weightlessness that produces perplexity and a humble attention, overwhelming and by far transcending any specific didactic role, and acquiring a type of endurance far more robust than that of a concept or a clear message. The irresoluble condition of its form maintains a melancholic feeling, mostly based on a state of discomfort.

29_Skill

The Mute Icon reverses the idea of skill by deliberately disregarding the value of technique for the sake of it, and by projecting it against itself in a clash that engenders new kinds and forms of experience. This clash irradiates a peculiar, inherently inharmonious form of virtue, more powerful than effective communication and more enduring than formal harmony.

30_Problem

The Mute Icon involves the construction of a problem whose attractiveness lies in the instability of its terms. This unintelligible problem manifests itself as a material experience, rather than as a logical theorem to be understood or a critical construct to be intellectually mediated. This problem is, by definition, both direct (empirically sensed) and indirect (tangentially posed).

31_In-between

The Mute Icon appeals to known architectural elements, obvious figures, common techniques, established stereotypes, and consolidated norms, but abstracts them out of their functional and communicational capabilities, which it mutes in order not simply to alienate them, but to suspend their presence in the limbo that lies in between architecture and its experience.

32_Materials

The Mute Icon frees traditional materials from their given frame of reference, not simply to generate novelty per se, as much as to constitute a form of architectural totality with more authority than the elements themselves, capable of exasperating experience to the point of becoming a mirage. Its ethics goes through convention and stops just before the threshold of innovation.

33_Negativity

The Mute Icon suggests a profound denial of the explicit iconic form, an active refusal of its functional ends, a dichotomization of their categorical basis, and an operative negation of its formal definitiveness. This involves an anti-axiomatic stance, a constantly inconclusive positioning that operates as a mechanism of retention and estrangement; that is, as a medium of suspense.

34_Principles

The Mute Icon stipulates principles driven by experience, rather than by categorical definitions. Carefully constructed to engender feeling, its concepts are transposed to the physicality of buildings and directed to a wide imaginary audience, assumed to approach the work of architecture in a low-brow state of distraction, rather than to a cultivated disciplinary public.

35_Audience

The Mute Icon does not presuppose, and actually avoids, save as an accidental consequence, any didactics in the reading. On the contrary, it dilates and problematizes communication, multiplying and contradicting the manifold forms of understanding a physical artifact to make them coexist in its radically impersonal and acritical medium without canceling each other.

36_Hermetics

The Mute Icon deliberately multiplies the understanding of form. It involves a conscientious hermetism. It does not pursue beauty or clarity but charm and darkness, engendering a particular form of respect, grounded on the threat and fear of silence. This respect provokes, generates anxiety, and incites the fury of having lost any trace of origin. It intimidates.

37_Threat

The Mute Icon imposes itself tangentially, never frontally. Its threat lies in its complicated earnestness and is threatening exactly as a result of not being so. Its threat is grounded on the uncertainty of its presence, which situates itself close enough to be felt and far enough to not be graspable, at a precise, suspicious, medium distance that takes the form of the loss of scale.

38_Visceral

The Mute Icon avoids facilitating and despises agreeing. Its politics is that of incorrection, its economy is that of difficulty. Its sociology is that of friction, without succumbing to rebel, bizarre, or reactionary forms. It assumes the duty of knowing how far to push form without falling into criticality and/or concept, just up to the point in which its mental construct remains visceral.

39_Physics

The Mute Icon tensely preserves the power of architecture as a primitive physical fact, nurturing it with multiplied resources and ineffable effects, perpetually proliferating differences and diluting expression. Its physics of dilution bypasses the dichotomy between tectonics and stereotomy, turning the first into a hollow mass and the second into an aggregation of tiny fragments.

40_Effects

The Mute Icon weighs effects and distributes them across the whole, involving them directly in the overall experience they create. It tensions diverse affirmations without privileging one over the other and confounds them in a heterogeneous, magmatic conglomerate, where they reverberate and give away their will to truth in favor of increasing their reach and capabilities.

41_Reciprocity

The Mute Icon bestows experience but does not provide knowledge. It rarely gives more than what is strictly necessary for a dark event to take place, and always expects astonishment in return, no more and no less. Demanding by definition, it does not evangelize through dogmas or teach through principles, but quasi-innocently persuades and induces through evasiveness.

42_Market

The Mute Icon models the insertion of architectural thought into the market and introduces the logics of practice into the world of academia. Through a gradient of intensities that joins the mental with the visceral, the ideological with the pragmatic, the general with the particular, and the organizational with the phenomenological, it joins high-brow form with low-brow experience.

43_Expertise

The Mute Icon sophisticates the forms of expertise in architecture in the third digital age without developing autonomously from practice. It engages new typologies and gives impulse to new procedures. Its aesthetics transcend theoretical camps, flirt with technical sources, navigate fluidly formal backgrounds, and learn promiscuously from philosophical frameworks.

44_Indifference

The Mute Icon neither constructs an image nor is the result of any specific ideology. It engenders an intangible effect by hiding its causes. It is as effective as it is damaging and destructive. It takes the materials beyond their traditional ethos, turns them insubstantial, problematizes their qualities, and diffuses their specificity. It satisfies by breeding dissatisfaction.

45_Technology

The Mute Icon assumes recent developments in the productive apparatus of architecture and guides their potentials by turning them into a technology of miscommunication, both resisting the mystification of them through the creation an autonomous realm and escaping from using them simply according to the demands, ethics, and mechanisms of traditional architectural representation.

46_Technique

The Mute Icon treats technique as second to the capability of generating a new form of iconicity, able to transform the sense of complex architecture in the globalized world. The relationship with advanced technology is therefore not fetishistic and is constantly evaluated in terms of impact, cultivating a raw relationship to technique and projecting architecture beyond its epoque.

47_Control

The Mute Icon takes the lack of measure of control techniques in contemporary architecture to a state of deliberate indefinition that diffuses (both distributes and maximizes) its power. It does not degrade techniques to the role of aiding sheer improvisation but rather potentiates them into a tight state of ductility, intense, sharp, and penetrating, and yet soft, flexible, and graceful.

48_Content

The Mute Icon is filled with stuff, not with content. Stuffing is generic, effective, pragmatic, and mutes the mass by means of nurturing it in content without quality. Stuffing is the ultimate anti-compositional, anti-organic condition: zero process, intangible meaning, indistinct parts, abstract materiality, slippery object, generic organization, void interiority, lack of function.

49_3d Billboard

The Mute Icon is an empty symbol, a 3d billboard with no message, loaded with noise and transmitting the paradoxically transcending power of tight nonsensicality. Any index and traces of meaning lying in its parts are dismantled by meticulously blurring their constituency and by carefully neglecting their recognizability in the continuum of abstract materiality.

50_Nonsense

The Mute Icon makes of materiality its medium, not one that reveals an authentic essence but one that expresses the nonsensicality of message, the substrate for a well-calculated, finely calibrated construction of nonsense. Opaque, latently aggressive, mottled materiality, unbound from the idea of agreeability and delight, placed between the banal and the sublime.

51_Character

The Mute Icon approaches character antithetically to the traditional ethics of the narrative of materials, here replaced by an abstract materiality: nonrepresentational representation, radically inessential, intensely flavorless, inconsequential, amoral, distasteful, veiled and yet naked, apparently immediate as a consequence of being graciously mediated.

52_Grain

The Mute Icon involves the low-res treatment of the fine grain, sharply imprecise, slickly rough, carefully careless, precisely sloppy. The medium grain corresponds to the medium scale and the median precision, under an overall ethics of the more-or-less. Chunks, not pieces; leftovers, not fragments; encounters, not details; clumsy intensities, not clear hierarchies.

53_Neutrality

The Mute Icon uses greys, blacks, off-blacks, whites, and off-whites to homogenize differences. Color unifies differences without producing fusion and flattens materiality into the domain of plasticity. The non-color is the superseding gloss that further rarefies materiality to lose any relationship to its material origin and make it acquire an artificial status of naturalness. Everything is imbued.

54_Same

The Mute Icon produces an overall effect of sameness. All becomes the same and loses discreteness in favor of contributing to the tightening of the continuum. The material becomes the substance of the natural condition of the building: free from the self-consciousness derived from the anxiety of understanding, it becomes intrinsic to the value of the whole.

55_Equalize

The Mute Icon proliferates differences to the point of neutralizing their value and equalizing their effect in the whole, intensifying continuity and rendering it singular in that context. Against the classical approach to coordination of parts and wholes, abrupt contrasts between zones and regions operate as shifts and interruptions in the overall game of change without change.

56_Plane

The Mute Icon levels up and down materials to inscribe them in the same plane of consistency that switches relevance away from the part and toward the leap in the spatial-material continuum. This leap is displaced from any didactic position and introduces counter-intuitive rhythms, syncopations, and unexpected counterpoints, corrupting the formal logic of the whole.

57_Embededment

The Mute Icon embeds the part in the whole without simply reducing it, creating a partiality larger than the part, which goes beyond the particularity of the element. The structure of the stuffing of the whole is neither autonomous, nor is it broken down, nor does it disappear. Rather, it gets complexified by being integrated into a three-dimensional camouflage.

58_Pattern

The Mute Icon uses pattern as a vehicle for the management of character rather than as a formally autonomous technique in and of itself. Pattern is a working means, not a formal resource, in the administration of the oblique, counter-intuitive relationship between particularity (not part) and whole. Pattern is the means for the peculiar mood of the abstract materiality.

59_Trends

The Mute Icon takes patterns to the higher level of noise, washing and cleaning up the whole to paradoxically make it dirty. The administration of pattern is quantitative, but its effect is qualitative and not simply organizational. It transcends the efficacy to control formal and geometric problems in favor of the gracious manufacturing of behaviors, habits, customs, and trends.

60_In (New Kinds of) Form We Trust

The Mute Icon nurtures motifs transversally to form, inorganically to its constituency, and filters within it a kind of convention of its own that collectively flips its structure upside down. The lack of exact correspondence between patterns subverts order and renders it problematic and fundamentally dubious, without relying on critique and profoundly trusting in the power of form.

61_Money and Value

The Mute Icon raises the value of architecture to a status where its added value coincides with its difficulty. Its inefficiency in its purpose of communication is thus taken to an affirmative level, where the new, along the lines of its subversive condition, coincides with sheer productivity and becomes paradoxically conservative, fluidly communicated, and, more importantly, everlasting.

62_Restraint Meets Transformation

The Mute Icon involves a formalism that transcends the form of the object and engulfs a whole series of habits within and around it. The difficult continuity between organization, form, pattern, and new form, articulated by partially neutralizing, carefully breeding, and consciously diverging all differences, unfolds deliberately into the realm where restraint meets transformation.

63_The Ethics of Doubt

The Mute Icon engages the mix of conservation and transformation by means of an ethics of doubt, a sustained form of doubt, careful, meticulous, tightly refrained, culturally framed, laterally determined, affirmative in its conscientious ethics. Here the notion of harmony is taken to a level where it contains imbalance, latency, uncertainty, skepticism, and even cynicism.

64_The Aesthetics of Obscurantism

The Mute Icon opens a new form of obscurantist aesthetics via difference, discrepancy, blurring, illegibility, indifference, counter-intuition, displaced pattern, and doubt. This form is relevant today simply because the affirmative idea of complexity must build up a new form of life, a problematic one, overcoming neoliberal illusion without a reactionary stance.

Doubt is its force.

Buenos Aires, November 2019

AUTHORS & CONTRIBUTORS

PATTERNS is a leading architectural practice led by partners Marcelo Spina and Georgina Huljich. The firm brings a critical and progressive approach to projects across scales, agendas, and geographies, insisting on the cultural and social relevance of architectural form, contemporary aesthetics, and emerging technologies. Based in the expansive city of Los Angeles, the firm takes advantage of the city's decidedly global stance and idiosyncratic identity to create equally engaging and speculative architectural content through formats as diverse as master plans, landscapes, buildings, projects, installations, objects, books, and exhibitions. With twenty years of building experience, PATTERNS has completed buildings and ongoing projects in the United States, Europe, South America, and Asia.

PATTERNS' most significant completed projects include Victory Healthcare in North Hollywood, CA; Jujuy Redux Apartment in Rosario, Argentina; Prism Gallery in Los Angeles, CA; Eye of Time Corporate Headquarters in Chengdu, China; FyF Residence in Rosario, Argentina; Jujuy 2056 Apartment in Rosario, Argentina; League of Shadows multipurpose event structure in Los Angeles; and Land.Tiles (temporary installation), among others. Current projects include A4H, an office building in Glendale, California; Olympia Towers, a mixed-use complex in Downtown Los Angeles; Karma Sanctum, a boutique hotel in Bali, Indonesia; and Casa del Sol, a summer residence in Mykonos, Greece.

PATTERNS has gained international recognition as one of the most intriguing and broadminded firms in contemporary architecture with work exhibited worldwide, most notably at the Venice Biennale in Italy, The Chicago Biennial, The Museum of Contemporary Art in Los Angeles, The Art Institute of Chicago, The San Francisco MOMA, The MAK Museum in Vienna, and The FRAC in Orleans, where it is also part of their permanent collections. Their work has been published extensively and has been the subject of numerous essays, books, magazines, newspapers, and exhibition catalogues internationally. The office's first monograph *PATTERNS: Embedded* was published in 2010 by Shanghai-based ACDCU.

PATTERNS has received numerous prizes and awards, including the American Architecture Award, five AIA LA Honor and Merit Awards, an AIA National Design Review Award; first prizes in the competitions for the SCI-Arc Graduation Pavilion, a Temporary Pavilion for MOCA, the Vertical Garden at the Schindler House, the New SCI-Arc Café; and the third prize in the prestigious Young Architect of the Year Award. PATTERNS was part of the Emerging Voices Series of the Architectural League of New York and *Architectural Record*'s Design Vanguard and was the recipient of the "Arch is" Emerging Practice Award by the AIA LA Chapter.

In 2013, Marcelo Spina and Georgina Huljich were the recipients of the prestigious USA Grigor Fellowship, a prominent endowment that recognizes America's most accomplished and innovative artists. In addition to their professional and academic careers, Spina and Huljich were the curators of "Matters of Sensation" at Artists Space in New York in 2008. Considered at that time to be the most important collective exhibition in architecture that Artists Space ever organized, the influential show opened to great acclaim and helped position an emerging generation of now-established architects, designers, theorists, and thinkers in the United States context.

Marcelo Spina (b. Rosario, Argentina, 1970) is an architect (AIA) and educator. He holds a Professional Degree from the National University of Rosario, Argentina and a Master of Architecture from Columbia University in New York. He worked for RUR / Reiser+Umemoto and Keller Easterling in New York and for Gerardo Caballero in Rosario before opening his own office. Spina has been part of the design faculty at SCI-Arc since 2001 and was the coordinator of the Architectural Technologies Program from 2011 to 2019. He has been a visiting professor at the University of Pennsylvania; Yale; Syracuse; Harvard; University of California, Berkeley; Tulane; Washington University, St. Louis; University of Vienna; University of Innsbruck; and Di Tella University, among others. Mr. Spina has been a member of the Board of Trustees at SCI-Arc since 2016 and has served in national juries for the Progressive Architecture Awards (P/A Awards), The Architectural League of New York, and Mies Crown Hall America's Prize, among others.

Marcelo Spina founded PATTERNS in Los Angeles in 2002 as a speculative platform to explore an increasingly global design culture.

Georgina Huljich (b. Rosario, Argentina, 1974) is an architect and educator. She holds a Professional Degree from the National University of Rosario, Argentina and a Master of Architecture from UCLA, where she graduated with Distinction and was the recipient of several design awards. She has previously worked at the Guggenheim Museum and the architectural firm Dean/Wolf Architects in New York, and at Morphosis Architects in Los Angeles. Huljich is an Associate Professor at the Department of Architecture at UCLA, where she has taught since 2006. She has been a visiting professor at Yale; University of Pennsylvania; Syracuse; University of California, Berkeley; University of Southern California; and Tokyo Institute of Technology (TIT). Her current research focuses on strange peripheries in Europe and Asia and the way they affect notions of type, form, and aesthetics. Ms. Huljich has been a member of the Executive Board at CAP UCLA since 2015. She has served in national juries for The American Academy Rome Prize and the AIA Awards.

Georgina Huljich joined PATTERNS as Partner in 2006.

Guillermo Martinez (b. Bahía Blanca, Argentina, 1962) is a novelist and author of short stories. Since 1985 he has lived in Buenos Aires, where he earned a Ph.D. in Mathematical Logic. He also has pursued postdoctoral studies at Oxford University. He is the author of the short story collection *Infierno grande* (*Vast Hell*, 1989), of the novels *Acerca de Roderer* (published as *Regarding Roderer*, 1992), *La mujer del maestro* (*The Master's Wife*, 1998), *Crímenes imperceptibles* (published as *The Oxford Murders*, 2003), *La muerte lenta de Luciana B.* (published as *The Book of Murder*, 2007), *Yo también tuve una novia bisexual* (*I Also Had a Bisexual Girlfriend*) and of the books of essays, *Borges y la matemática* (published as *Borges and Mathematics*, 2003), *La fórmula de la inmortalidad* (*The Immortality Formula*, 2005), *Gödel para todos* (*Gödel for Everyone*, 2009) in collaboration with Gustavo Piñeiro, and *La razón literaria* (*The Literary Reason*, 2016, literary essays).

The Oxford Murders was awarded the Argentinean Planeta Prize and has had international success. It has been translated into 38 languages and made into a film by Spanish director Alex de la Iglesia, starring Elijah Wood and John Hurt. His novel *The Book of Murder* was selected by the Spanish critics as one of the ten books of the year. One of his stories ("Vast Hell") was published in *The New Yorker*. He was awarded the Gabriel García Márquez Hispanoamerican Prize for his book of short stories *Una felicidad repulsiva* (*A Repulsive Happiness*, 2014). His last novel, *Los crímenes de Alicia* (*Alice's Murders*) was awarded the Spanish Nadal Prize (2019). He was visiting professor of Spanish Literature at the University of Virginia (USA) and is currently a part-time professor of Creative Writing at the Universidad de Tres de Febrero (UNTREF) in Buenos Aires.

Ciro Najle (b. Buenos Aires, Argentina, 1966) is an architect who holds a Master of Advanced Architectural Design with honors from Columbia University GSAPP, in addition to a degree with honors from the Universidad de Buenos Aires. He is currently Dean and Professor of the Escuela de Arquitectura y Estudios Urbanos at the Universidad Torcuato Di Tella in Buenos Aires. His theoretical production, academic work, and research practice develop organizational models and design methodologies in architecture under the influence of digital culture and complexity theory in the age of globalization. He has been Diploma Unit Master and Director of the Landscape Urbanism Graduate Program at the Architectural Association in London, and Visiting Professor at Harvard University GSD, Cornell University AAP, Columbia University GSAPP, the Berlage Institute, the Universidad Federico Santa María, and the Universidad de Buenos Aires. Director of General Design Bureau in Buenos Aires, and previously of Mlab and of MID, he was awarded the Young Architect of the Year Second Prize in London, and his work has been widely published by international media. He is the author of several books, including *The Generic Sublime* (Actar / Harvard GSD, 2016), *Suprarural* (Actar, 2017) with Lluís Ortega, and *Landscape Urbanism, A Manual for the Machinic Landscape* (AA, 2002) with Mohsen Mostafavi, as well as editor of *Superdigitalismos* (CPAU, 2019). His additional publications include writings in *Quaderns, Space, Oris, Praxis, Harvard Design Magazine, UR, i+t, Egg, Plot, and Summa+*; the interview series *Out of Time* (Plot, 2012–present); and the introductions to the 2G Monographs on FOA (GG, 2000) and MGM (GG, 2009).

Brett Steele (b. Boise, Idaho, USA, 1962) was appointed Dean of the UCLA School of the Arts and Architecture in August 2017. A teacher, writer, and recognized leader in arts and architecture education—as well as a leading voice on architecture and urbanism—he is a frequent lecturer, presenter, and critic at universities, cultural centers, and offices worldwide. He has served on numerous arts and architecture commissions and juries and has participated in policy planning initiatives worldwide. He holds an Architectural Association diploma, and his academic experience and scholarly interests focus on the modern and contemporary conditions of arts education and culture. He has also written extensively on the expansive circumstances of today's electronic, computational design studios. Prior to this appointment at UCLA, Brett was the director of the Architectural Association School of Architecture (AA) in London, where he led a decade-long transformation and expansion of one of the world's most renowned schools of architecture. His awards include an Honorary Fellowship from the Royal Institute of British Architects (RIBA) and an outstanding achievement award and fellowship from the Royal Society of Arts (FRSA).

Constance Vale (b. Raleigh, North Carolina, USA, 1985) directs the Factory of Smoke and Mirrors, an experimental research practice that undertakes aesthetic and conceptual investigations in the territory between architecture, art, and theatre. She is an assistant professor of architecture at Washington University in St. Louis and has previously taught at SCI-Arc and UCLA AUD. Vale's work has been exhibited at the A+D Museum in Los Angeles and Des Lee Gallery in St. Louis and published in the *Journal of the American Institute of Architects*, the *Los Angeles Times*, *Archinect*, and *CLOG*. In 2019, Vale curated an exhibition and organized a corresponding symposium entitled *Decoys & Depictions: Images of the Digital*, an event exploring how architects and artists construct images today and the social and political effects of images in the contemporary world. Vale earned a Master of Architecture from Yale School of Architecture, where she received the Moulton Andrus Award for Excellence in Art and Architecture and two Feldman Nominations; her Bachelor of Fine Arts is from Parsons School of Design. She has practiced at nationally and internationally recognized offices in Los Angeles, New York, and Pittsburgh.

BIBLIOGRAPHY

BOOKS

Alberti, Leon Battista. *De Re Aedificatoria*. Munich: Prestel, 1975 [o.p. 1452].

Alberti, Leon Battista, Joseph Rykwert, Neil Leach, and Robert Tavernor. *On the Art of Building in Ten Books*. Cambridge, MA: MIT Press, 1997.

Aristotle. *Poetics*, trans. Anthony Kenny. Oxford: Oxford University Press, 2013.

Borges, Jorge Luis. *El Aleph*. Barcelona: Lumen, 2019 [o.p. 1949].

Boullée, Etienne Louis. *Architecture, Essay on Art*, ed. Helen Rosenau, trans. Sheila De Vallée. London: Academy Editions, 1976.

Dal Co, Francesco and John Zukowsky, eds. *Mies Reconsidered: His Career, Legacy, and Disciples*. Chicago: Rizzoli and Art Institute of Chicago, 1986.

De Oliveira, Olivia. *Subtle Substances: The Architecture of Lina Bo Bardi*. Barcelona: Editorial Gustavo Gili, 2006.

Deleuze, Gilles and Félix Guattari. *A Thousand Plateaus*. Minneapolis, MN: University of Minnesota Press, 1994.

Ferriss, Hugh. *The Metropolis of Tomorrow*. New York: Ives Washburn, 1929.

Fried, Michael. *Art and Objecthood: Essays and Reviews*. Chicago: University of Chicago Press, 1998.

Gargiani, Roberto. *Rem Koolhaas, OMA: The Construction of Merveilles*. Lausanne: EPFL Press, 2008.

Harman, Graham. *The Quadruple Object*. Winchester, U.K.: Zero Books, 2011.

Kant, Immanuel. *Critique of Judgment*, trans. Werner S. Pluhar. Indianapolis, IN: Hackett, 2010.

Kaufmann, Emil. *Three Revolutionary Architects: Boullée, Ledoux, and Lequeu*. Philadelphia: American Philosophical Society, 1960.

Le Corbusier and Pierre Jeanneret. *Œuvre Complète*, eds. W. Boesiger and O. Stonorov. London: Thames & Hudson, 1964.

Le Corbusier and Frederick Etchells. *Towards a New Architecture*. Connecticut: Martino Publishing, 2014 [o.p. 1923].

Lemagny, Jean-Claude. *Visionary Architects: Boullee, Ledoux, Lequeu*. New York: S.W. Swan Services, 1968.

Lepre, J.P. *The Egyptian Pyramids: A Comprehensive, Illustrated Reference*. Jefferson, NC: McFarland, 2006.

Machado, Rodolfo and Rodolphe el-Khoury, eds. *Monolithic Architecture*. Munich: Prestel, 1995.

Martinez, Guillermo. *La muerte lenta de Luciana B*. New York: Harper Collins/Rayo, 2008.

———. *Crímenes imperceptibles*. Buenos Aires: Planeta, 2003.

Mertins, Detlef. *Mies*. London: Phaidon, 2014.

Neutelings, Jan Willem and Michiel Riedijk. *At Work: Neutelings Riedijk Architects*. Rotterdam: 010 Publishers, 2005.

Ngai, Sianne. *Ugly Feelings*. Cambridge, MA: Harvard University Press, 2007.

Painter Jr., Borden W., *Mussolini's Rome: Rebuilding the Eternal City*. New York: Basingstoke, 2007.

Perrault, Claude. *Ordonnance for the Five Kinds of Columns after the Method of the Ancients*. Los Angeles: The Getty Center, 1993.

Rossi, Aldo. *A Scientific Autobiography*. Cambridge, MA: MIT Press, 2010.

Turnock, Julie A. *Plastic Reality: Special Effects, Technology, and the Emergence of 1970s Blockbuster Aesthetics*. New York: Columbia University Press, 2015.

Virilio, Paul. *Bunker Archeology*. New York: Princeton Architectural Press, 2009.

Wang Shu and Hsieh Ying-Chun. *Illegal Architecture: Wang Shu and Hsieh Ying-Chun*. Taipei, Taiwan: Garden City Publishers, 2012.

Wright, Frank Lloyd. *Frank Lloyd Wright: An Autobiography*. Petaluma, CA: Pomegranate, 2005.

ARTICLES IN BOOKS

Eisenman, Peter. "Strong Form, Weak Form." *Re:Working Eisenman*. London: Academy Editions, 1993.

Gooden, Mario. "_orm is a Four-letter Word (that Starts with 'F')." *Perspecta*, Vol. 43: Taboo. Cambridge, MA: MIT Press, 2010.

Mertins, Detlef. "Open Contours and Other Autonomies." *Monolithic Architecture*, eds. Rodolfo Machado and Rodolphe el-Khoury. Munich: Prestel, 1995.

Neumann, Dietrich. "Three Early Designs by Mies van der Rohe." *Perspecta*, Vol. 27. Cambridge, MA: MIT Press, 1992.

Rhodes, John David. "The Eclipse of Place: Rome's EUR from Rossellini to Antonioni." *Taking Place: Location and the Moving Image*, eds. John David Rhodes and Elena Gorfinkel. Minneapolis, MN: University of Minnesota Press, 2011.

Shklovsky, Viktor. "Art as Technique." *Theory of Prose*. Normal, IL: Dalkey Archive Press, 1991 [o.p. 1925].

Somol, R.E. "12 Reasons to Get Back into Shape." *Content*, eds. Rem Koolhaas and OMA. Cologne: Taschen, 2004.

Spurr, David. "Figures of Ruin and Restoration: Ruskin and Viollet-le-Duc." *Architecture and Modern Literature*. Ann Arbor: University of Michigan Press, 2012.

Vidler, Anthony. "The Architecture of the Uncanny: The Unhomely Houses of the Romantic Sublime." *Assemblage*, No. 3. Cambridge, MA: MIT Press, July 1987.

ARTICLES IN PERIODICALS, PRINT

Altshuler, Joseph. "Animate Architecture: 12 Reasons to Get in Character." *Log*, No. 33 (2013).

Carpo, Mario. "The Duck's Swan Song" from "Letters to Log." *Log*, No. 9 (Winter/Spring 2007).

Chakroff, Evan. "Recasting History: The Ningbo Historic Museum." *Log*, No. 24: Architecture Criticism (Winter/Spring 2012).

Cousins, Mark. "The Ugly (Part 1)." *AA Files*, No. 28 (Autumn 1994).

———. "The Ugly (Part 2)." *AA Files*, No. 29 (Summer 1995).

———. "The Ugly (Part 3)." *AA Files*, No. 30 (Autumn 1995).

Ferriss, Hugh. "The New Architecture: Evolution of a City Building Under the Zoning Law." *New York Times* (March 19,1922).

Hilberseimer, Ludwig. "Konstruktion und Form." *G Materialien zur elementaren Gestaltung*, No. 3 (June 1924).

Ito, Toyo. "Liquid Space and Fractal Boundary." *El Croquis: Toyo Ito 2005–2009*, No. 147 (2009).

———. "Za-Koenji Public Theatre." *El Croquis: Toyo Ito 2005–2009*, No. 147 (2009).

Jencks, Charles. "Eisenman Ducks" from "Letters to Log." *Log*, No. 9 (Winter/Spring 2007).

———. "The Iconic Building Is Here to Stay." *City*, Vol. 10, No. 1 (April 2006).

Kipnis, Jeffrey. "Towards a New Architecture." *Architectural Design* 102: *Folding In Architecture* (1993).

Lynn, Greg. "Architectural Curvilinearity: The Folded, the Pliant, and the Supple." *Architectural Design* 102: *Folding In Architecture* (1993).

Payne, Jason. "Variations on the Disco Ball, or, The Ambivalent Object." *Project: A Journal for Architecture*, Issue 2 (Spring 2013).

Pearson, Clifford A. "At New York's Smart New Museum of Contemporary Art, Tokyo-based SANAA Creates an Unambiguous Icon for an Area in Transition." *Architectural Record*, Vol. 196, No. 3 (March 2008).

Powell, Eric A. "Petra's Sister City," *Archaeology*, Vol. 63, No. 4 (July/August 2010).

Schweizer, Rahel Hartmann. "Historisches Museum Bern, Bern, Switzerland." *Architectural Record*, Vol. 198, No. 12 (December 2010).

Scott, K. "Inside the Breuer Building, After the Whitney and Before the Met." *The New Yorker* (March 12, 2016).

Somol, R.E. "Green Dots 101." *Hunch*, No. 11 (2007).

Sudjic, Deyan. "Wrong about Rem." *Log*, No. 6 (Fall 2005).

Vidler, Anthony. "The Theatre of Production: Claude-Nicolas Ledoux and the Architecture of Social Reform." *AA Files*, No. 1 (Winter 1981–82).

Warke, Val K. "Type — Silence — Genre." *Log*, No. 5: *Postcriticality* (Spring/Summer 2005).

Whiting, Sarah and Peter Eisenman. "I Am Interested in a Project of Engaged Autonomy." *Log*, No. 28 (2013).

Zaera Polo, Alejandro. "Eisenman's Machine of Infinite Resistance." *El Croquis*, No. 83 (1997).

Zambenedetti, Alberto. "Filming in Stone: Palazzo della Civiltà Italiana and Fascist Signification in Cinema." *Annali d'Italianistica*, Vol. 28, *Capital City: Rome 1870-2010* (2010).

ARTICLES IN PERIODICALS, ACCESSED ONLINE

Cousins, Mark. "The Ugly." *AA Files*, Vol. 29 (Summer 1995).

Hyde, Timothy. "Piles, Puddles, and Other Architectural Irritants." *Log*, No. 27 (2013).

Martinez, Guillermo. "Decálogo," El Malpensante. elmalpensante.com (no date).

Mcguirk, Justin. "Caixa Fórum." *Icon Magazine* (July 8, 2008).

Stott, Rory. "Why China's President Says 'No More Weird Buildings'." *ArchDaily* (October 21, 2014).

Stinson, Elizabeth. "How They Made *True Detective*'s Opening Credits So Eerie." *Wired* (June 22, 2015).

ARTICLES AND FEATURES ON WEBSITES

"Death Star & How the Death Star Got Its Trench." Colin Cantwell. colincantwell.com.

"Death Star I." *Wookieepedia: The Star Wars Wiki*. starwars.wikia.com.

"icon, n." OED Online. Oxford University Press. oed.com.

"New Museum: Building." New Museum. newmuseum.org/building.

"Parametricism as Style — Parametricist Manifesto." Patrick Schumaker. patrikschumacher.com/texts.

"*Star Wars* 40th Anniversary," Empire Movies. empireonline.com/movies.

"*Star Wars* Episode VI: Death Star II Under Construction Model Featurette," YouTube. youtube.com.

"Wang Shu Jury Citation," The Pritzker Architecture Prize. pritzkerprize.com/laureates.

INTERVIEWS AND TRANSCRIPTS OF INTERVIEWS

Martinez, Guillermo. Interview with Marcelo Spina. Buenos Aires. August 16, 2017.

LECTURES

Kipnis, Jeffrey. "Sherman and Koolhaas, or how to see through a mirror clearly, face to face." Wexner Center for the Arts. November 8, 2017.

———. Untitled lecture. A. Alfred Taubman College of Architecture and Urban Planning, University of Michigan, Ann Arbor. November 12, 2010.

EXHIBITION CATALOGS AND PROJECTS

Johnson, Philip and Mark Wigley. *Deconstructivist Architecture*. New York: Museum of Modern Art, 1988.

Riley, Terence and Guy Nordenson. *Tall Buildings*. New York: Museum of Modern Art, 2003.

Tschumi, Bernard. *Advertisements for Architecture*. 1976–1977.

Venturi, Robert. *Complexity and Contradiction in Architecture*. New York: Museum of Modern Art, 2002 [o.p. 1966].

FILMS

Blackwood, Michael. *Mies*. New York: Michael Blackwood Productions, 2005.

Lewis, Peter B., Frank O. Gehry, Jeffrey Kipnis, Brian Neff, and Thomas Ball; prod. Jennifer Frutchy. *A Constructive Madness: Wherein Frank Gehry & Peter Lewis Spend a Fortune and a Decade, End Up with Nothing and Change the World*. Columbus, OH: The Ohio State University, 2003.

Scott, Ridley. *Gladiator*. Hollywood, CA: Paramount Home Entertainment, 2010.

MUTE ICONS—and Other Dichotomies of the Real in Architecture

Published by
Actar Publishers, New York, Barcelona
www.actar.com

Authors
Marcelo Spina, Georgina Huljich

Edited by
Constance Vale

Graphic Design
Jessica Fleischmann / Still Room Co.

With contributions by
Brett Steele, Constance Vale, Ciro Najle, Guillermo Martinez

Printing and binding
Arlequin

Printed in Europe

Distribution
Actar D, Inc. New York, Barcelona

New York
440 Park Avenue South, 17th Floor
New York, NY 10016, USA
+1.212.966.2207
salesnewyork@actar-d.com

Barcelona
Roca i Batlle 2-4
08023 Barcelona, Spain
+34.933.282.183
eurosales@actar-d.com

English ISBN: 978-1-945150-86-9
PCN: Library of Congress Control Number: 2017960630

Publication date: 2021